HAVE THE MOUNTAINS FALLEN?

April 2018

Dear Michael,

Hope you enjoy the
book.

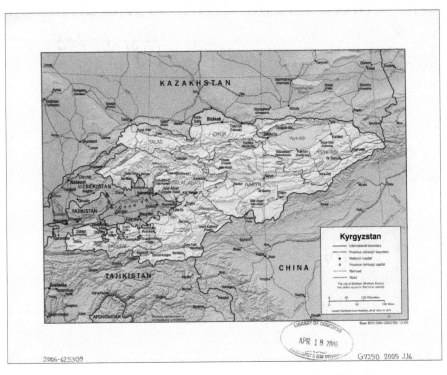

Map 0.1: Kyrgyzstan. Source: Library of Congress, Geography and Map Division.

HAVE THE MOUNTAINS FALLEN?

Two Journeys of Loss and Redemption in the Cold War

Jeffrey B. Lilley

INDIANA UNIVERSITY PRESS

This book is a publication of

Indiana University Press
Office of Scholarly Publishing
Herman B Wells Library 350
1320 East 10th Street
Bloomington, Indiana 47405 USA

iupress.indiana.edu

Cataloging information is available
from the Library of Congress.

ISBN 978-0-253-03242-3 (hardback)
ISBN 978-0-253-03244-7 (pbk.)
ISBN 978-0-253-03446-5 (MOBI)
ISBN 978-0-253-03243-0 (web PDF)
ISBN 978-0-253-03445-8 (ePub)

1 2 3 4 5   23 22 21 20 19 18

For Lynn and Mom. Thank you.

CONTENTS

PREFACE

This book was sparked by a desire to explore one of the major events of the twentieth century, the Cold War, and one of the defining moments in my life, the collapse of the Soviet Union. I studied Russian and later lived in Moscow during the years spanning the fall of the Soviet Union and the rise of the independent states.

The sense of elementary survival in the Soviet Union in those days was palpable. It usually had to do with food. Like Soviet citizens, I carried a bag everywhere I went because I never knew what might suddenly turn up. Hustlers would appear on a street corner, unload cardboard boxes full of produce, and start hawking their goods. It might be Ecuadorian bananas, Cuban grapefruits, or Polish jam. Whatever it was, I bought a lot of it and carted a sagging backpack home.

Procuring food was a metaphor for scratching out a life in those topsy-turvy days of change. A Russian sports entrepreneur captured the mood in the early 1990s when he said: "It's a difficult time but an interesting time. I like it very much. Each day I'm like a hunter. Where will I get my food? Who will I kill?"

The longer I spent in the former Soviet Union, the more I was drawn in. Traveling across the former Soviet republics in the 1990s and 2000s, I met people overcoming hardships to live meaningful lives. A woman sewing new clothes for her daughter out of discarded clothes. People flocking to Eastern religions after prohibitions on worship were eased. Like the food, you would find them in surprising places.

Like Kyrgyzstan. That's where I met Chingiz Aitmatov in 2007, a writer little known in America but one of the leading literary figures of the twentieth century.[1] Researching Aitmatov's life, I learned about his countryman Azamat Altay, a broadcaster for Radio Liberty who fled the Soviet Union after World War II. The more I studied the two men, the more I understood that their life paths were part of a wonderful and tragic tapestry of the twentieth century. Paths connected by a kindred struggle for more freedom for their people. Paths linked by poplar trees.

—〰—

Altay was born in a mountain village near the border with China. Marooned outside his homeland for more than half a century, he outlasted his archenemy the Soviet Union. Upon his return to Kyrgyzstan in 1995, he went immediately to the site of a cluster of poplar trees that he and his father had planted when he was a young boy, and embraced them. The trees towered over the aging Altay, silent markers to his fifty-year odyssey as a Soviet dissident in Europe and the United States.

During the decades Altay was building a life for himself in the West, Chingiz Aitmatov was cultivating a remarkable literary persona in Soviet Kyrgyzia. Spurred to write by the disappearance of his father during Stalin's purges, Aitmatov penned compelling stories featuring spirited characters with a thirst for freedom. His stories were a far cry from the stilted products of Soviet socialist realism demanded by the state.

In one of Aitmatov's first short stories, a teacher plants two poplar trees to inspire a student to spurn an arranged marriage and continue her education. "While they will grow and get stronger, you will grow too," the teacher says to the student. "You will become a scholar."

The story of Chingiz Aitmatov and Azamat Altay—two men from a mountainous land in the middle of the Asian continent—is a story of a captive people's aspiration for freedom. One fights from the outside, a dissident hardened by war and steeled by privation; the other struggles from the inside, an intellectual warrior who rises in the Soviet system even as he skewers it in coded prose.

They fought for freedom not with guns but with words and ideas. Their lives are proof that lies live on for only so long; that the truth, as evidenced by the attainment of justice and redemption, is achievable; and that the search for a meaningful life is based on individual freedom.

Defying the Iron Curtain, Aitmatov and Altay met and pursued a shared dream—to preserve their culture and help make the Kyrgyz people more free and independent. This is the untold story of two men from an unfamiliar land whose lives were connected like poplar trees growing side by side, their branches intermingling and overlapping with the passage of time.

NOTE TO READERS

Altay was known by two names: Azamat Altay (Al-tai), which he adopted in the early 1960s in the United States, and his birth name Kudaibergen Kojomberdiev (pronounced Hoo-dye-bear-gen Ko-zhom-bear-dee-yeff). Chingiz Aitmatov's name is easier to pronounce: Ching-geez Ait-matt-off. A note on transliteration appears following this preface.

The second clarification has to do with their homeland. When it was part of the Soviet Union, it was a Soviet republic, known officially as the Kirghiz Soviet Socialist Republic, or Kyrgyzia for short. After Kyrgyzia became an independent country in 1991, it changed its official name to the Kyrgyz Republic but is commonly known today as Kyrgyzstan. Using an *i* or a *y* has to do with transliteration. For simplicity's sake, I spell the root word "Kyrgyz" when referring to the country or its people.

And, finally, on pronunciation, via a bit of personal history, since people are usually befuddled when it comes to pronouncing the country's name. When I landed a job in Kyrgyzstan in 2004, my father, a diplomat who himself had traveled to far corners of the world, congratulated me on the upcoming adventure with my young family in tow: "So, you are taking Lynn and the boys to Gurkistan?" He was passable on the last syllables but got fouled up on the first. Others mistake it as Kurdistan. In 2013, Secretary of State John Kerry called it Kyrzakhstan, and in 2015 the *New York Times* issued what someone called "the greatest correction" in the newspaper's history after it referred to Kyrgyzstan as Kyrzbekistan. The error kicked off considerable Twitter banter and resulted in the creation of the hashtag #kyrzbekistan for the mythical country.

So, just to be clear, it's not the land of the Gurkhas or Kurds, and it's definitely not Kazakhstan, its oil-rich neighbor to the north, or Uzbekistan, its authoritarian neighbor to the west. It's Kyrgyzstan, pronounced somewhat like Keer-gihs-taan. Go heavy on the gutturals. I hope you enjoy getting to know a bit about a beautiful country, its spirited people, and their struggle for freedom and independence.

ACKNOWLEDGMENTS

The journey toward this project started long before it was conceived in 2007. It began when I started studying Russian in 1982 at Williams College. So I'd like to thank my Russian professors at Williams, the late Nicholas Fersen and Darra Goldstein. Darra, an accomplished author in her own right and a source of encouragement since I sat in her classes in Williamstown, launched me on my lifelong study of Russian, the language I used to access Aitmatov's world. Languages truly are the door to a richer experience and a key to building bridges on this divided planet.

So many other people to thank:

Among family, I am grateful to my wife, Lynn Alleva, and my mother (and editor), Sally Lilley, for their creative approaches to life, appreciation of the arts, and support along the curves, descents, and ascents of this ten-year journey; my brother Mike for helping to make the Lewes, Delaware, beach house a haven for writing; the Rumson Lilleys and Aunt Beth for fun and games at the beach; my late father, Ambassador James R. Lilley, who gave me the "international bug" and got me started on books when we wrote his memoirs; and my late brother, Douglas Lilley, who was a writer inside.

As for my Kyrgyz colleagues, thank you to Iliyas Mammadiyarov for a memorable trip to Sheker with his father in June 2013 and for being my man-on-the-ground—with Ermek Adylbekov—in Bishkek throughout the writing process; to Tyntchtykbek Chorotegin, Venera Djumataeva, Peter Baumgartner, Gulya Ashakeeva, and Amirbek Usmanov, for helping me with sources, the Radio Liberty story, and contacts; to Kyrgyz Ambassador to the United States Kadyr Toktogulov for reading and helping promote the manuscript; to former Kyrgyz ambassador to the United States Zamira Sydykova for helping arrange a 2008 event at the Library of Congress commemorating Chingiz Aitmatov, and for helping get me in touch with Azamat Altay's family in the United States; to Abi Pazylov, who in August 2007 arranged a phone call with Chingiz Aitmatov; to Jyldyz Bakashova, director of the Kyrgyz National Library in Bishkek and an Aitmatov scholar in her own right; to Gulnara, Ken, and Mira Mahendru for opening their house (Azamat Altay's house) to me during a blizzard in January 2016 and sharing Altay's letters, photos, and scrapbooks; and to the staff at the Central Archives of the Kyrgyz Republic for access to photos of Chingiz Aitmatov, which go back decades.

Thanks as well to Bob Karlowich, Kathleen Kuehnast, the late Edward Allworth, Ed Kasinec, and Timur Kocaoglu for helping to bring alive Altay, a man I never knew; to Ken Peterson and friends for putting me on the trail of Boris Arapovich; to Don Lamm (via dear family friends Susan Conway and Patrick Oliphant) for reading an early version of the book and providing tactical advice in tackling the world of publishing agentless; to Belle Yang, family friend and veteran writer, for connection and support; to Baktygul Aliev, Darra Goldstein's successor at Williams College (who, of all things, is Kyrgyz), for help with transliteration; to my brother-in-law Mark Caceres for help on the photos; to Joe Mozur, the American Aitmatov scholar, for reading the manuscript and providing needed shots of optimism; and to Enders Wimbush, Ross Johnson, and Gene Parta, a hall of fame of Radio Liberty, for their support and information on Altay and Radio Liberty.

Much research was done sifting through archives at various institutions, either in person or remotely. Indeed, when I travel abroad, I am reminded by comparison of the wonderful academic institutions we have in America. Thank you to the Library of Congress, for being open, helpful, and a treasure trove of books, a direct manifestation of America's democracy; to Columbia University's Robert Davis, librarian for Russian, Eurasian, and East European studies, as well as the university's Rare Manuscript Library for helpful documents; to the Hoover Institute for access to its Radio Liberty archives; to my alma mater Johns Hopkins SAIS for its quiet library; to the Central Asia Caucasus Institute at SAIS, and its director Fred Starr for advice along the way; to George Mason

Fenwick Library, Special Collection and Archives Division, for Arena Stage archives; and to the late Zelda Fichandler, a gem of a person, for sharing her memories of Arena's 1975 production of Aitmatov's play.

Among friends, I send hearty appreciation to Billy Amoss and Adam Kahane, for their friendship, support, and keen readers' eyes, as well as a shout out to the Silver Spring YMCA. A good swim can cure much of what ails us. Thank you to close friends John Knab for laughs and pro bono legal consulting, and to Paul Asel and John Forster for camaraderie, conversation, and a good game of basketball.

Deep gratitude goes to the Aitmatov family, Eldar and Maria, for being generous with their time on a June day in 2013 in sunny Kyrgyzstan and for answering my e-mails and queries over the ensuing years, and to other members of the Aitmatov family (Roza, Ilgiz, Japarbek, Askar, and Asan) for sharing their memories of Chingiz.

Three people in Kyrgyzstan whom I met briefly also come to mind: Eric, who came out on the street one night in Bishkek to give me copies of films based on Aitmatov's books because he was so excited a Westerner had taken an interest; Regina Helimskaya, an intrepid journalist in whom a fire burns to uncover the truth and keep the powers-that-be accountable; and Jyldyz Masalbekova, my translator on my first trip to Sheker in 2007, who remains in my memory as an uncanny mixture of the book's two protagonists.

And, finally, thank you to the International Republican Institute for sending me to Kyrgyzstan in 2004 to head up its office in Bishkek; and to Jennika Baines and Indiana University Press for saying yes, some thirty years after publishing Chingiz Aitmatov's most famous novel in English.

NOTE ON TRANSLITERATION
AND TRANSLATION

For transliteration from Kyrgyz to English, I have been guided by the BGN/PCGN Romanization system, mostly because it has the fewest letters with diacritical marks.

To be faithful to those markings, I have included uniquely Kyrgyz vowel sounds Ü and Ö as well as an additional guttural vowel. To help with pronunciation, table 1 provides a key.

Kyrgyz Vowel Pronunciation Key

Kyrgyz alphabet	Transliteration	Pronunciation
Ɵ	Ö	"u" as in *turn*
Y	Ü	"ew" as in *flew*
Ы	Y	long, between an *i* and *e*

However, for some names and some letters, I have sought to use whatever version is most familiar to an English-speaking audience rather than contorting them with confusing transliteration. Thus, you will see Chingiz Aitmatov and Issyk Kul instead of Chynggyz Aitmatov and Ysyk-kül. Regarding Issyk Kul, which literally means "warm or sacred lake" in Kyrgyz, I will call it Lake Issyk Kul despite the redundancy. The following Kyrgyz words appear in the text:

Agai—respectful way to address an older man
Aitish—improvisational oral poetry competition
Aksakal—respected elder, literally "white beard"
Bozüi—yurt

Eje—respectful way to address an older woman

Jailoo—high mountain pasture

Kalpak—traditional felt hat worn by men

Komuz—three-stringed instrument

Kymyz—fermented mare's milk

Manaschi—oral storyteller of the Manas epic in the Kyrgyz language

Ürkün—mass flight to China by the Kyrgyz people in 1916 (as well as Kazakhs, Dungans, and Uighurs) after a failed rebellion against Tsarist Russia

LIST OF NAMES

Family of Chingiz Aitmatov	Family of Azamat Altay (born Kudaibergen Kojomberdiev)
Aitmat Kimbildiev (grandfather)	Kojomberdi Teke uulu (father)
Törökul Aitmatov (father)	Kargadai (sister)
Ryskulbek (uncle)	Gulshara (sister)
Karakyz (aunt)	Toichubek Turgambaev (nephew, Gulshara's son)
	Gulnara Turganbaeva (niece, Gulshara's daughter). Married name: Gulnara Mahendru
Birimkul Kimbildiev (grand uncle)	Saniye Altay (wife)
Alimkul (father's cousin)	
Ozubek (father's cousin)	
Nagima Abduvalieva (mother)	
Gulsha (aunt/mother's sister)	
Hamza Abduvaliev (maternal grandfather)	
Ilgiz (brother)	
Lutsia (sister)	
Roza (sister)	
Urmat Alimkulov (nephew/Roza's son)	
Kerez Shamshibaeva (wife)	
Sanjar (son)	
Askar (son)	
Maria Aitmatova (second wife)	
Shirin (daughter)	
Eldar (son)	

TIMELINE

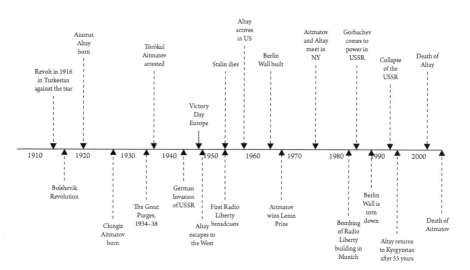

Figure 0.1

HAVE THE MOUNTAINS FALLEN?

PART ONE

1

Flight

In June 1941 the Soviet conscript Azamat Altay found himself in the crosshairs of the Nazi blitzkrieg. His staff sergeant, a man named Belov, had been one of the first to fall when German forces rolled into Soviet-occupied Lithuania in the early morning hours of June 22. Ordered by his commanding officer to retrieve Belov's identification documents, Altay crawled on his belly across an exposed field. As bullets whizzed overhead, he pulled Belov's Komsomol membership card from his bloody clothes.

Groveling back to Soviet lines, Altay shielded himself with Belov's corpse on his back. He edged forward on the ground for what seemed like an eternity. When he arrived at the Soviet trenches, he discovered that his platoon had disintegrated under the German onslaught and that his commander had fled. When he gave Belov's card to his platoon leader, the man shrugged as if Altay had given him theater tickets: "Who needs this membership card now?" he asked in the din of war.[1]

Altay's birth name was Kudaibergen Kojomberdiev, and as his nine-syllable name attested, he was not the average Soviet soldier.[2] He was a Muslim from Kyrgyzia, a republic in the Asian part of the Soviet Union. His village in the foothills of the Ala-Too Mountains was just a few days' hike from the border with China. With Asian eyes, high cheekbones, and dark hair, he looked Mongolian, and it seemed that the indomitable spirit of Genghis Khan ran through his veins.

Over the following few years, Altay would suffer torture, starvation, and solitary confinement. He would escape from Nazi prisons three times and eventually make his way to the West to escape Joseph Stalin's barbarism.

Altay had arrived in Soviet-occupied Lithuania in September 1940, during a time of peace for the Soviet Union. The Molotov-Ribbentrop Pact, which in 1939 had divided up Poland and the Baltic nations between Germany and the Soviet Union, was holding steady. Stalin's gamble of pacifying Hitler while the Nazis battered France and England appeared to be paying off.

On his own as a young man, Altay soaked up the experience of being out of his landlocked native republic for the first time in his life. With more than three thousand miles separating European Lithuania from his home in Soviet Central Asia, he must have felt as if he had landed in another world.

In spite of not being able to communicate, Altay felt a natural affinity with his hosts. While Lithuanians were generally hostile to Soviet soldiers, whom they saw as occupiers, they welcomed the curious Altay, who asked questions about their daily life and history. It was Altay's first lesson that ethnic groups on the edges of the Soviet Empire had a natural bond.

Lithuanian farmers would invite him into their houses and feed him when he was on military training exercises with his platoon. Communicating with his hosts using hand gestures, Altay began to understand that many Lithuanians, far from feeling liberated by the Soviets, were seething under occupation. Altay was also struck by the cleanliness and coziness of Lithuanian houses; these were signs to him of a happy people, not the forlorn, starving masses portrayed by Soviet propaganda. Altay realized that Soviet propaganda was telling bald-faced lies. Loath to keep quiet, he told his fellow soldiers how he had socialized with Lithuanians. "These people aren't dying of hunger in their capitalist country," he said.[3]

Altay's dissenting views had no place in the Soviet system. He was summoned to a meeting of his military unit's political committee, reprimanded for socializing with Lithuanians, and kicked out of the Communist Party. Already a minority in the Soviet army as a Muslim from Central Asia, Altay had become an outcast. The young Soviet conscript began to survey the world around him suspiciously. People were not to be trusted, or personal views shared. Altay's hardening exterior would serve him well in the coming years.

Germany's surprise attack on the Soviet Union on June 22, 1941, decimated the Red Army. Supported by planes, tanks, and heavy armor, the Nazi invasion apparently so distressed Stalin that he refused to speak with the Soviet people about it. Instead, it was left to Soviet foreign minister Vyacheslav Molotov to make a radio address at noon, a full nine hours into the blitzkrieg. Molotov tried to rally a traumatized Soviet people by uttering the now-famous words: "We are right. The enemy will be defeated. Victory will be ours."[4]

Despite his misgivings about the Soviet Communist Party, Altay, who was posted on the border between Soviet-occupied Lithuania and German-occupied Poland, threw himself into the fight with invading Germans. He had given an oath to defend the homeland, however imperfect it was, and his country was under attack. "It is not a Kirghiz custom to avoid fighting for one's native soil," he wrote some years later.[5] And that soil was being gobbled up at an impressive clip—the Germans would make it all the way to Moscow in just four months.

On the battlefield, in the face of overwhelming German firepower, Soviet forces were in chaotic retreat. Altay would lament later that the Soviet soldiers were not taught how to retreat in an orderly manner. Instead, all was chaos. After finding that his platoon had disintegrated, Altay ran for his life through an open field, with bullets clanking off his shovel and grazing his military coat.

He eventually located remnants of his battalion on the other side of the Neman River in the Kaliningrad region, and together they headed northeast to Russia. Cut off from supply lines, Altay and some of his battalion mates joined forces with other Red Army stragglers and rallied to fight against the German juggernaut. Somehow they survived Nazi bombs, tank shells, and gunfire for two months, and at the end of August, after crossing hundreds of miles of territory, they ended up in the besieged city of Veliki Luki in western Russia, near the border with the Belorussian Soviet Republic. Reunited with their regimental commander, they prepared for a last stand. Just 42 men of the original 2,500 soldiers in Altay's regiment answered the muster call.

Surveying the decimated ranks of troops, a Soviet colonel ordered Altay, just a cadet, to lead the remaining soldiers in a desperate counterattack to break the siege. Altay gathered himself for what must have seemed like a futile mission. "Attack," he cried, leading his bedraggled troops into battle. At his signal, his men followed, yelling, "For Stalin, for the motherland!"

The counterattack failed miserably, with German troops advancing relentlessly against the outmanned Soviets. When the retreat signal was given, Altay hid in low bushes with ten other soldiers while German soldiers on motorcycles rumbled by just feet away. "What do we do now?" he despaired. "Where do we go?" His commander slipped away into nearby woods and—in an act that Altay knew from military school signaled the desperation of their situation—wrapped the platoon's banner around his torso under his shirt, so it could not be captured. He was never seen again. Altay was captured a short while later while searching for food in a village.

He and his fellow soldiers were actually captured by Spanish soldiers fighting with the Nazis and turned over to the Germans. From that fateful day, Altay began an ordeal of capture and escape during which he would spend thirty months in prisons across 250 miles of Nazi-occupied territory in present-day Lithuania, Latvia, Belarus, and Russia, and eventually make it to France to fight with French partisans until the end of the war. Altay's travails as recounted in his memoirs are fantastic and some say improbable given the difficulty of surviving three years behind Nazi lines. But dates and descriptions of places and wartime conditions accord with other accounts.[6]

After his capture by the Germans in late August 1941, Altay and other prisoners of war were imprisoned in a temporary camp swelling with those who had been captured. The onset of winter brought cold weather and wind, and there was little food. Prisoners stood in line from morning until noon to get food; even then, their hunger pangs were not satisfied. In his memoir, Altay recounts how when German guards shot a dog, prisoners pounced on the creature, tearing it to pieces. Altay's friend managed to get a leg, and they cooked up a soup to feed five people. "Hunger robs a man of his pride," Altay would remark many years later. "And he turns into an animal."[7]

Shortly thereafter, Altay endured a ten-day forced march with thousands of other Soviet POWs, during which the weak and failing were shot if they could not keep up with the eighteen-mile daily regimen. The march took the group farther from the front lines and deeper into German-occupied territory, ending in November 1941 in Latvia. There, humiliation continued, with sadistic German guards tossing pieces of bread down into the makeshift pens that confined the Soviet POWs. While the guards laughed, starving POWs grabbed at the morsels so desperately that the bread disintegrated before any of it hit Altay's hands. But the saving grace was two fellow Kyrgyz POWs who, no doubt recognizing a "brother Kyrgyz," shared their heavy military coats with Altay to keep warm at night in the frigid temperatures. It was not the last time brotherly Kyrgyz would come to his aid.

At Camp Valeyko, a German concentration camp near the Belorussian-Russian border to which he was transferred in late 1941, Altay endured what he later described as "hellish torments," including sleeping in animal pens surrounded by barbed wire and starvation rations. The five-foot-seven, broad-shouldered Altay was wasting away. "If we don't escape, we'll die," he said to a fellow Kyrgyz.

In fact, the German policy toward Soviet POWs was calculated. Just months before, the German Army had set a ration of a mere 2,200 calories per day for working Soviet prisoners of war, an amount insufficient to sustain life for long. But in practice many Soviet prisoners of war received a ration of only seven hundred calories a day, the equivalent of about three candy bars. It was death by starvation. Because the Soviet Union had not ratified the 1929 Geneva Convention on prisoners of war or declared its commitment to the 1907 Hague Convention on the rules of war, the Germans justified their actions by saying they had no obligation to care humanely for POWs.[8]

Under the cover of a rainy night in early December 1941, Altay and a fellow Kyrgyz prisoner approached the barbed-wire enclosure surrounding the horse pen they were living in. Hastily covering the metal spikes with rags and bags they had collected, they slipped their emaciated frames through the barbed wire. "No more humiliation by German guards," Altay thought. "No more tearing a dog to pieces for morsels of food."

Altay and his fellow prisoner ran into the darkness, crossing fields of frozen cabbage plants, some of which they scooped up and nibbled on as they tried to put distance between them and the camp. Hiding by day in the forest and moving by night, Altay lived like a fugitive behind German lines, begging food from friendly Polish and Belorussian peasants and taking refuge in their barns. Occasionally, he traded chores, such as chopping wood, cutting hay, and watering animals, in return for a hot meal and bath. The two Kyrgyz learned to navigate to friendly villages and houses that were not along main roads, which the Germans and their local collaborators traveled, often searching for escaped POWs. They always moved eastward, toward Soviet territory that had not yet been occupied. For Altay, his suffering as a POW ended for the time being, and the trials and tribulations of flight began.

He got separated from his Kyrgyz fellow escapee, who would eventually make it back to Soviet Kyrgyzia and write Altay some fifty years later recounting their joint escape. For Altay, fortunately, there were good Samaritans along the way, like Stefan, an elderly Polish man whose own son had been exiled to Siberia by the Soviets when they occupied land under the Molotov-Ribbentrop Pact with the Germans. Stefan would bring a blanket to Altay, who was sleeping in his barn, but his wife, bitter about her son's imprisonment, would take the blanket right back, muttering about lice as she walked away. While Stefan offered Altay meat and tea, his wife countered with potatoes and water. The wife seethed and took every opportunity to demean her unwanted guest. When German planes flew overhead on their way to bomb the Soviet Union, the wife coldly remarked to Altay: "Hey, Asian communist, today your Moscow will be destroyed."

Altay had gotten used to words like "communist," "komsomolets," and "Bolshevik" being used as pejoratives by Poles and others whose territory had been occupied by the Soviets. "When you live a cursed life, you have to accept such humiliations," Altay told himself. Living with Stefan and his wife for several weeks was a lesson for Altay on how to respond to misfortune. You can act with kindness and sympathy like Stefan, who saw in Altay his own son's plight, or you can respond with stinginess and anger as his wife did. Indeed, good and evil existed side by side during this peripatetic period of Altay's life, like variable winds on a sailing day. Altay tacked to the good whenever he could.

Traveling by night and taking refuge in barns and outdoor pens, Altay survived for a year before he was apprehended walking along a road at night by police in Nazi-occupied Belorussia and taken to a prison in the village of Ashmyani in central Belorussia. He was fortunate to be taken to a local prison, not a German military camp. The food was better, and given that winter was under way, he reasoned that he was better off with a roof over his head than braving the elements outside.

But with the local prison filling up with POWs, Altay feared that he and other POWs would be transferred to a concentration camp. He escaped a second time in December 1942—this time on his own—while repairing a road outside of Ashmyani as part of a prison work gang. Encouraged to flee by some Jewish prisoners who, he says, gave him rations of bread and milk, Altay broke from the work gang while the guards were warming themselves by a fire. Under cover of a heavy fog, he ran to a snowy forest and forded a freezing river. A helpful Polish peasant let him dry his clothes at his outdoor stove but then advised Altay to leave immediately because his Asian face would arouse suspicion among locals. His Asian looks, which had actually helped him early on in Lithuania, seemed to have become a liability. "They'll see you are from another people and country, and they'll punish us," he was told by his Polish host.

Following the advice of locals, after traversing thirty miles on foot, Altay ended up of all places in a Muslim village in Poland, one of very few such places in the region. Tracing their ancestry back to waves of Tatars who had arrived in the region as early as the fourteenth century, the Polish Tatars had maintained their religion and many customs, and they greeted a fellow Muslim warmly. Altay cleaned himself at the mosque, ate a meal, and attended prayers. The prayers took Altay back to his childhood during Muslim holidays when he had joined fellow villagers at the makeshift mosque in his home village. It was a welcome respite from life on the run. Seemingly at home among a fellow Turkic people, Altay nevertheless couldn't stay for long because the village was on a main road traveled by the German military.

Altay eventually joined up—or was forced to join up—with Belorussian partisans, who spirited him to eastern Belorussia on a sleigh. The partisans turned out to be a savage lot, robbing people, stealing horses, and preying on villages along the way. Altay commandeered a horse and galloped away, only to be captured by an even more savage group of bandits preying on defenseless villagers during wartime. This group was led by a commander who ate only meat and drank vodka for sustenance and spoke little. For food his subordinates would shoot cows and drag them to the forest to be dismembered and cooked. Altay watched as the partisans, lacking a shred of sympathy, forced an elderly grandmother to stand barefoot in the snow while her granddaughter pleaded with the partisans not to shoot the family cow. Sick to his stomach about being a party to such crimes, Altay lagged behind the group one night and fled on his horse in the other direction. For weeks, he wandered by foot, short on food and with a gun in hand to guard against the Germans or being taken away again by partisans.

—◊—

There was little time for child's play in the village of Sheker in Soviet Kyrgyzia once World War II broke out in June 1941. As Chingiz Aitmatov would later write: "The war demanded total commitment. It was each person's destiny, the lot of anyone who lived at the time, and the measure of one's actions and moral values."[9] That captured the effect of the war on tiny Sheker, which, though located thousands of miles from the front lines, was pulled into the colossal war effort. The village mirrored the vicissitudes of the war, responding like "a sensitive membrane to every blow."[10]

After meetings about the war in the first days of the German blitzkrieg, male members from the community of Sheker went straight to the regional center to sign up for the army. The departures came in waves. First, the village emptied of its teenage sons and younger men. Then, as the draft broadened to include men up the age of sixty, its fathers and even some grandfathers departed, some for the front lines, others for work in steel mills near the Ural Mountains or the mines and forests of Siberia.

As one of the few educated people left in the village, Chingiz Aitmatov was forced to quit school to work as the secretary of the village council. Just fourteen years old, he worked as the assistant to the sixty-year-old head of the village council, Kabylbek Turdubaev, a former shepherd who could write only the first four letters of his last name. "Besides you there is no one else suitable," Turdubaev told him. "We only have old people and children left." At the start, Chingiz couldn't even mount his horse without help.

Chingiz collected statistics on village life, analyzed them, and wrote reports—heavy stuff for a teenager. But that work did not compare to having to deliver "black papers," the official military document that certified the death of a soldier. By the time Chingiz would arrive at a front door, the houses were usually already in mourning, having heard earlier from the village elders of their family's loss.

The teenage postman would open the envelope and quietly read the black paper to the family, in the process translating the Russian into Kyrgyz. After he finished, silence would descend. Then there was a solemn transfer of the letter, with Chingiz advising the family members to store the letter in a safe place as proof of their loss.

Chingiz would then stare at the ground, uncomfortable, shifting his feet. Usually, he would hear a heavy sigh from the mother, then whimpering or heaving. And finally crying would rend the air like a plate shattering. Chingiz would stand there, a young boy, with nowhere to run and no way to console.

Villagers began associating the young village assistant with bad luck. As soon as households saw him riding down the street, they would shun him like an evil spirit. "Don't come to our house," they would say. "Pass by. Don't bring us bad news."

Such a young boy shouldering such heavy responsibilities—to suffer the village's grief as the messenger of bad news. A piece of paper in exchange for a son. But this was how Soviet society endured during World War II, or the Great Patriotic War, as it is known in Russian. Ironies overwhelmed: a distant war wreaking havoc in an isolated village, teenagers running village affairs, and a boy not big enough to mount his horse delivering death notices.

—␣␣␣—

World War II was a crucible for the Soviet people, a nightmare of loss that took the lives of twenty-seven million Soviet citizens, including ninety thousand men and women from Soviet Kyrgyzia alone. Altay and Aitmatov's separate war experiences would define the rest of their lives, ultimately leading Altay to forsake his country for the West and launching Aitmatov on a path to become one of the Soviet Union's most famous writers.

In today's independent Kyrgyzstan, both men are regarded as worthy descendants of their nomadic forefathers, who honed their own survival skills through centuries of fighting and intermingling with invaders in the middle of the Eurasian landmass. While nearby ethnic groups were wiped from the earth or assimilated, Kyrgyz tribes used a combination of a warrior spirit and flexibility to preserve themselves.

In his life, Aitmatov tended toward the intermingling side of the Kyrgyz character, paying heed to communist authority while penning scathing critiques of the Soviet system. Altay, in contrast, in his odyssey from traitor to national hero, was a lonely warrior. Together, the two men kept the dream of freedom alive during the dark years of Soviet communism and lived to see the birth of independent Kyrgyzstan in 1991.

This is the story of Aitmatov and Altay's remarkable lives on either side of the Cold War, the cord of devotion that linked them to the Kyrgyz people, and their unpublicized meetings during the days of division between east and west. This is the story of the survival of a small people surrounded by bigger, often hostile powers.

—w—

Napoleon supposedly said if you scratch a Russian, you will find a Tatar. If you scratch a Kyrgyz, you will find a Mongolian, Chinese, Persian, Arab, and perhaps even a Russian or two. And if you rub a bit more, their red-haired, blue-eyed forebearers from Siberia might pop out.[11]

The Siberian Kyrgyz were a feisty people, ruling the area around the Yenisei River in the ninth century. But they met their match in the Mongols, who cut a wide swath across the Eurasian landmass, and submitted to them without much of a fight. Around the middle of the ninth to the middle of the thirteenth centuries the Kyrgyz migrated south to their historical homeland in the center of Eurasia. The migrating Kyrgyz ended up in what became known as Mogulistan, or "country of the Mongols."

The conquering Mongols ended what one historian has called "Central Asia's Golden Age of Enlightenment"—a period of several hundred years from the eighth to the twelfth centuries that preceded the European Enlightenment. During that time, in centers of learning from Persia to western China, resourceful and worldly thinkers made remarkable advances in astronomy, mathematics, philosophy, architecture, painting, and poetry.

The Mongols made their own imprint. The Kyrgyz people's broad faces and Mongolian eyes, no doubt, got a head start when two hundred thousand Mongol nomads streamed in with their cattle after victorious Mongol warriors subdued the Central Asian tribes.

While the Mongols may well have influenced the looks of the Kyrgyz, the mélange of other cultures that washed over the region introduced religion, Islam via the Arabs in the seventh century, and language, Turkic through a succession of Turkic rulers. Both define the region to this day.

Over the ensuing centuries, the Kyrgyz clung stubbornly to their cattle, yurts (or *bozüi*, as they call their movable dwellings), and animism despite their more powerful neighbors. A Chinese chronicle from the 1700s records the Kyrgyz as being passive Muslims, with just two men praying out of a hundred, and leading a rudimentary daily existence. Their life was simple to describe: "Felt yurts—their home; herding—their job; meat—their food."[12]

Russia's colonization of Turkestan—roughly today's Central Asia—started around 1860. That's when northern Kyrgyz tribes asked for Russia's help in throwing off the yoke of the Kokand Khanate, a Turkic state that had ruled the region for 150 years. Over the following decade, Tsar Alexander III's army secured—others would say occupied—Central Asia as a production center for cotton and other agricultural products, as well as a buffer zone against disturbances in nearby China.

Migrants streamed down from the European part of Russia and Siberia, enticed by offers of free land. The terms were attractive: each settler received twenty-five acres of choice land, subsidies for fifteen years, and exemptions from taxes and military service.[13] News spread so rapidly of abundant water, fertile soil, and good hunting conditions that between 1903 and 1911 the Slavic population of the Semirech'ie region, which included much of the northern portion of present-day Kyrgyzstan, al-most doubled to 175,000.[14]

———

The Russian presence in tsarist Turkestan ultimately led to a societal explosion. Seared into Altay's childhood memory were his father's stories about the 1916 rebellion in Turkestan and the people's ensuing flight to China, or Ürkün, as it is called in the Kyrgyz language. Like the Arab uprising against the Ottoman Empire and the Irish rebellion against England at roughly the same time, Ürkün sparked a national awakening among the indigenous people of tsarist Turkestan. Altay's father Teke uulu described the revolt as "a rebellion against the Russian Tsar and the Russian people."[15]

The uprising was triggered by the calling up of tens of thousands of Kyrgyz to serve in labor units of the tsarist army, which at the time was fighting the Germans in World War I. The mandatory conscription on June 25, 1916—or "thunder on a clear day," as Altay would himself call it years later—enraged the Kyrgyz because they believed it reneged on the promise of tsarist authorities in the 1870s not to draft Kyrgyz for military duty.[16] But the seeds of rebellion had been nurtured by decades of steady Russian encroachment, corrupt practices, and increasing resentment on the part of the Kyrgyz and other Central Asians at being treated like a colonized people.

The tsarist conscription in June of men between the ages of nineteen and forty-three hit poor Kyrgyz families the hardest, depriving them of their most able-bodied male family members at harvest time, and bypassed richer families who had the money to pay a bribe for someone else to take their father's, husband's, or son's spot.

———

Though not coordinated, the uprising spread rapidly across tsarist Turkestan, starting in urban centers in today's Uzbekistan and then gain-ing a foothold in villages to the east. Ultimately, it engulfed the eleven million inhabitants of Central Asia in some form or another, although the triggers for rebellion differed depending on the location. But the source of tension in almost all cases was land.

Among the settled peoples of Uzbekistan, Tajikistan, and Kyrgyzstan, the focus was on the usurpation of land used for cotton by Russian farmers and on government demands that local farmers turn over a portion of their crop to the state and pay taxes. In mountainous areas of Kyrgyzstan and eastern Kazakhstan, the local farmers objected to being forced to cultivate poppies for use in medicine for tsarist soldiers on the European front and local herders opposed being allocated subpar land.

Some of the fiercest fighting was around Issyk Kul, an enormous alpine lake on whose southern shore Altay's father lived with his parents and siblings. Over the years, tensions between locals and settlers had been stoked by unfair land allotment policies, according to which Russian and Ukrainian settlers had gained the most sought-after plots of land near the lake's shore, while the mostly nomadic Kyrgyz had been forced to accept land in the foothills that was less suitable for grazing livestock.[17]

The Russian authorities declared martial law on July 17, 1916, and gave locals a last chance to give up their men to military service. But the decree backfired. Local officials who had pledged loyalty to the tsar switched sides to their ethnic kin, and Kyrgyz guerilla fighters seized rifles and ammunition from Russian soldiers at the west end of the lake. Russian villages on both the northern and southern shores of the lake, largely undefended because most working-age Slavic men were fighting in World War I, were attacked and burned by the Kyrgyz. Women and children were taken hostage.[18]

In early August, the uprising turned savage, so savage, in fact, that nearly one hundred years later the Russian and Kyrgyz governments still avoid discussing it, and sensitive documents in the national archives are available only with the permission of the Kyrgyz security service.[19]

At the eastern end of the lake, Kyrgyz laborers working as hired hands for Slavic landowners suddenly dropped their hoes and plows and withdrew into the mountains. Concerned about a lack of workers to collect the upcoming harvest, Russian Orthodox monks at the nearby Holy Trinity Monastery raised the alarm with Russian officials that something seemed amiss, but Russian officials and the state-controlled press ignored the entreaties.[20] Most of the monks remained at the monastery, trusting that the local Kyrgyz, many of whom had worked the monastery's fields for years, wouldn't hurt them. One monk, however, took shelter in catacombs on a nearby island. He lived to tell the tale.

On August 10, with the uprising igniting in villages around the lake, the Kyrgyz came down from the mountains. Using a young Kyrgyz who studied at the monastery school as an interpreter, they shook down the monk Rafael when he came to greet them at the gates of the monastery. They took his shoes, shirt, and wallet; before departing, they promised not to touch the monastery's icons. A relieved Rafael returned to his brothers, who were taking refuge in the monastery's sanctuary. But shortly thereafter, the mob returned. Kyrgyz men broke down the gates of the church where the monks had taken refuge and, armed with sharpened sticks, axes, and hunting rifles, stormed into the religious sanctuary. Amid yelling and screaming by the marauders, the monk Rafael, singing prayers in a deep bass voice, led the monks in procession to the church's altar, where each was handed an icon and a cross.

But the mob would not be restrained. After forcing the monks to take off their outer religious robes, the intruders led the religious men, dressed in their undergarments and still carrying holy objects and singing homilies, out to the church's porch. There the mob set upon the holy men one by one. Rafael was the first to die. The bloodthirsty mob urged on the young translator as he chopped off the monk's head and right hand, in which he was holding a Bible. Other monks were stabbed and bludgeoned to death with blunt spears. The massacre took the lives of eight monks.[21]

In response to the brutality around Lake Issyk Kul, with the burning of Russian homesteads, murders, and hostage taking, Russian authorities announced a scorched-earth policy of pacification, forcing the Kyrgyz to flee their homes or perish. Disorganized and lightly armed Kyrgyz villagers wilted in the face of the vengeful counterattack by Russian forces. The tsarist governor of Turkestan ordered that there be no mercy for rebels from Karakol, the main city at the eastern end of the lake then known as Prezhevalsk, where almost all Russian settlements had been destroyed (see map 1.1).

With reinforcements sent in from the war front, Siberia, and other parts of Central Asia, Russian troops overwhelmed the insurgents. Part of the pacification policy included distributing weapons to Russian set-

Map 1.1: Map of the Kyrgyz Republic. Source: ©d-maps.com. http://d-maps.com/carte .php?num_car=26704&lang=en

tlers. "Do not spare cartridges," ordered Governor-General Kuropatkin of Turkestan. Entire villages were leveled by artillery fire or burned to the ground. Russian soldiers—and villagers—brought little credit upon themselves with their conduct, forcing Kuropatkin to complain that "many Russians are depraved to the core."[22]

In a testament to the lopsided nature of the conflict, one historian estimates that, while about 2,100 Russians were killed in the Semirech'ie region, nearly 263,000 Kyrgyz and Kazakhs died, with close to 124,000 fatalities in and around Karakol alone.[23] It was a massacre.

One story filtered down to Altay about a massacre several days after the monastery murders. While on the way to market outside Karakol with a Russian military escort leading them, Kyrgyz and Dungan residents were set upon by armed Russian peasants once the military escort had passed by.[24] In an article that he himself wrote on the 1916 revolt many years later, Altay reported that five hundred Kyrgyz and Dungans had been killed.[25]

———————

No longer feeling safe in their village down the shoreline from Karakol, Altay's father fled east with his parents and several siblings in the fall of 1916. They joined what is estimated to be 100,000 to 120,000 Kyrgyz fleeing for their lives over the mountains into China before winter set in. Many refugees were pursued by Russian soldiers through rocky gorges. Higher up into the mountains, they had to navigate narrow, slippery paths across centuries-old glacial ice. They were part of a continuous procession of ragged and destitute Kyrgyz—some steering animals, some with just the clothes on their backs—desperate to cross the mountain passes, some towering nearly thirteen thousand feet. Thousands didn't make it, with whole families, along with their camels and other livestock, sliding down to their deaths in deep gorges.

After a ten-day journey across the Ala-Too Mountains, Teke uulu and his family arrived in the oasis town of Aksu in China's westernmost Xinjiang Province. The welcome in China was harsh, with the Kyrgyz receiving little sympathy from the native Uighurs and local Chinese who themselves were struggling to survive in the hardscrabble frontier—not to mention that the arrival of the exiles sent food prices soaring.

To procure food and shelter, Kyrgyz families were forced to sell what possessions or heirlooms they had. Some families lived in animal quarters, spreading hay on the dirt floors. Lucky children found work as houseboys, while others were sold into servitude. Desperate Kyrgyz were forced to steal, making the plight of all Kyrgyz even worse.[26] Fleeing Kyrgyz made up a song to describe their pitiful condition as refugees in China:

> Hapless people on camel and horse,
> You are so thin, you wear shoes made of human skin
> Of those who have died on the way.
> You traded *bozo* [a mildly alcoholic grain beverage] on the way and
>   sold all that is good and bad, repainted the old and sold it as new.[27]

Unable to find work, family members started to weaken from hunger. Desperate and losing strength, Teke uulu's parents decided to return home so at least they could be buried on native soil. Determined to fulfill his parents' wish, Teke uulu, the oldest male child in the family, led the trip back in 1918. He clothed his parents warmly, fashioned a makeshift sleigh out of poles, and procured a horse. When he couldn't find enough food for the ten-day journey, his sister Kaldyk stepped forward, selling herself into marriage for thirty-two pounds of flour. "I will be satisfied if this sack of flour is enough to get you back to Kyrgyz soil," she told her teenage brother. "Leave now or the flour won't last, and then where will we find more flour?"

The return trip brought no solace. Both of Teke uulu's parents perished on the way, with his father dying on the ascent back into the mountains. Urging on the exhausted horse pulling the sleigh that carried his traumatized mother and his father's dead body, Teke uulu and his brother Mukhambet managed to traverse the Bedel Pass and bury their father on Kyrgyz soil. Ailing and stumbling refugees were also making their way back, some falling by the wayside. Their mother expired on the way down to the lake.

The 1916 rebellion and ensuing flight to China led to a sharp fall in the population of Turkestan, with one source reporting that approximately 270,000 Central Asians died. Exact figures are hard to come by. A high school textbook published in Kyrgyzstan in 2007 notes that the population of what is today the northern part of Kyrgyzstan decreased by 42 percent. But more recent research raises the numbers significantly, with claims that the Kyrgyz lost 40 percent of their population and that, had the tragedy not occurred, the population of Kyrgyzstan would today be twice what it is.[28] It's probable that between seventy thousand and one hundred thousand people perished in the mountains or in China. Recent visitors to the remote Bedel Pass report seeing the bones, skulls, and soles of shoes that still mark their ancestors' fateful route.[29]

—⁓—

Living far to the west, near the border with Uzbekistan, the Aitmatov family was out of harm's way when the national rebellion broke out in 1916. Situated in the Talas Valley, their home village of Sheker had natural protection. Mount Manas, a fifteen-thousand-foot-high snowcapped natural barrier, walled the village off to the south, and a span of the Ala-Too Mountains formed a barrier to the east.

In fact, natural boundaries and a lighter Russian footprint—which meant fewer forts and even fewer settlers than around Lake Issyk Kul—had helped insulate the Talas region from the excesses of the 1916 revolt. While villages around the lake had been razed and tens of thousands Kyrgyz forced to flee to China, Sheker had continued its mostly peaceful existence, a safe haven in turbulent times.

Known for thinking in new ways and taking risks, the Aitmatov family represented the Sheker clan's "progressive" wing. At the turn of the twentieth century, patriarch Aitmat, the grandfather of Chingiz Aitmatov, earned the nickname "machinist Aitmat" for having brought the first foot-pedal sewing machine to the village.

Restless and in search of a grander idea to further raise their families' economic fortunes, Aitmat and his brother Birimkul invested their life savings in a mill on the banks of the Kürküröö River, which coursed through the village from its source at Mount Manas. They enlisted family labor to dig the canal to the site and raise the mill's walls and roof. Business was brisk the first year, with some farmers even crossing the border from Kazakhstan to crush their wheat at the mill.

But misfortune struck when the mill burned to the ground one night in 1913. The brothers suspected that jealous relatives, in cahoots with a competitor, had set the fire. To this day, the abandoned millstone lies on the bank of the Kürküröö River—a testament to the Aitmatov family's snuffed-out dreams. Aitmat and his twelve-year-old son Törökul—Chingiz's father—were forced to take work on a nearby tsarist railroad project in 1915.

———

Upon arrival back at Lake Issyk Kul in the spring of 1918, Altay's father learned that the Bolshevik Revolution had overthrown the tsar. Information to this remote part of the tsar's former holdings traveled slowly and only with sketchy details: "The power of the poor has been established; the power of the rich has ended."[30] His father, an illiterate farmhand, hoped a new day was dawning.

The Bolshevik Revolution had roared through Central Asia like a desert storm, wiping away vestiges of the previous society and leaving in its place a revamped landscape. Whereas before a feudal order had reigned, with Kyrgyz society effectively controlled by a small group of wealthy landowners, now there was the Communist Party, alone at the top after the Bolsheviks had seized power in November 1917.[31]

Working through armed soviets, or workers' councils, the Bolsheviks quickly established control over the main cities of tsarist Turkestan. The revolution was a time of great hope for the Kyrgyz people, who—still

reeling from the war, the rebellion, and the ensuing flight to China—
believed they had been quite literally saved from extinction.

The Bolshevik appeal to the Muslims of Central Asia in December
1917 promised them freedom: "From this time, all of your beliefs and
customs, your national and cultural institutions are declared to be free
and inviolable. Establish your national life according to your own pattern
and wishes. This is your right. We carry on our banner the liberation of
the enslaved peoples of the entire world."[32] For many poor Kyrgyz who
were working as de facto slave laborers, the Bolshevik appeal was infec-
tious. They were told they could toss away their sharecropping life and
gain land, peace, and bread.

—⁓—

The revolutionary appeal struck a chord in Sheker. With the Bolsheviks promising to lift poor peasants out of poverty, Aitmat believed the
family had another chance to improve its standing. He also knew the Bolsheviks needed young aspirants. Aitmat's nephew Alimkul was blazing
a trail as the first chairman of the village soviet, commanding authority
as the man who had picked the location for the village when the Soviets
decreed that the Sheker clan settle into permanent housing. Törökul was
an aspiring communist pioneer, young, fervent, and bilingual in Kyrgyz
and Russian, which he had learned thanks to Russians at the railroad construction site who encouraged him to study at a Russian-language school.

Opportunities ensued, and in 1920 Törökul, just seventeen years old,
accepted work as the secretary of his district's party committee in Talas
Province. He then was picked to study in Moscow at the premier training
ground for young party cadre destined to work in Central Asia.

Aware that "backward" Central Asia needed special attention because
peasants oppressed by feudal lords fell outside Marxist theory of a struggling urbanized proletariat, Moscow was putting considerable resources
into training a cadre of local specialists. Törökul Aitmatov would return
a polished product from three years of study at the Communist University for the Toilers of the East, as comfortable in a Russian wooden house
drinking tea as he was in a Kyrgyz yurt drinking *kymyz*.[33] He was ripe
for grassroots party work—spreading the gospel of communism to his
fellow Kyrgyz.

Hoping to gain a parcel of land, Altay's father, Teke uulu, trekked eighteen miles by foot from the village of Korumduu in the foothills of the Ala-Too Mountains to Bokonbaevo, the nearest administrative center. He had heard that communist authorities were redistributing land and cattle expropriated from so-called kulaks, or wealthy landowners.

Teke uulu had struggled since returning to Issyk Kul in 1917. Without his own land or animals, the daily circumstances of his life had not changed much, and he mourned for his family. Not only had he lost both parents on the fatal trip back to Issyk Kul in 1918 and his sister Kaldyk to marriage in Xinjiang; he couldn't locate an older sister and brother. He hoped they had found refuge in the mountains but feared that they, too, had lost their lives in the 1916 revolt.

The next morning, Teke uulu got a windfall: nineteen acres of land, ten lambs, farm animals, and a horse. The horse was especially dear, a black colt that gave him a means of transport and, equally important, a measure of dignity in a society that revered men on horses.

The promise of the revolution was being fulfilled. Lenin was addressing some of the chief causes of the 1916 rebellion by redistributing land to local Kyrgyz, and the Kyrgyz in China were returning in droves. With land and animals, Teke uulu was well-off enough to get married and start raising a family.

Born in 1920, his son Azamat was a child of the revolution. His birth name, Kudaibergen, means "God given," and after the family losses he had endured, Teke uulu felt truly blessed to have a child, not to mention a boy in a traditional society that honored patriarchal lineages. Fortune was also smiling on the family's economic conditions. In just two years of work, Teke uulu became an independent farmer. The family moved into a house, five sisters followed, and ten lambs became sixteen. As they said in those days, if the ox didn't die and the cart didn't break, you would be okay, which meant you would never starve.

2

Seeds of Rebellion

As a young boy in the village of Korumduu, Azamat Altay would wake up to a vista of snowcapped mountains surrounding the village on three sides. The open side gave out onto Lake Issyk Kul, a hundred-mile by sixty-mile body of water that looked like an inland sea.

His family lived a nomadic life in tune with nature's rhythms: moving with their animals to high mountain pastures, or *jailoo*, in the summer and returning to their yurt by the Korumduu River in the fall. Located some ten thousand feet above sea level, Korumduu was a place of snow, hail, and thunder, and young Azamat loved to stand under a hailstorm and feel the burning sensation of the stones bouncing off his face.

Nature was Altay's playground. He told time by the sun, and his toys were pebbles, whips, and handmade dice and tops. From the age of six he helped his hardworking father with homesteading chores, like shepherding the family's hundred sheep and harvesting hay for the winter. While completely obedient to his father and elders in the village, as was tradition, Altay developed an independent spirit. One day Altay helped his father plant two poplar trees near the mud-walled house they lived in during the winter. The trees would grow up side by side with Azamat, marking his life as the first son of his father, the first member of his family to grow up under communism and the first generation to be educated. After the losses of 1916, a life of hope beckoned.

Like his nomadic forbearers, Azamat grew up in the saddle, roaming the foothills and, as was the tradition for Kyrgyz boys, competing in races during festivals. The Kyrgyz believe that God made horses with leftover clay from man, and to this day, horses hold a sacred place in

Kyrgyz culture. It's rare to find a Kyrgyz who hasn't ridden. "If you are only going to live one day," Kyrgyz say, "spend half of it in the saddle."

Horses have long been seen as fellow travelers with man through life, carrying him over mountain ridges, transporting him into battle, and providing nourishment. Their meat, packed into sausages, is considered a delicacy, and fizzy, fermented mare's milk is the closest thing to a national beverage.

—⁓—

By the mid-1920s, people in the village had enough to eat, and, importantly, there was peace. Villagers traded mostly with the Chinese, sending opium and grain over the mountain passes in return for clothes and shoes. Medical care was dispensed in the traditional way in line with Tengriism, the ancient religion of the tribal people of Central Asia that has features of shamanism, animism, and ancestor worship.[1]

Long into his old age, Altay would recall a particular episode. After a sleepless night, he awoke with a high fever. For the next few days, searing pain in his toe increased, and pus started to ooze from the swelling digit. Villagers were summoned, but their incantations to spirits proved fruitless.

With no one in the village able to help, the family summoned Teke uulu's younger sister, an illiterate woman from a village a day's journey away who was known as a healer. When Altay's aunt arrived, she took a sharpened piece of bone, heated it, and, while Altay was being held down by four men, pushed the makeshift knife into the affected toe. Amid the blood and pus streaming from the infection a white, inch-long worm crawled out. The pain immediately ebbed, and Altay was better in a few days.

Ignorance of modern medicine often meant life was unforgiving. Illnesses treated routinely today could be fatal. Even when more modern medical care started to arrive, courtesy of the Soviets, there was great suspicion. Epidemics ebbed, but barriers of ignorance were stubbornly resistant. Villagers unaccustomed to syringes and painkillers believed doctors to be guilty of killing a person if they administered medicine to a person who ultimately died; some even sought revenge.

In 1931, with just faith healers in the village and no trained doctors, Altay's five younger sisters died during a typhoid epidemic. Then in 1932, a week after giving birth to his sister Kargadai, his mother died. Altay himself may well have died of typhus if his father, seared by the loss of five daughters, hadn't relented and allowed doctors to treat his only son. At the age of eight, Altay started school, the first member of his family ever to do so. He studied well—in the whitewashed school building that was formerly the village landowner's house—and gained entry into a vocational boarding school located at the east end of the lake that specialized in horse breeding. He became known in his village as the boy who could read and write. In the summer at *jailoo*, at the end of the day he would read aloud some of the first published Kyrgyz-language books in Cyrillic script. When he got to the sad parts, the grandmothers and young girls would weep.

The early Soviet years brought needed peace and some prosperity, especially to landless peasants like Altay's father. But in the realm of politics, the rosy promises of Lenin and Stalin were coming up empty.

The Bolsheviks intended to create a completely new type of society, premised on a citizen indoctrinated in a communist way of life. That meant a fusion of the many different nationalities of the Soviet Union into a "Soviet man," one who spoke Russian, rejected religion, disavowed private property, and submitted to the directives of the Communist Party. The end goal was worldwide revolution. It was a recipe that rode roughshod over the individual, not to mention the extended family or clan structure of the nomadic Kyrgyz. Communist miscalculations, excesses, and brutality would ultimately mean the loss of millions of innocent lives over the ensuing decades.

There turned out to be little space in Bolshevik social engineering for Central Asians' own aspirations. The Soviet government created Central Asian communist republics out of tsarist Turkestan in 1924 and accorded each the trappings of statehood, such as its own government, national language, university, and academy of sciences. But in reality Moscow's long hand, exercised through obedient republican-level Communist Party organizations, controlled most facets of life.[2]

It was a deeply centralized system that quashed Central Asian hopes for freedom and independence, particularly sentiments for an independent Turkestan.[3] Then, just as they were doing in other parts of the Soviet Union, communist authorities sealed off Central Asia from its neighbors. Borders with Iran, Turkey, and Afghanistan were closed and wouldn't reopen for nearly seventy years, and the border with China was tightly controlled. Central Asia became enveloped in the Soviet system.

The Soviets reacted to threats outside and inside—many trumped up, some real—by clamping down. The broken revolution had sent opponents of the Bolsheviks fleeing to Siberia, where, with the support of foreign powers, they had established an alternative government and army. To support the ensuing civil war against the White Russians, as their opponents were known, the Soviets requisitioned farmers' produce, a policy that contained within it the seeds of Soviet authoritarianism to come.

Draconian policies in Turkestan, compounded by a decrease in arable land due to cotton cultivation and Slavic farmers' preference to export their produce, precipitated a widespread famine in which hundreds of thousands died.[4] Angling to take advantage of the chaos, British agents operating in Tashkent and across the border in lawless Xinjiang agitated for the upper hand in the struggle between British colonial India and Soviet-occupied Central Asia, in the last stages of what was known as the Great Game.

In their arrogant march toward a communist future, the Bolsheviks swept aside rival political currents in Central Asia, such as the Jadid movement, which, while it had roots in Islam, championed schools that taught secular curriculums. The destructive force was the Bolshevik-inspired Tashkent Soviet, Slavic in makeup, which treated the native populace with disdain.[5]

When Mustafa Chokai, the heir to the Jadid movement and head of the Muslim Provisional Government of Autonomous Turkestan, called for the creation of a united Turkestan, the Tashkent Soviet moved aggressively against it in January 1918. Filling its ranks with desperate World War I POWs from Germany and the Austro-Hungarian Empire who had been stranded in Central Asia, the Tashkent Soviet gave its soldiers free reign in the battle for Kokand, near the present-day Kyrgyz-Uzbek border. Rape and plunder followed, with homes, mosques, and caravanserai burned to the ground.[6]

The massacre of up to fourteen thousand Muslims by Soviet forces in Kokand helped to sow the seeds of rebellion in what became known as the Basmachi Revolt, a Central Asian offshoot of the civil war of the 1920s. Lenin's special emissary to Central Asia, Georgi Safarov, who later wrote a critical review of the Soviet takeover of Central Asia, described the bloody arrival of communism with a sardonic quip: "Will Russian freedom never come to an end?"[7]

The 1920s and 1930s brought more man-made calamity. With the rise of Stalin to power after Lenin's death in 1924, moderating tendencies to jump-start the Soviet economy were discarded. In its place, Stalin embarked on industrialization and forced collectivization, mass movements that caused more upheaval in the Soviet Union's Muslim republics.

—·—

In his first years of party work, Törökul Aitmatov's grassroots efforts were bolstered by the Communist Party's support of new cultural and educational institutions in Kyrgyzia. Newspapers, schools, theaters, and clubs of various sorts were accessible to the masses. Those innovations, coupled with remarkable gains in literacy, proved to be positive contributions of Soviet communism.[8]

But after working on the ground in Kyrgyzia for a few years, Törökul began to chafe at micromanagement from Moscow. The most glaring example was in educating youth about the Communist Party and its plans for Kyrgyzia. Believing that the work had to be undertaken by people who understood the local culture, he openly advocated for the training and advancement of local Kyrgyz cadre.

But, insistent on directing the building of communism from the center, Moscow sent specialists who neither understood the local situation nor spoke Kyrgyz. Törökul's views reflected frustration among the Kyrgyz elite, many of whom like Törökul had been educated in Moscow and thought of themselves as dedicated communists. They were becoming increasingly disappointed by Soviet retrenchment on independence.

Fed up with policies carried out by non-Kyrgyz imports, a group of progressive-minded Kyrgyz intellectuals and party officials drafted an alternative platform—called the Letter of Thirty—in 1925 and sent it to top party officials in Central Asia and Moscow. The letter criticized the dominance of the Communist Party in the governing of Soviet Kyrgyzia.

In theory, government ministries were supposed to conduct day-to-day affairs in Kyrgyzia, but in reality they had become "water carriers" for the party. Specifically, the letter objected to official business being done in Russian, demanded the ouster of Russian communists from leading posts and called for an overhaul in personnel appointment, with more Kyrgyz trained to work in government and hiring to be done regardless of class origin. The views of the Letter of Thirty reflected Törökul's concerns, but he himself was not a signatory.

The response was swift, mostly because spies had infiltrated the group. Influential signers were removed from their posts and punished: one was executed, two sentenced to long jail terms, and others exiled to far regions of the Soviet Union. There would be no opposing voices or debate in Stalin's Soviet Union.

In 1926 at the east end of Lake Issyk Kul in the city of Karakol, where he was working, Törökul Aitmatov's own dissenting statements caught the attention of the local police, who accused him of promoting a "nationalist line." It was a potentially career-ending charge. But Törökul was too effective a party operative to sideline. When the Kyrgyz Communist Party needed a "fireman" for volatile Jalalabad District in the south in 1927, they called on Törökul.[9]

To the dismay of Törökul Aitmatov and others in the Kyrgyz elite, the Soviet government steamrolled ahead with controversial policies: accelerating the building of communism at home by instituting a planned economy, where decisions on the production and distribution of food and goods were made by ministries in Moscow.

A key driver of the planned economy was forced collectivization, which undid the most progressive reforms of the early Soviet period—such as granting land and farm animals to landless peasants like Altay's father—in favor of herding peasants onto collective farms, where they worked for the state. The holdings of large landowners were wiped out, and many of the wealthiest landowners were deported to Ukraine and Russia.[10]

In 1929 Altay's father was assigned to work in the village kolkhoz called the Lenin Collective Farm, which had been built on the expropriated holdings of a wealthy kulak who had been deported to Ukraine.

Doubts about the course of communism troubled the highest-ranking Kyrgyz official in the republic. In September 1928, Jusup Abdrakhmanov, the twenty-eight-year-old chairman of the Government of Kyrgyzia, despaired about the corroding effect of Moscow party domination. "Uncertainty and doubts about policy of the day are leading to a fall in the mood of the middle rank of party workers," he wrote. "I personally have a bad mood towards Moscow and am struck by the bureaucracy and hopeless pessimism of party activists."[11]

Abdrakhmanov concluded that Stalin's policy of building socialism throughout the Soviet Union was impoverishing the Kyrgyz people. He was particularly incensed by Moscow's decision to transform Central Asia into a cotton-producing region, thus marginalizing the production of wheat. In 1933, when that policy contributed to widespread famine, he countermanded Moscow's requisition of wheat, directing that the grain be used instead to bake bread locally to feed starving people pouring over the border from Kazakhstan.

In southern Kyrgyzia, Törökul Aitmatov walked into a powder keg. Tension over collectivization was exploding. Rich settlers, wealthy landowners, and religious clerics, who together held about 80 percent of the land in Jalalabad, were opposing land redistribution and changes to water rights that undergirded collectivization. Some Kyrgyz preferred to slaughter their livestock rather than deliver them to state collective farms. Others fled with their herds to China, and the most desperate took up arms and replenished the ranks of the Basmachi rebels, who would fight against Soviet power from hideouts in the mountains until 1933.

In Jalalabad, which fronts on the Uzbek border, Basmachi rebels were stirring up divisions between local Uzbeks and Kyrgyz and making raids on villages before retreating into the mountains, all in attempts to torpedo land reforms that had worked successfully in the north. The situation threatened to spin out of control, with rumors gaining traction among the local Uzbek population that, under the pretense of land reform, the local Kyrgyz were taking land from Uzbeks in order to drive them across the border into Uzbekistan.

As the head of the commission on land and water reform, Törökul Aitmatov sought to communicate with all parties. During meetings with peasants in both communities, he explained how plans to bring in agricultural equipment, dig better irrigation canals, and consult agronomists would increase agricultural production. The situation quieted down, and, by April 1929, once water problems had improved and peasant collectives had gained access to tractors and plows, villagers were lining up behind the policy.

Törökul's successes did not go unnoticed. In 1931, impressed by Törökul's crisis management skills and willingness to buck the system, head of the government Abdrakhmanov made a bid for Törökul to be the No. 2 person in the government. But the Communist Party won out over the government and again dispatched Törökul to the south. This time, he was sent as the top party official to calm the situation in Aravan, near Kyrgyzia's second-largest city, Osh, where the collectivization process was lagging.

Using a combination of organizational skills and exhortation, and introducing new agricultural machinery and techniques, Törökul Aitmatov turned the situation around in favor of the Communist Party. Some claim that in Aravan he advanced collectivization too eagerly by subjecting middle-class families—in addition to wealthy landowners—to confiscation of property and exile from their home regions.[12] Whatever his methods, he was in accord with party policy of the day, called dekulakization, which was to wage "an offensive against the kulaks."[13] Törökul was a sensitive soul, but also obedient.

When Törökul left Aravan in 1934, the district was at the top of the Kyrgyz Republic for fulfilling plan quotas in cotton and wheat. Villagers named the new collective farm in Aravan after Aitmatov and even made up a song about him:

> Hey, you, peasant on a white horse.
> Aitmatov cares like the father of the people and calls on you
> To take the fate of the people into your hands
> And become the master of your land.[14]

In part due to the efforts of Törökul Aitmatov, by 1933 nearly 70 percent of peasant households in Kyrgyzia had been absorbed into the kolkhozes, or collective farms, of the state system.[15] In the name of communist progress, a nation of nomadic herders had been forced to settle into permanent dwellings. A pastoral way of life was in retreat, and a reign of terror was ahead.

———

A few years after Altay's father joined the collective farm, the purges in Kyrgyzia took root. Opposition to the radical policy measures of recent years, coupled with Stalin's increasing paranoia about a hostile world, pushed the Communist Party's demonization of opponents to new heights. The first stage of the purges in 1932–1933 targeted so-called counterrevolutionaries and supporters of local nationalism.

The Soviet secret police blackened the names of leading lights of Kyrgyz society by associating them with the Socialist Turan Party (STP), which they charged was a counterrevolutionary organization intent on overthrowing Soviet power. The secret police connected the party to shadowy groups over the border in Xinjiang and to revolts inside the republic sparked by opposition to collectivization.

In fact, the STP was a pretext for removing disgruntled individuals who had openly challenged Soviet power.[16] Signers of the Letter of Thirty were prime targets, including head of government Abdrakhmanov, who at the end of 1933 was expelled from the party and jailed. Kasym Tynystanov, a beloved literary figure and editor of the first newspaper in Kyrgyzia, was accused in 1933 of membership in STP and jailed.

The purges took a bloody turn nationwide following the Kirov Affair in 1934, when Leningrad party boss Sergei Kirov was murdered, allegedly by spies working to undermine Stalin's leadership. But the whole affair was likely concocted to launch a purge of Stalin's enemies, perceived and real, inside and out of Soviet ruling structures.[17] No longer satisfied with public denunciation or imprisonment of opponents, Stalin and his allies embarked on a campaign of physical annihilation and mass terror, which led to one of the greatest human tragedies in the twentieth century.

———

The Great Purges dominated the thinking of a maturing Altay. From reading regional newspapers—which carried the party line on the purges to villages around Lake Issyk Kul—he believed that bourgeois nationalists, saboteurs, and the homegrown Basmachi in the nearby mountains were enemies of the common people. In debates with his fellow students, Altay, a rising star in the communist youth movement, took the party's side.

Like Törökul Aitmatov, as an educated boy from the village, Altay was just the kind of person the Communist Party wanted to influence to strengthen its position in the countryside. He rose quickly in the Pioneers, which was akin to a politicized Boy Scouts. A successful stint in the Pioneers led to membership in the highly selective Komsomol, which captivated Altay with its strong ethos of community service in the Kyrgyz countryside. "Was it not my dearest wish, too, to get an education so that I might do all in my power to save Kirgiz mothers from starvation and Kirgiz children from epidemics, and to introduce culture into Kirgiz villages, not as a strange monstrosity, but as help to the Kirgiz people," he wrote years later about his time in the Komsomol.[18]

Altay himself had a personal stake in bringing change to the countryside. As was often the custom in villages, he had been betrothed at birth to an infant girl in the village. That contract saddled his parents with an annual dowry payment, called *kalym*. When that girl died at age thirteen, her elder sister became Altay's bride-to-be. His parents tried every means to drive him into marriage, but the teenage Altay squirmed away, saying he had to continue his studies in Frunze.[19] Eventually, he faced down his father in a generational battle, telling him that he would not marry the villager and that all the money his father had paid over the years in *kalym* should be considered a loss.

Freed from such obligations, Altay studied well at a vocational school for teachers in the capital of Frunze, where he was encouraged by the Komsomol to write articles about his hometown for the Komsomol newspaper. He set the goal of becoming part of the educated elite of his generation to help address the lack of genuine intellectuals in Kyrgyzia.

But as a loyal Komsomol member who read the Kyrgyz-language *Pioneer* newspaper cover to cover, Altay feared that the gains of the revolution might be wiped out by the party's enemies. Playing on such fears, the People's Commissariat of Internal Affairs, or NKVD, which became the engine of the bloody purges under Stalin, snatched up individuals across the Soviet republics.

In Soviet Kyrgyzia, specially briefed party workers would do the NKVD's bidding during meetings in schools, government offices and collective farms. Drawing on informers at the local level and dossiers of information compiled over years, the party workers "unmasked" people with only the slightest connection to higher-ups who had already been arrested. In Altay's own village, teachers were arrested for merely using an arrested writer's books in their classes.

A sense of powerlessness spread across Kyrgyzia. A person could be arrested on the slightest pretense. Altay's close friend Saken Koichubaev, a twenty-year old who worked in the kolkhoz warehouse, was hauled away one night in 1936 and imprisoned. His offense: suggesting to a visiting party official that instead of criticizing the kolkhoz for delayed grain deliveries the official should offer some help.

The arrest of Kasym Tynystanov cast a pall over Altay and his idealistic friends. As one of the creators of the Kyrgyz alphabet and a respected poet, Tynystanov was the pride of the nation, a man who personified the possibility of a poor boy from Issyk Kul becoming learned. After having battled his opponents for years through newspaper articles and public declarations, Tynystanov was a broken man at the age of thirty-two. But that didn't deter the NKVD. Thousands of Tynystanov's colleagues and acquaintances were also arrested, including some who had visited him in the hospital. Not content with breaking the man, communist authorities set up a special commission to confiscate Tynystanov's books.

The arrests of Kyrgyzia's most famous writers followed Tynystanov's detention. Eventually, the purges confiscated textbooks and swept up most of the teachers at Altay's vocational high school, leaving Altay and his fellow students to wait in classrooms for the few teachers who were still available to arrive from teaching lessons at other schools.

Was the gift of reading and writing, one of the accomplishments of Soviet power, actually a curse that could land an educated and patriotic Kyrgyz in jail? Altay stated to feel uneasy. In a hint of counterrevolutionary sentiment bubbling up, he asked a friend to conceal his own collection of Tynystanov's books from the commission's prying arms. When Altay returned home in the summer, he buried the books in the ground in an iron box.

Indeed, the seeds of rebellion were stirring inside Altay. He and his fellow students could no longer distinguish truth from lies. Endless discussions in the dormitory left him questioning what was happening. The answers of feckless bureaucrats infuriated him more. When Altay and his fellow students dared to question the chairman of the Frunze City Education Department about the treatment of a fellow student, they were told, "There are state agencies to discover who is an enemy or a friend, and they know their business better than any of us."[20]

⸺⁂⸺

In the tense and dangerous atmosphere following Kirov's murder in 1934, while working as the number two party official in Kyrgyzia, Törökul Aitmatov clashed with his superior, Communist Party chief Morris Belotski, about the mass arrests of leading party and government officials in 1935, including the rearrest of Kasym Tynystanov. "How is it possible to call these people 'enemies of the people?'" he protested to Belotski's charges when they requested that he confirm a list of future arrests. "These are true patriots of their people."[21]

While it was clear to Belotski that Törökul was sympathetic to some of the demands of the so-called opposition, there was insufficient evidence to link Aitmatov to them. And his stellar record of serving the party in troublesome spots in Kyrgyzia had pushed him up to the powerful second secretary position. Unable to remove the efficacious Aitmatov, Belotski arranged for him to be transferred to Moscow where he was assigned to study at the Higher Institute of Marxism-Leninism and the more famous Institute of Red Professors.[22]

For the Aitmatov family, Moscow was a pleasant interlude during a grim time. The privileges that came with Törökul's studies made the family feel special: they had a comfortable two-room flat in a student dormitory in central Moscow and maid service to help with cleaning and errands. The adult students in the dormitory came from other Soviet republics, making life on a daily basis a bit like being at the League of Nations, with different languages spoken, food cooked, and holidays celebrated. The older Aitmatov boys, seven-year-old Chingiz and younger brother Ilgiz, played with the "international" contingent of children from other Soviet republics. At school in Moscow, Chingiz became adept in reading, writing and speaking Russian, just like his parents.[23]

Törökul and Nagima Aitmatov met in Karakol in 1926. Törökul's appearance at the doorway of the local Komsomol office had stunned the twenty-one-year-old Nagima. Even though dressed in the faded, quasimilitary garb of a party official, Törökul cut a dashing figure, with a shock of black hair above a broad face and sparkling eyes. Törökul would later describe their chance acquaintance—not hatched by parents like most weddings at the time in Kyrgyzia—as a meeting arranged by God.

Nagima was an educated woman from a prominent Tatar family in Karakol.[24] With brown hair, aquiline features, and a light skin tone, she looked European, and like many Tatars, she straddled two cultures: Europeanized Russian culture on the one hand, and Turkic Muslim culture on the other. In fact, because they possessed business acumen and spoke a Turkic language very close to the Kyrgyz and Kazakh languages, Tatars had been used by tsarist authorities as liaisons between Russians and Central Asians since the 1700s. Many Tatars had worked as teachers of Russian in the first schools opened up under tsarist rule in Central Asia. Others, like Nagima's father, saw business opportunities on the fringes of the Russian Empire and became successful merchants.

Nagima's father, Hamza Abduvaliev, built a leather factory, buying rawhide from the nomads and producing leather for belts, boots, and shoes. In his spare time, Hamza became a Tatar Johnny Appleseed, collecting different kinds of apples from Russia and breeding them with local sorts in an orchard at the edge of town that is still known as "Abduvaliev's garden."

But the Abduvaliev family fell on hard times after the Bolshevik Revolution. Hamza was targeted as a wealthy kulak; his two-story house lined with Persian rugs in the center of Karakol was confiscated, his department stores and savings nationalized, and his land expropriated as part of the land reform campaign carried out in the 1920s. He and his wife moved into a modest two–room house near the orchard. A graduate of the Women's High School in Karakol, Nagima was denied a chance to take entrance exams for medical school because she was the daughter of a so-called *bai*, or wealthy merchant.

In spite of the pain the revolution had inflicted upon her family, Nagima became a secretary in the Karakol Komsomol office and took up the cause of communism. After her marriage to Törökul in 1926, she set an example as a liberated Soviet woman in Jalalabad and Aravan, speaking out against polygamy, the wearing of veils, and domestic violence.

———

Befitting their allegiance to the Communist Party, Törökul and Nagima were bringing up their children in a new way—to become model Soviet citizens. Törökul refused to strike Chingiz or his siblings if they misbehaved, preferring to admonish them verbally (see figure 2.1). Nagima was raising the children herself instead of leaving them in the care of relatives in the village as was often done in Kyrgyzia. To prepare the

Figure 2.1: Törökul Aitmatov with son Chingiz, date unknown. Source: Central State Archives of the Kyrgyz Republic.

children to go to school at an early age, she set specified times for meals and put the children to bed on a regular schedule. That was a far cry from the normal life of children in Kyrgyzia, whose lives revolved around seasons, not clocks, and whose time was taken up by caring for animals and daily chores, not textbooks.

In other ways, too, the Aitmatov family was exemplary. Both Törökul and Nagima understood that knowledge of Russian, the lingua franca of the republics of the Soviet Union, meant connection with a wider world and could open up opportunities far beyond landlocked Soviet Kyrgyzia, with its population of just a few million people. Both spoke, read, and wrote Russian fluently, and they imparted to Chingiz and his siblings a love of Russian literature and culture. In Moscow, Törökul would take Chingiz to watch the latest films and visit the famous House of Writers and the House of Film Actors.

Young Chingiz's knowledge of Russian was already paying dividends. A few years earlier when he was spending the summer in the mountains outside Sheker, village elders had called on him to translate their conversation with a Russian veterinarian. The elders were in a panic because the kolkhoz's newly purchased stallion had suddenly keeled over and died. The local shepherds in the kolkhoz had been counting on this particular stallion from Russia to improve their stock of horses.

And now it was dead, its eyes glassy and stomach bloated out. To avoid punishment for losing such prized property, the kolkhoz would need an official document attesting to the cause of death. For this they had to explain to the visiting veterinarian that the imported horse had eaten poisonous grass that local horses knew to avoid.

Ready to discuss his findings after inspecting the deceased horse, the red-haired veterinarian began to speak, but his five-year-old translator ran away and hid in the family yurt. Chingiz's relatives reprimanded him: "What will this Russian man say about how badly we are raising our Kyrgyz children?" A chastened Chingiz made his way back to the group and interpreted back and forth as the shepherds explained the cause of death to the animal doctor. The visitor completed the official form, and the kolkhoz was off the hook. Chingiz had bridged the communication gap, and he scampered off with a piece of boiled meat as his reward.

But the halcyon days of the pastures and Moscow were in the past. Now it seemed poisonous grasses were surrounding the communist experiment all over the Soviet Union, including Soviet Kyrgyzia.

———

Between 1934 and 1938, the Stalin-directed purges decimated the ranks of the Communist Party hierarchy, the armed forces, and the country's scientific and intellectual elite, and reduced Soviet citizens to a supine people. In terms of total human loss, one American historian put the number at eight million purge victims in camps and another one million in prisons.[25]

Up to forty thousand Kyrgyz citizens are believed to have lost their lives as a result of the purges, including nine of fourteen of the republic's Communist Party general secretaries, all of whom were executed in 1937 or 1938. In an account he wrote in 1961 on the purges in Kyrgyzia, Altay described Kyrgyz citizens during the time as "silent witnesses to a savage nightmare."[26] In Altay's village, thirteen people were arrested; only one was seen alive again. That was 1939, and the lone survivor returned to the village, gaunt and skeleton-like. When Altay pressed him about his experience, he said, "I wouldn't wish my worst enemy to experience what I've seen and been through."

If the arrival of Soviet power had restored confidence in Russian-Kyrgyz relations that was lost during 1916, then the purges, with their decimation of the ethnic Kyrgyz elite, sent the Kyrgyz people reeling backward again.

The purges nearly swallowed up Altay himself. Returning home from Frunze for the summer holidays in 1936, he and his fellow students discovered they were on the same steamer as one of the most decorated party officials in the republic, Abdykadyr Orozbekov. The ride across Lake Issyk Kul took several hours, and the students sang to pass the time. Orozbekov, then in his twelfth year as the chairman of the Kyrgyz Communist Party's executive committee, joined in, singing and sharing food with the group of young students.

A year later, Orozbekov was fired from his job and declared an "enemy of the people." He was executed later that year. As part of the campaign against Orozbekov, a teacher from Karakol alleged in a newspaper article that Orozbekov had trained students to be "bourgeois nationalists." The article even mentioned the trip on the steamer in the summer of 1936. Fortunately for Altay, the author didn't mention any names of students. He continued his rise in a party he had begun to doubt.

During his studies in Bishkek, on account of his good record and correct class origin, Altay had been asked to become a reporter for the *Young Pioneer* newspaper in Frunze. He became quite an investigative reporter, particularly in his native Issyk Kul region, writing revealing articles about unprepared schools and absent principals. On a reporting trip to his home village in 1939, he exposed a local Communist Party official who had married three young girls in quick succession. Altay joined the Communist Party in the summer of 1940, and his life took a familiar trajectory when in the fall of 1940 he was drafted into the Soviet Army and sent to Soviet-occupied Lithuania to guard the border (see figure 2.2).

Later in life, he would rue his youth spent in service of the Komsomol as "a symbol of my naïve and fruitless hopes, and as a symbol of my delusion."[27]

Figure 2.2: Azamat Altay (born Kudaibergen Kojomberdiev), center, as a young Soviet Army conscript in the early 1940s. Source: Photo courtesy of Gulnara Turganbaeva.

In 1937 Communist Party plenums in Kyrgyzia, taking their lead from Stalin's directive to wage more hostile class struggle, launched attacks against "unfavorable elements" in the Kyrgyz Communist Party. Following events closely from Moscow, Törökul saw how vague accusations, including terms like "disloyalty," "Trotskyism," and "world revolution," were being wielded like sharpened swords.

Törökul knew he was in trouble when the man who had recruited him into the Communist Party, Minister of Health Khodshahan Shorukov, was targeted not for his work in the health field but because of his friendship with former head of government Abdrakhmanov. To charges of disloyalty had been added accusations of mere association: if a person was arrested, that meant that ten of his colleagues could be snatched up for merely having had comradely relations.

Sensing that his arrest was imminent, Törökul prepared an escape plan for his family. He needed a remote place to hide Nagima and the children. In August 1937 he told Nagima to pack for a trip to Sheker. "Tell the children they are going to the dacha," Törökul said.[28]

Törökul knew that in remote Talas his children had the best chance of survival as offspring of an "enemy of the people." There, shielded by mountains and protected by layers of family, the children could best avoid being deposited in orphanages, given name changes, or separated.

In the face of a widening witch hunt, however, Törökul—a loyal party member to the core—refused to believe that Soviet communism was at fault. Rather, he insisted that an unsupervised NKVD running amok was the cause of the chaos and that the out-of-control internal security service would soon be reined in. "I am not guilty, and will be freed soon," he told Nagima before the family's departure in August 1937. "I believed in Soviet power and the Bolsheviks. The October Revolution saved the Kyrgyz people from genocide. The whole race would have been exterminated. Soviet power opened our eyes and liquidated illiteracy. That's why I am thankful."[29]

3

Have the Mountains Fallen?

On an August day in 1937, Chingiz Aitmatov pressed his cheeks against the window to catch a final glimpse of his father in the cavernous Kazan Train Station, the passenger depot in Moscow for trains heading to Central Asia. As the locomotive gathered speed, Chingiz watched as Törökul ran to keep up with the train and then faded into the distance.

Inside the train cabin, holding six-month-old baby Roza, Nagima wiped tears from her eyes, and turned her attention to her three older children. The younger ones were giddy over the news they were headed to the dacha. On the upper bunk, though, nine-year-old Chingiz was inconsolable. He remembered his parents' farewell embrace moments before in the compartment: his father's quivering lips and his mother's tears. Something was horribly wrong.

Sobs continued from the upper bunk. "We are not alone, son," Nagima comforted her eldest child. "Not alone. Just look and see how many people are around you." But Chingiz couldn't be fooled. His father was gone, and filled with dread, he feared he would never see him again.

After a seven-day journey, the Moscow train pulled into Maimak Station in the northwest corner of Soviet Kyrgyzia in the early morning hours of September 1. Nagima gathered the family's luggage, corralled her groggy children, and cradled Roza. With help from fellow passengers, one after another members of the family jumped to the ground. The train was off a few minutes later.

For Nagima, the last days in Moscow had been a hazy blur of packing and panic. Her last words to Törökul before he exited the train in Moscow still echoed in her head: "I leave you in God's hands. We have no other hope." With her feet on the ground in Central Asia, the realization hit Nagima that she was on her own, solely responsible for her four children. In a chill wind, Chingiz and Ilgiz dragged the family's suitcases and bags to the one-story station house, sticking close to their mother who was holding Roza and leading three-year-old Lucia by the hand. The family waited in the hall of the station house until morning, when relatives arrived in a horse-drawn cart to take them back to Sheker.

Sheker as a safe haven made the only sense in the crazy world surrounding the Aitmatov family. It was isolated and full of family. High mountains rose to protect it, and friendly territory stretched for miles around. Relations with Kazakhs across the nearby border were familial because the Kyrgyz and Kazakhs shared a similar language, culture, and religion.

Talas's tribal structure—which was an obstacle to the Soviet idea of creating a modern man—was a boon for beleaguered Nagima and her family. The Soviets wanted to socially engineer a man devoid of class sensibilities, but they could not—and would never—replace the hierarchical and patriarchal nature of Kyrgyz society, which had been protecting individuals and families for thousands of years.[1]

The tribal structure in Sheker centered on the Sheker clan, which was part of a larger tribe called Kitai. Over the centuries, families in Sheker had consolidated through annual treks to high mountain pastures, sharing food in hard times, and marrying their sons and daughters off to one another in better times. Benefits of the clan were several: it gave a young man a ready-made identity, bonded him together with his neighbors, facilitated pooled labor, and provided a safety net. Families instructed their boys from a young age about the history of preceding generations. Only by knowing his family's lineage would a boy be considered a worthy descendant, youngsters were told. Village elders took pride in testing them, occasionally tweaking them on the ears as they passed by: "Hey, little warrior, who is the father of your father? What kind of person was he, and what did he do?" If a boy did not know the names of seven preceding generations of male descendants in his clan, called *sanjira* in Kyrgyz, he was an embarrassment to his family. Worse, he could be derided as a slave, the lowest insult for freedom-loving nomads.

———

Aunt Karakyz was the bedrock of the Aitmatov family in Sheker. Though just in her early thirties, Karakyz-apa, as she was called, had sad eyes and a lined face, testament to the hardship she had had to overcome in Sheker's traditional society. Two decades earlier, when she was thirteen years old, Karakyz—with long eyelashes, black hair hanging in sixteen braids and skin the color of ripened wheat—had caught the eye of a wealthy married man from the next village. His name was Minbai, and he was on the prowl for a second wife to bear him children.

With her father Aitmat working away from the village on the railroad, Karakyz's uncle Birimkul had stepped in to handle family affairs. That was bad luck. Whereas Aitmat had only one wife and had bucked tradition by allowing his oldest daughter, Ayimkul, to marry at the "late" age of nineteen, Birimkul was more steeped in tribal ways: a polygamist himself, he didn't care if Minbai was more than three times older than his niece. Hoping to offset the damage done to the family's livestock by freezing temperatures, Birimkul agreed to marry off Karakyz to Minbai in exchange for a substantial dowry that would help the Aitmatov clan survive until summer.

In the accepted tradition of the time, Karakyz had no say in the matter; she was a commodity to be bartered for the betterment of the family. And at thirteen she was deemed ready for marriage. As the Kyrgyz saying went, "If a teenage girl doesn't fall from being struck by a man's fur hat, she can withstand marriage."[2]

After the wedding ceremony, Karakyz escaped from her new husband and jumped into bed with her mother and sister, as any scared teenager might do. But women relatives, doing the bidding of the groom's first wife, worked as enforcers—a second wife can lessen the workload for female members of the family—and dragged a shrieking Karakyz back to the wedding yurt. When Karakyz escaped again, the rich groom threw up his hands in disgust. The ugly scene repeated itself, but eventually Karakyz had to submit. She untied her braids in the morning in a sign she was no longer a virgin.

After her childhood marriage in 1917, Karakyz had remained with the wealthy merchant for ten years, but she never bore him any children. Only in the late 1920s, when Soviet power had taken a strong stand against polygamy, did she return to Sheker, where of her own accord she married Dosali, a hunter.

Willful and scarred, Karakyz had strong opinions that she wasn't afraid to air, even in the middle of the Great Purges. Though unschooled, she was wise, and she possessed a fighting spirit that influenced young Chingiz as he embarked on life without a father.

——~~——

In 1937, communist authoritarianism was shaking the foundations of Kyrgyzia with its assault on defenseless and guiltless people. Its face in Soviet Kyrgyzia—an NKVD agent named Valeri Khodakov who was working as a journalist—arrived in Frunze in early September 1937. Taking his lead from Stalin's directive to wage class struggle, Khodakov wrote articles in *Pravda* that excoriated "bourgeois nationalists" in the Kyrgyz party leadership and government, accusing them of being slow in removing "fascist agents" from party ranks. By naming specific people in power, Khodakov's article gave the green light to the NKVD to pursue so-called enemies of the people.[3]

Only in a totalitarian system could a single journalist's written words gain the power of an executioner's sword.

The accusations rippled across the mountains and valleys of Soviet Kyrgyzia, all the way to the Talas Valley. "I have bad news," Alimkul said to Nagima as he handed her the September 13, 1937, edition of *Pravda*. There, in an article entitled "Rotting Policy of the Communist Party of Kyrgyzia," Nagima saw Törökul's name among thirteen high-ranking Communist Party officials incriminated by Khodakov.[4]

Over the next several weeks, in cryptic writing designed to evade censors reading the mail, Törökul informed Nagima he had been kicked out of the party at a meeting at the Institute of Red Professors in Moscow and that he expected to be arrested and sent to Frunze. He kept a brave face. At a gathering with fellow Kyrgyz students studying in Moscow before he was deported, he did not waver: "I don't like this story," he told fellow students of the ongoing witch hunt. "But justice sooner or later will win."[5]

Then the dominoes started to fall in Sheker. The first person taken from the family was Alimkul, the bearer of bad news to Nagima. A month after the family's arrival, three NKVD agents dismounted from horses in front of Alimkul's house, tied his hands, and rode him away on a horse like an outlaw in a western movie. Except Alimkul had committed no crime: he had merely extended help to his relatives, like any caring human would do.

Törökul's younger brother Ryskulbek was next, expelled from the Frunze Teacher's Institute. Shortly after he returned to Sheker and moved in with Karakyz, he was arrested and sent to Siberia. Hoping to escape arrest, Alimkul's younger brother Ozubek, who worked as a policeman in the village, fled. But he was caught, arrested, and sent to prison. Three male relatives of the Aitmatov family had disappeared within two months for helping the family of an enemy of the people. Sheker was isolated but not impregnable.

In what turned out to be his last letter, Alimkul informed the family that he was working in lead mines at a labor camp near the border with Kazakhstan. He expressed more concern about his cousin Törökul's fate than his own. But it was the fate of eighteen-year-old Ryskulbek that broke the family's heart. Just a student at the time, Ryskulbek was dealt with in an inexplicably harsh way. He was sent to a Siberian labor camp where prisoners were worked to death. In his last communication with the family, he told them he was building roads near the border with Manchuria. Suffering from kidney problems, he couldn't fulfill his workload and was being punished with reduced food rations in the bitterly cold winter.[6] He was wasting away. "I understand your situation," he wrote to his family in Kyrgyz, "but if you can, please send me a packet of talkan. I promise I won't make such requests often. I just need some to get me through the next five or six months."[7]

None of the men—Alimkul, Ozubek, or Ryskulbek—was ever seen again.

Törökul's letter to Nagima, dated November 26, closed out with a message for his children, whose well-being was always on his mind: "Be strong for the children. I will send school notebooks [for them] the next time."

No package ever arrived. Unbeknownst to his family, Törökul was arrested five days later. He arrived in Frunze prison on January 14, 1938, traveling by train through the same railroad tunnel he had helped build as a young boy, at a spot just twelve miles from his family in Sheker. The heartbreak must have been excruciating: to know his family was just miles away but unreachable.

In November 1938, when the time came for his trial on charges of disloyalty to the Soviet Union, Törökul had prepared for any outcome. Denied permission to communicate with his family, he asked a fellow prisoner from Talas, Tenirberdi Alapaev, to pass word.

"Explain to my family that I was wrongly accused," he told Alapaev. "My oldest son Chingiz—he's a very good boy, tender and responsible. He can't tolerate a person suffering," Törökul continued. "Humanism, kindness, these are good traits, but you have to know how to courageously oppose injustice. What's going to happen to him? I ask you, please speak with him, tell him to be courageous, strong and prepared for any difficulties. And explain to him that if I don't return, he will be the oldest male in the family, the first helper of his mother."

Törökul explained to his cellmate a signal system that would work in the event he didn't return after his sentencing. If Törökul asked through a militiaman for soap from his toilet kit, that meant he had been transferred to another jail and would likely be executed. If he asked for a comb, he had been exiled to Siberia, and if asked for his toothbrush, he had been sent to the Urals.

Then he handed Alapaev a handmade toiletry bag he had stitched together from towels. On the front, as if to remind the fellow prisoner of his duties, Törökul had sewn the names of his two sons, Chingiz and Ilgiz, and the Cyrillic letters for *T, A, L,* and *A* for Talas. He didn't have enough thread to finish the word.

"If we don't see each other again in this world," Törökul said in parting, "then I'll see you in the next life."[8]

———

Törökul Aitmatov was at the tail end of a cruel and systematic process that unfairly victimized tens of thousands of Kyrgyz. Indeed, the Soviet penchant for planning took on a sickening twist during the purges. The local NKVD branch in Kyrgyzia would receive its operational orders from Moscow in quotas: for example, for the first quarter of 1938, 35 people were to be shot, 1,250 to be jailed for twenty-five years, and 3,740 to be given a ten-year jail sentence. NKVD employees would then begin their "harvest" according to the plan.

In a testament to the inhumanity of the system, a former NKVD employee in Soviet Kyrgyzia admitted the easiest part was executing the smaller numbers of people in the first group. It was more difficult to meet the quotas for the second or third groups; in the case of underfulfillment, NKVD employees themselves faced the penalty of death. Completing a vicious circle, special sections of the NKVD spied on its own employees.[9] It is estimated that across the Soviet Union fifty thousand NKVD employees were murdered during the purges.[10]

More than a year and a half passed before the Aitmatov family was informed by the NKVD that Törökul had been sentenced to ten years in prison for trying to overthrow the Soviet government.

That was the first lie.

In October 1939, Nagima herself wrote to the head of the NKVD Lavrentia Beria, requesting that Törökul's case be reviewed because it had come to light that many people had been wrongly accused of being enemies of the people. The NKVD's reply was swift and blunt: Törökul Aitmatov had been sentenced properly and had been sent to the gulags without the right to communicate with his family.

That was the second lie. Others would follow, giving Nagima false hope that her husband was alive and might one day return.

—◌◌◌—

In the middle of the horror that had engulfed the Aitmatov family, there was a measure of respite in Karakyz's house, where Nagima and her family had moved after the arrest of the male relatives. The family made a quick survival calculation: as a simple hunter with no political ties and little dependence on the government, Karakyz's husband, Dosali, was less likely to be tainted through association with the family of an enemy of the people. The two families lived under one roof, with each allotted a room for sleeping and sharing a common room with a rudimentary kitchen and fireplace.

In humble surroundings, out of the range of prying eyes and diaboli-
cal minds, ten-year-old Chingiz found a salve. Already fearing that he
had lost his father, he had become increasingly withdrawn after the disappearance of his three Sheker "uncles." When not helping his mother,
he would pass the hours playing with Ilgiz and his cousin Japarbek, Karakyz's oldest son. But much of the time he appeared to be lost in his own
thoughts, an innocent child pondering the cruel twists of fate that had
befallen his family.

The laconic Chingiz came alive, however, when Karakyz would tell
stories. It was usually at bedtime in the common room, with heat from
the day's wood fire warming the mud-walled house. Nagima might be
in one corner nursing infant Roza and consoling herself by humming
Tatar melodies, while Dosali was hunched over in another corner, likely
cleaning his rifle after a day of hunting deer and geese.

By the light of the fire—there was no electricity in the village in those
days—Karakyz would gather the boys on the felt rug in the center of the
room and entertain them with Kyrgyz fairy tales and epic poems, including the exploits of Manas, the hero of the eponymous epic known to all
Kyrgyz. In rich and flowing Kyrgyz, Karakyz would bring history alive:
muscled Manas climbing to the summit of what came to be known as Mt.
Manas to see if enemies were approaching, strong man Kozhumkul carrying his tired horse down the mountain through a snowstorm. Dosali
might chime in with stories of his hunting exploits, of wolves giving birth
and defending himself against a hungry snow leopard in the mountains.
Eager to be transported to times of great battles and brave heroes saving the day, Chingiz would beg for more—"greedy for more words," as
Japarbek remembered.[11]

The times at the hearth balanced Chingiz's Russian-educated side.
Here, in the stillness of dark nights, in the company of his illiterate aunt
telling stories that had been passed down through generations, Chingiz
connected with the Kyrgyz people's timeless way of life, where quite
often Mother Nature was the adversary, not other men. The stories told
of a nomadic existence in which the Kyrgyz people strived to live in harmony with their surrounding environment. Man in this world was not
in control of his journey but a mere traveler alongside animals and the
natural elements. If Mother Nature was cruel, you couldn't get revenge;

you could only appeal to the spirits that supported life: the sky, trees, water, sun, moonlight, and fire.

In fact, in those troubled years in Sheker, one might say that the pastoral way of life healed Chingiz's crippled spirit. Karakyz's stories gave him a straight line to the past, and Chingiz himself made treks into the mountains, observing and participating in nomadic rituals passed down from his ancestors. People in the village still remembered the prerevolutionary years when Aitmat and Birimkul had led the clan on spring journeys into high mountain pastures, or *jailoo*.

Those trips would start out with a caravan of families and animals winding its way up the mountainside, like a huge snake. Children and village dogs would run alongside camels, horses, and oxen loaded with collapsible yurts, pots, felt rugs, and food supplies, clanking all the way. The sound of tinkling goat bells would ping off the walls of gorges as they ascended. At rest stops, while the women set up tables with samovars and snacks, Aitmat and Birimkul would play music on the three-stringed *komuz*. On special occasions, they would engage in *aitish*, spontaneous poetry competitions. Sitting across from one another on small rock outcroppings and, to the deep-toned chords of their *komuz*, they would improvise verses like rapping bards.

The end of the often treacherous two to three-day journey was usually a green meadow, invariably crisscrossed by streams fed by melting snow from surrounding glaciers. The packed yurt parts were assembled into stand-alone structures, with family members gathering around for the raising of the *tunduk*, the circular "center board" that keeps the window-less yurt open to the sky.[12] In less than ninety minutes, the yurt could be up, with smoke escaping out of the stovepipe and a meal of boiled lamb and tea ready to serve.

On the summer treks, young Chingiz would shepherd the sheep, goats, and horses as they roamed the lush spring grasses, which hold an almost sacred place in Kyrgyz culture. For it is those grasses that fatten the livestock—the sustenance of nomadic families—and help mares produce milk, or *kymyz*. The Kyrgyz believe the mare's milk, fortified by new meadow grasses ingested by the horse, is highly therapeutic. Shaking the milk up and down in a smoked leather pouch tinges the contents with a smoky flavor. The result after fermentation is a strong, fizzy beverage that Kyrgyz are convinced can cure any ill, from the common cold to digestive problems. In today's Kyrgyzstan, professionals in the cities often take a week's vacation in the summer to head to the mountains for a diet of sun, wind, and *kymyz*. Just *kymyz*, morning, noon, and night. They return to the city ruddy-faced and energetic.

For many Kyrgyz, going to *jailoo* is like a pilgrimage. Life can take on a more spiritual quality in the high mountains, the senses titillated in the rarefied atmosphere. There is the smell of spring grasses and flowers, the feel of refreshing wind blowing from a glacier, the taste of water from burbling streams, the sound of wildlife in the morning, and, of course, the sight of soaring, snowcapped mountains. And there is direct connection with manifestations of life and death: new grasses feed foals born during the summer encampment while dangers lurk nearby, be it a camel falling off a narrow ridge or a family stolen away by a sudden landslide. Indeed, a stay at *jailoo* underscores human insignificance in the face of powerful and capricious nature. For in a second or two—the time it takes to hear a splitting sound and the whoosh of cascading snow—life can change irrevocably.

Just as parishioners offer up prayers for protection in church, the Kyrgyz pray for safe passage in the mountains: "O, spirits, we ask you to keep the mountain pass open for us. Withhold cold rains and snowstorms. Please grant happiness to our children and safe passage for our animals so they can partake of the juicy grasses of your meadows. We earnestly hope that in the morning the song of birds and rays of the sun will wake us through the tunduk of our yurts."[13]

Observing the nomadic way of life in the 1930s, Swiss adventurer Ella Maillart wrote of the nomads: "They are more at ease in their world which they understand perhaps better than we understand ours. They understand and accept the natural rhythms of life, like hunger and the contentment that comes with satisfying hunger. Each person is not a lonely individual struggling against the whole world, but a member of a clan or tribe. He is part of an organic whole, part of something bigger than himself. He is not an end in himself. We westerners suffer, unable to integrate ourselves into a living concept bigger than ourselves."[14]

During the summers of his youth, Chingiz Aitmatov caught the tail end of authentic nomadic life. With the settlement of the Sheker tribe in the early 1920s and the onset of collectivization a bit later, the annual treks were a fading way of life. People became more rooted in houses and communities around the Kurkureyu River, thanks in part to the efforts of Uncle Alimkul. Life began to take place in the valley where the collective farm gathered residents into new roles of accountant, secretary, political organizer, and, above all, party members. To be sure, there were still a good number of shepherds, but the flocks and herds were communalized, along with farm equipment and feed, thus requiring fewer shepherds.

Though suffering from asthma and racked by arthritis that was deforming her hands, Nagima became determined to find work to release her relatives from the daily stress of supporting the family of an "enemy of the people." But she had to venture outside Sheker because her breathing problems prevented her from working with tobacco, the kolkhoz's main crop in the 1930s.

When she interviewed for a job at the Kirovka District Office about twenty-five miles from Sheker, she was ridiculed by a young party official, whom she recognized as having fawned over Törökul when he had appeared in the district office as a ranking official. The once-obsequious official, who had likely been promoted in the wake of the purges, forced Nagima to come back time and again to inquire. Finally, irritated by her pleas, in the presence of a European-looking visitor sitting in his office, the official stared her down.

"Aren't you sick of coming here?" he asked rhetorically. "Even if you were three times smarter than you are, I wouldn't have any work for you."

Gathering her strength, Nagima took a different tack. "Ok, let's say Törökul and I are enemies, but what about our children? What have they done? I have four children. I need to feed them."

The coldhearted official shot back: "I could care less about your children. If you can't feed them, disburse them among your relatives or send them to an orphanage."

Nagima slammed the door and rushed outside. Hugging a tree for support—for some sort of consolation—Nagima grieved for the hardship she had had to endure and feared for the children she had promised to protect.

Then came a tap on her shoulder. A kind face and gentle voice.

"Can you work as an accountant?" asked the European-looking man, who had witnessed the ordeal with the party official. He turned out to be an ethnic German named Otto Zyuderman, who worked as the representative of the Kyrgyz Ministry of Supply in Kirovka District.

As a result of Zyuderman's intervention, Nagima got a job as an accountant at a butter factory in Kirovka. She moved the children from Sheker into two rooms in workers' barracks. They were joined by Nagima's sister Gulsha, whose own husband had been exiled to northern Kazakhstan, and Gulsha's son Asfandiar. The sisters split responsibilities: Nagima was the breadwinner; Gulsha took care of the home.[15]

—♦—

Although he was living in Kirovka, impressionable Chingiz continued to take his cues from Aunt Karakyz-apa. She was a moral compass for him in the way she related to the world around her. Chingiz was especially struck by her connection with the animal world. Once, when one of the family's ewes inexplicably rejected her lamb, refusing to nurse it and even fighting with it, a distraught Karakyz tried to cajole the mother to care for the forlorn lamb by whispering incantations into her ears and hanging amulets from her neck. But her interventions proved fruitless.

So, in the evenings, around the fireplace, Karakyz would appeal to the sky. Lost in her own thoughts, she would raise prayers upward, hoping for some kind of explanation for this unnatural injustice. What was happening in the world, she would ask, for a mother to reject her defenseless child? Were the rivers running backward? Were the mountains falling?

As for the Great Purges, which had robbed her of two brothers and two male cousins, Karakyz-apa was unintimidated and even cursed Stalin by name in the presence of family members. She insisted that what was happening was all a lie. It was as if this illiterate woman's sixth sense had intervened to tell her not to accept the totalitarian doctrine. It was against the natural order of things.

While others cowered—village residents avoided mentioning Törökul's name for fear of association with an enemy of the people—Karakyz-apa counseled Chingiz and his siblings to not be shy about their family's name. Their father Törökul was worthy of praise, she instructed them, no matter where he might be or whatever people might say about him. She was determined to save the children from the corroding effects of being labeled the family of an enemy of the people, from low self-esteem, and, most importantly, from slavish obedience to the false powers-that-be. Many years later, Chingiz Aitmatov would write of his aunt: "Karakyz-apa showed us that no matter what calamities may befall a person, he will never be lost as long as he lives among his own people."[16]

Chingiz tried to find his own ways to set the record straight. Unlike Karakyz-apa, Chingiz could read the newspapers. The articles against his father and the disappearances of his uncles were reminders of his outsider status, of a deficiency that he longed to correct. He would read books about Soviet spies and daydream about catching a foreign agent and dying in the process. If the son turned out to be a selfless servant of Soviet power, that would surely prove his father's innocence, Chingiz reasoned.

Sensitive and unsure of himself, Chingiz wanted to please. He even reprimanded his aunt for her anti-Stalin views. As the male head of the family at age twelve, he didn't want any more upheaval, so a part of him was inclined to get along with authority, a trait he would carry into adulthood. At the same time Karakyz's doubts resonated, and, while he hadn't internalized them, he began to perceive the duality of human endeavor: things weren't always what they seemed.

4

The Burdens of War

It is often said that a writer is born during his childhood. That was the case with Chingiz Aitmatov. Karakyz-apa's storytelling contributed to a fairy-tale turn of mind that found expression in Aitmatov's later use of Kyrgyz fables and legends in his literary works. His wartime experiences became fodder for character development and plotlines, and, as a product of a nomadic way of life, he strove to integrate his readers into a larger living concept, to make humanity itself the world's clan or tribe.

It was, however, a chance meeting on a winter night in the middle of World War II that most closely connects Aitmatov's childhood with his future métier. In the story of the stolen cow, one can glimpse seeds of the writer's humanistic approach to life and his reverence for mankind's meandering path from experience through understanding to wisdom.

After Nagima Aitmatova took a job as an accountant at the butter factory on a collective farm, the family moved to Jiyde a dusty village near the border with Kazakhstan. The job at the kolkhoz provided some security during wartime scarcities. But the family was barely scraping by, with Nagima's salary coming in payments of food that depended on the kolkhoz's overall production. Relatives in Sheker sent flour and corn when they could. The Aitmatov family rented a shepherd's primitive house with a flat roof and dirt floor.

It was the bleakest time in their lives. Nagima was a fish out of water. Her fellow villagers saw in her an elite, sophisticated woman suddenly living in a backwater. "You came to this shit hole from Moscow?" they would ask incredulously. One of the few literate people in the village, Nagima would read the Russian and Kyrgyz-language newspapers out loud and then, using the simplest language possible, translate for the villagers what was happening in the war. Other times, she would read them letters sent from the front and explain to them where their sons or husbands were fighting. They had no idea where Europe was.

The family's most important possession—that for which they were most thankful—was their cow, given to them by relatives before the war. They kept the milking cow, named Zukhra, in the kolkhoz's animal pen. The children doted upon Zukhra, who was due to give birth to a calf in the spring. They would take turns feeding her hay and scraps of food and walk her to the nearby stream. Come springtime, if they took good care of Zukhra, the children knew they would be rewarded with fresh milk, sour cream, and yogurt. That meant that no matter how bad the situation with food supplies, the family would be able to survive.

While visiting Jiyde from Sheker in February 1943, Chingiz woke up early to check on Zukhra. But the pen was empty, with just her rope leash lying in the corner. In a panic, Chingiz checked the outside areas and went down to the river where she watered. No sign. Then he roused the stable hand who was sleeping in the corner of the pen, but he was no help. Fearing that Zukhra had been stolen, Chingiz told Nagima that he would go in search of the thieves. Then he ran to the house of his friend, the village tractor driver, who had a hunting rifle. An agitated Chingiz explained what happened and asked to borrow the rifle.

Chingiz set off in the early morning, with the loaded rifle slung over his shoulder. He searched for shoe prints and scoured familiar bunkers and hidden places, reasoning the thieves would be waiting until night fall to abscond with the pregnant cow. The more he paced forward, the more bent on revenge he became.

Surely, the thieves had targeted the family cow because they knew the Aitmatov family had no man of the house to defend them. Fiery anger rose up inside Chingiz's fourteen-year-old body. He imagined the sensation of sweet revenge once he had shot the robbers.

But he found no one, and the day stretched into the cold evening hours. All around was grassless steppe and in the distance the lifeless hulks of mountains. He changed direction to head to the main market in the region, where, he speculated, the men would likely sell the cow. Suddenly at an intersection in the snow, Chingiz crossed paths with an elderly man riding a donkey. His head lowered, Chingiz hurried by with the rifle over his shoulder. He didn't bother to greet the white-bearded man in a faded skullcap coming from the direction of an abandoned cemetery.

"Wait, son," the elderly man startled Chingiz. "Are you on your way to kill someone?"

Raising his head, Chingiz grunted in assent. The two strangers' eyes met, and, despite the pursuit of revenge that had seized his mind, Chingiz was struck by the man's weathered face and gentle, understanding expression.

The man halted his donkey. "Tell me what happened."

Chingiz related the story of the stolen cow.

"Listen to me," the man said. "I understand your anger, but don't ignite revenge inside yourself. Life itself will punish those who have committed this evil deed. Punishment will stalk their every step, when they lie down to sleep and when they wake up."

The old man paused. "Return home. This world is just. You will have peace and reward if you return home. Don't think I am just trying to calm you. There will come a day when you will remember my words and understand I was right."

The old man continued on his way. But his calm, penetrating voice had dissipated the anger inside Chingiz, who slung the then-useless rifle over his shoulder and headed home, with the sun retreating behind the mountains. Sobs shook his body, and tears ran down his face.[1]

A nameless man in the dark of winter had steered a wayward lad away from destruction. Chingiz would forever be grateful for the life lesson that heartlessness breeds more heartlessness until there is understanding.

A world away in Nazi-occupied Lithuania, Azamat Altay found himself trapped in a house in April 1943. Lithuanian police working for the Nazis threatened to lob a grenade into the house. After giving his watch to the Lithuanian woman who had shielded him, Altay exited with his hands up in the air holding his rifle. Preoccupied with concerns about what might happen to his Lithuanian protectors, he wasn't able to brace himself when a policeman bashed him in the face with the handle side of an unexploded grenade. Blood poured from his eyebrow. For the rest of his life he would wear the scar, with its distinctive curve like a question mark above his right eyebrow. It was more heartbreak for the war-weary Altay.

Altay found himself back at the Nazi prison in Ashmyani in a cell in Nazi-occupied Belorussia with twenty-three other prisoners. He changed his name to avoid being discovered as an escaped POW from that very camp five months earlier. He became Kadyr Asanov, the first of several name changes he would undergo in his eventful life. At the prison, Altay learned how to heal his wound by bathing it with his salty tears. But new wounds soon appeared, with prewar amity with Lithuanians giving way to outright hostility. Lithuanian police who saw Soviet soldiers as occupiers beat up Altay during interrogations, calling him a "Stalinist bandit." That beating was the beginning of an eleven-month ordeal in the Belorussian prison and in a Gestapo prison in nearby Vilnius, much of it spent in solitary confinement. Stuck in a cell on the top floor of the three-floor prison in Vilnius with little to do, Altay would climb on a chair and peer through a small window to get a glimpse of life on the street below. When lucky, he would catch sight of birds flying.

Altay survived using his wits. He read Chekov in Russian, though at first he understood nothing. In prison, he started to learn Russian, which had become a necessity as a language of survival for it was through Russian—not Kyrgyz, which very few people knew—that he could communicate with the Russian-speaking locals who had been his lifeline and through translation with French and German speakers. Indeed, a Russian-French dictionary would become as important to Altay's survival as a gun. He also befriended an elderly Polish inmate from Vilnius who shared food packets sent by his family. To procure extra food, the resourceful Altay fashioned a "fishing pole" out of rags and old socks that he would lower down several floors to sympathetic residents, who would fasten a loaf of bread to the pole.

In February 1944 Altay and the other inmates from the Gestapo prison in Vilnius were transported to France when the country was still under German occupation. There the prisoners worked to build a wall near the seaside city of Brest. France was a breath of fresh air. Unafraid of the German occupiers, the locals were happy to give the prisoners food, and even the German guards were less severe. Altay and others POWs even found time to wander the city. But with the Allies closing in, the Germans were transferring POWs, who served as a labor force and possible bargaining chip, to Germany.

Because food was more plentiful in France and the population more welcoming to Soviet escapees, Altay decided his best chance for survival was to remain in France. He made his break in May 1944. While German soldiers guarding his train were drinking from barrels of wine, he jumped from the open doors of the slow-moving train onto French soil. After explaining in Russian and broken French that he was an escaped Soviet POW—that dictionary was key—Altay was sheltered, fed, and given a change of clothes by French sympathizers.

The D-Day landing followed in June 1944 on the coast of Normandy, not far from where Altay had jumped from the train. Tying a red ribbon on his arm, Altay joined a group of French partisans assisting the invading Allied troops as they pressed inland. He manned a machine gun when his group of partisans fired on retreating German troops. In his memoirs he writes that he fought with the French partisans until the liberation of Paris in August 1944.

Announced in Moscow in the early morning of May 9, 1945, news of the German surrender spread "like the wind" across the vast territory of the Soviet Union. In Central Asia radio broadcasts set off celebrations in population centers. Like ripples in a pond, the momentous announcement radiated outward, with mounted horsemen delivering the news to isolated villages.

Sheker was one of the last villages to get the news; residents gathered on top of a hill at the foot of Mt. Manas, anxious to hear the news in person. Some women snuck away to milk their cows but then rushed back to the knoll. Standing on the hill, Chingiz Aitmatov tingled with nervous excitement. Like other children forced to take on adult burdens during the war, he had matured quickly over the previous four years, steeled by privations and tempered by the losses he had witnessed among his fellow villagers.

When at last residents saw dust rising from the messenger's galloping horse, they rushed forward. As if shot from a cannon, they flowed down the hillside, the moving mass of humanity extended in the front by excited children and stretched in the rear by wounded veterans, some hurrying as fast as they could on crutches. Released from their sacrifice and their grief, the villagers enveloped the messenger. Now, they knew for sure the war was over.

"Oh, Victory, we waited for you for so long."[2]

Expected to crumble within months of the German blitzkrieg, the Soviet Union had prevailed by becoming a unified military camp, stitched together by the planned economy that oversaw the rebuilding of 1,500 factories from frontline territories in the interior. Thirty of those factories had been evacuated from Russia and Ukraine and reestablished right off the rails in Kyrgyzia, including Torpedo Factory No. 150 on Lake Issyk Kul and the Frunze Mortar Factory. Close to 150,000 evacuees had been resettled in Kyrgyzia, and mercury from the mines of southern Kyrgyzia had filled virtually every piece of ammunition and explosive made for the successful war effort.

The victory over fascist Germany had come as a result of a patriotic surge across the country. In Soviet Kyrgyzia, the reforms of the 1920s—the orderly return of their compatriots from China, land reform, and the literacy campaign—had given the Kyrgyz people a stake in a system that was worth defending. Just twenty-five years earlier they had revolted when asked to provide men for the tsarist army; this time they had answered the call of the Soviet commissars, with four hundred thousand people from Soviet Kyrgyzia serving in the army or mobilized to work in factories. Close to forty-two thousand received medals for bravery.[3]

But Altay saw victory from the other side, and it left a strong impression. He had seen how much the French despised the Germans and how the military force the United States sent, including tanks and transport vehicles, had helped to turn the tide. "We won because of these things," he wrote in his journal on Victory Day in Paris.[4]

Back in the Soviet Union, victory writ large stifled any outrage about the perversions of the Stalinist system that had crippled the country before and during the war. Dissenting voices would remain muffled until

1956. But people knew, and everybody died a bit inside when they remembered the system-inflicted losses that had ripped families apart.

Inside Chingiz, Karakyz-apa's anti-Stalin barbs had found a home, and a tendency to question percolated at a low boil. What of the political prisoners who had labored and died in inhuman conditions in support of the war effort? How about Ozubek and Alimkul at the lead mines of Ak Tuz near the border with Kazakhstan? Poor Ryskulbek. Unfair. Unjust.

Their fates were a reminder to Chingiz of the disappearance of his own father. Possessed of his father's gentle nature, Chingiz was developing an awareness of the plights of his fellow men and a sensitivity to the pursuit of freedom and justice.

———

Determined to return its scattered citizens to the homeland, the Soviet government set up repatriation camps in Europe for displaced citizens and soldiers following the defeat of Germany in May 1945. Although he had heard rumors during his partisan days about ill treatment of Soviet POWs upon their return to the Soviet Union, Altay was eager to return to his beloved Lake Issyk Kul and be reunited with his family. In his mind, he had nothing to fear: he had fought bravely, escaped from his German captors and then joined the resistance. In the year following the liberation of Paris, he had returned to work with the Soviet military in Paris to help document and organize Soviet citizens scattered around Europe for repatriation.

In August 1945 Altay himself boarded a train, one of thousands of Soviet citizens heading eastward. The train cars leaving Camp Beauregard outside Paris were festooned with congratulatory banners, such as "We achieved freedom. Our country won." Other slogans addressed POWs directly: "Prisoners of Nazism, your motherland awaits you." POWs on the trains started to cry when they saw the slogans, their difficult passage coming to an end. American soldiers in France offered Altay and other departing Soviet POWs their food rations as a token of solidarity.

But Altay noticed the situation changed the farther east the trains traveled, with Soviet soldiers surrounding the trains once they entered the Soviet zone of occupied Germany. Cheery slogans were torn from the sides of the trains, and nice words were replaced by curses and insults.

At Camp Eisenach in the Soviet zone, men were separated from women and women from their children. Heads were shaved, food was scarce, and anyone who questioned their treatment was called a fascist by Soviet guards. Fearing confiscation by the guards, Soviet citizens, pretending they were warming themselves at a fire, began burning the gifts they had brought with them. Returning Soviet POWs, who were deemed to be traitors, were especially furious about the unexpected humiliations at the hands of their own soldiers. Nazi camps were one thing, but the vast majority of POWs had served bravely for the Red Army.

Altay recounts in his memoir that things got worse after Camp Eisenach. At Soviet Camp 237 near Magdeburg, a former German prison that had become a holding station for twenty-five thousand Soviet repatriates, tension escalated. When a fight broke out between inmates over food, Soviet guards sprayed machine-gun fire over the prisoners, killing eighteen people and wounding another twenty. The next week, despairing of ever returning to a normal life, thirty camp residents hung themselves. Altay's options were narrowing.

After a failed escape attempt, in which a quick thinking Altay and two fellow escapees convinced Soviet border guards they were former Soviet soldiers actually crossing from the English zone into the Soviet zone to return home, he was sent to Camp Brandenburg, a processing depot for Soviet soldiers returning home. There, because he knew how to write, he earned a job as a clerk, one of thirty clerks for twenty thousand repatriating soldiers. His Soviet education kept on returning dividends. The clerk's job bought him a bit more time to mull another escape attempt.

———

It was as if Tengri, the sky god revered by nomads, were watching over Azamat Altay, delivering him a godsend from his native Kyrgyzia as he wrestled with whether to return home. "Kudaibergen, are you really alive?" the elderly Asian-looking man exclaimed upon seeing Altay's face in the clerk's office at Camp Brandenburg.

Altay looked up. "Yes, it's me, the son of Kojomberdi Teke uulu."

The elderly man, himself a POW, had good reason to believe Altay was dead. He had mourned with Altay's father in late 1940 when, after learning of his son's capture by the Germans in the first months of the war, Teke uulu had held a funeral in the village.

Speaking in Kyrgyz, which the snooping Red Army guards couldn't understand, Altay and the elderly Kyrgyz man shared stories over the next few days. The older man warned Altay that a harsh fate awaited returning POWs and related what he had witnessed in their own village before he himself had been drafted: just two to three days after returning, former POWs were picked up by a black car and taken away, never to be seen again.[5]

In fact, the Stalin regime was petrified by the prospect of returning citizens turning against the Soviet system. Concerned that Soviet citizens stranded during the war in Europe had been seduced by higher living standards and a sense of freedom, Soviet military authorities and the NKVD set up strict "filtration" commissions, with even stricter controls for former POWs. Because they aroused suspicion, around 273,000 Soviet citizens were sent to the NKVD camps or gulags upon their return to the Soviet Union, some for clearly having collaborated with the Nazis, but others merely because they had the misfortune of having been taken prisoner alive.[6]

"It's better for you not to return home" the village elder advised him. "If you return, your life will be very difficult."

Fortune continued to smile on Altay. For his good work as a clerk on demobilization, he was assigned to a border guard regiment. While on duty at the border he fed himself by shooting deer and dreamed of freedom. "When you stand on the border, you have just one thought: how to flee to the West," he would write years later. "I understood that the Stalin regime, even though it had won the war, humiliates its own citizens, that it is a government against the people."

———

After midnight on January 1, 1946, as revelers in cities around Europe were raising their glasses to the end of World War II, Soviet border guard Azamat Altay tossed aside his rifle, threw off his military overcoat, and stole across the border into the English zone of recently liberated Germany.

Altay headed south from the English zone in Germany. He was determined to get to France, the only country that had welcomed him and where he had friends from his partisan days. Using a smattering of French, German, and Russian, he begged a ticket off an elderly station worker at the Saarbrucken train station. Lacking permission to cross the still-militarized German-French border, he stowed away, hiding in the first-class bathroom.

Altay arrived in Paris, a free but penniless man, with not a French franc to his name. A passerby gave him two francs to ride on the subway. It was a humble start to a new life, but with each mile he traveled—on foot, by train or subway—he was leaving behind the tragedies of the past.

PART TWO

PART TWO

5

Chinese with a Dog

Radio Liberty's headquarters in Munich buzzed with excitement on March 18, 1953. A gaggle of languages from far corners of the Soviet Union—among them Armenian, Azeri, Chechen, Georgian, Kyrgyz, and Tatar-Bashkir—reverberated down the hallways as journalists prepared for inaugural fifteen-minute broadcasts. Staff members finalized translations about the biggest news of the month: the sudden death of Soviet dictator Joseph Stalin on March 5.

In glassed-in studios, broadcasters cleared their throats during practice runs through scripts. Seated in front of a microphone, newly minted radio journalist Azamat Altay's mind wandered. Seven years ago he had arrived in Paris, a destitute Red Army deserter. Now, clean-shaven and well-dressed, he rehearsed his report for Radio Liberty's Turkestan department one last time.

But practice runs couldn't allay his anxiety. After thirteen years of "silence" with his homeland, Altay would soon be talking directly to the Kyrgyz people. Would his voice carry over thousands of miles? Would he stumble over his words? And what of his father? Would his father be listening and recognize his voice?

After a Kyrgyz melody opened the show, Altay began his broadcast in Kyrgyz. "This is Radio Liberty speaking, the free voice of your compatriots abroad," Altay announced in Kyrgyz.

The first-time broadcaster fumbled, losing his place in the text, but regained his poise: "The monster Stalin has died, the man who destroyed the best of the Soviet people."

The signal carrying Altay's voice gained time as it headed east across the Eurasian landmass. After bouncing off transmitting towers on Taiwan, it broke through Soviet radio frequencies and alighted above mountainous Kyrgyzia. Dachas in the foothills of the Ala-Too Mountains picked up the signal.

—⁓—

Altay had scrambled to survive during his first years in Europe. In France, without a diaspora to rely on and lacking knowledge of French, he had crisscrossed the country, picking up menial jobs wherever he could. He harvested wine grapes in the fall, cleaned out chicken coops in the winter, and cut down trees in the spring. There were long days and few friends.

To keep himself company in southern France, he got a puppy, whom he named "Dos," the Kyrgyz word for "friend." Happy to have a companion, Altay fashioned a carriage for the dog and took him wherever he went. The pair became a familiar sight in the town, with Altay pulling the carriage like a rickshaw driver. Dos sat in the carriage, his hind feet on the seat and his front paws on Altay's shoulders. French villagers took to calling Altay "the Chinese with a dog."

Dos provided a pleasant interlude in an otherwise uncomfortable time. In those days, a hostile environment constrained Altay's movements, particularly in the big cities where French communists were reporting to the Soviet embassy on Soviet citizens stranded in France. As a stateless Soviet Army deserter, Altay feared that any minute he could be swooped up by a communist dragnet.

Altay had seen the lengths to which Soviet authorities were prepared to go to ensure control over their people. He had lived through the horror of the Soviet repatriation camps, and he had heard stories of Soviet agents operating in France. With the help of local informers, they were seizing Soviet citizens hiding in France, transporting them to repatriation camps, and murdering them—all under the nose of the French police.[1]

Fearful that he, too, could be captured, Altay wrote his life story. But, really, he was writing his own obituary. Should he be deported to the gulags, he wanted to make sure that people understood why he had escaped to the West. Above all, he wanted his father to know the truth in the event he had to hold a funeral service for his only son.

"I am yesterday's half-savage despot who helped despotic powers," Altay began. "If I had known what I was doing, I wouldn't have helped the Stalinist terrorists."

He then recounted the turn of mind he had experienced when living in France after the war: "I saw real life. I lived among French workers and peasants, socialized with them, and saw how they lived. Now that's life and living."

The young Kyrgyz closed out his personal manifesto with a raison d'être: "I want to fight for the truth and freedom of my people."[2]

Inside Altay burned with anger over separation from his people, which he blamed on the Soviet system. The article was an outlet for his rage. It was as if he were shouting from the Kyrgyz mountain tops. He imagined the echoes reverberating in the mountains passes where his grandparents had died in 1918, floating down to the foothills where the unfairly persecuted had sought refuge during the Great Purges and then carrying across the prison camps of the Soviet Union where repatriated Russian POWs were being worked to death as he wrote.

———

Altay's article was published under the heading *Testament of a Young Kyrgyz* in the November 23, 1946, edition of the *Socialist News*, an anticommunist émigré newspaper in New York.

Just months before, British statesman Winston Churchill had uttered his famous warning: "From Stettin in the Baltic to Trieste in the Adriatic, an iron curtain has descended across the Continent."[3] Churchill's speech to an audience of forty thousand people in Fulton, Missouri, demarcated a line between the free world and the captured world under Soviet domination. His words on a March day in 1946 prodded the democratic West to change the way it viewed the communist East. No longer was the Soviet Union an ally who had helped to end the war against Germany and a partner in peace for the reconstruction of Europe. It was a menace to the free world.

———

Fearful of being seized, Altay schemed. Through a contact, he met a Kazakh forester, who introduced him to a French government official in the small town he was working in. That acquaintance produced the police signature Altay needed to work officially as a lumberjack. To get an international refugee passport, he schemed more, lying that his father had been born in Poland in order to avoid any claim the Soviets might have on him. The Nansen passport allowed him to remain in France under the status of a refugee.

With the two documents in hand, Altay breathed easier. But he remained on the lookout for destructive forces, as he would for the rest of his life. When Altay had called himself a half-savage despot in his article, he was revealing. He had scratched his way to freedom but remained suspicious—and rightly so—of the outside world. Like a savage guarding his territory in the forest, he was always on the lookout for people working against him. Hostile forces included the Soviet government which had branded him a traitor and, worse, the people back home blackening his name by saying he had suffocated a communist while in a German POW camp.

People in Altay's narrow world came with agendas that could be dangerous. That had been true during the purges in the Soviet Union, when informers could overhear a complaint, and turn a tranquil life into hell, as they had done with his village friend. And it was true in France, where he was desperate to break free of the hold of the Soviet system. As a Soviet soldier, POW, and illegal immigrant, he had learned the harsh lessons of survival: keep your head down, say little and distrust people. There was no guarantee of goodness in the world if you had been raised in Stalin's Soviet Union.

———

In France there was freedom. For every Soviet sympathizer or NKVD agent who lurked around the corner, there were countless opportunities to learn. Altay took advantage of a rich intellectual atmosphere, populated by philosophers and writers who years earlier had fled the Bolshevik Revolution and settled in France.

While working in a fruit orchard outside Paris, Altay met the Russian philosopher Nikolai Berdyaev while he was shopping for fruit and vegetables. At the fruit stand, the peasant boy from Lake Issyk Kul engaged the anticommunist philosopher from Kiev. The basics of Berdyaev's philosophy of personalism—which put a primacy on individual freedom and the human capacity for self-improvement—clicked with Altay. At his lectures, Altay heard the elderly Berdyaev denounce the Soviet concept of a classless society as unachievable and destructive. Here was a Russian man, thought Altay, who spoke openly about the ills of Soviet society and charted a way forward.[4]

Altay started to associate with the Russian diaspora, Ukrainian separatists, and the tiny Central Asian community in Paris. Through a contact, he got a job in a tooth-powder factory. The factory was in the house of a prominent Russian émigré. Next to the laboratory where Altay worked was a library with a huge collection of books. In between washing his daily quotient of 250 bottles, Altay would sneak off to the library and read Russian classics.

His studying continued in the evenings. Through dissident social circles, he met the widow of Mustafa Chokai, the Kazakh-born president of the Turkestan Republic, also known as the Kokand Government, which had been a center of Turkestan independence after the Bolshevik Revolution. After the Tashkent Soviet violently suppressed the Kokand Government in 1918, Chokai and his wife, Maria, had fled to Turkey. They ended up in France in 1921, where the erudite Chokai wrote articles, published newspapers, and made speeches in support of an independent Turkestan

So, after a day's work in the laboratory scouring bottles, Altay would ride his bike to Chokai's house. In Chokai's voluminous library, he would peruse issues of the journal *Young Turkestanets* that Chokai had founded, scan newspapers from Soviet Central Asia, and read books on the history of the Turkic people.[5]

Reading issues of *Young Turkestanets*, Altay learned things prohibited in the Soviet Union, like the historical roots of independent Turkestan and an alternate version of the 1916 revolt that had so shaken his father's family. He tucked away the information for future use. At midnight he would ride home to the boardinghouse where he rented a room.

And even then he might not go to sleep, preferring to read and write his thoughts down or just think. It was a pattern of little sleep that Altay would follow for the rest of his life. "I sleep badly," he would say, "but read well."

Altay also got freelance translation jobs from Alexandre Bennigsen, a French civil servant at the time. As head of the Russian documentation service in the Office of the French Prime Minister in the late 1940s, Bennigsen called on Altay when he needed translations of newspapers from Soviet Central Asia. Work on translation jobs for Bennigsen led to invitations to share meals, and eventually Altay was spending vacations with Bennigsen and his family in the south of France. With a shared experience fighting the Nazis and an intense dislike of the Soviets, the two men would form a bond that would last a lifetime. Bennigsen would go on to become one of the world's foremost Turkologists and the preeminent authority on the Muslim peoples of Soviet Central Asia.

In his memoir, Altay wrote that during those days of studying and reading, he became completely absorbed in the struggle on behalf of the Kyrgyz people, as if transported to "another world." Influenced by the writings of men like Chokai and friendship with Bennigsen, Altay supported the establishment of a united Turkestan, comprising five Soviet republics. His stance dovetailed with the emerging US foreign policy toward the Soviet Union, and in particular towards the Soviet Muslim republics.

———

American government organizations arrived in Europe in the early 1950s to support a growing anti-Soviet movement of which Altay was a part. The American representatives were overseas tentacles of the policy of containment, which US diplomat George Kennan had articulated in his famous "X Article" in 1947.

Based on Kennan's close observations of the Soviet system, the article, which was published in the July 1947 issue of the authoritative journal *Foreign Affairs*, provided the ideological underpinnings for a new US policy toward Moscow. Kennan argued that the West should combat Moscow's expansionism—ultimately more a political threat than a military one—through political means and wait the Soviets out since Western institutions of democracy and the free market would prove more resilient.

In Kennan's view, war was not inevitable if the United States and its Western allies were firm in response to Soviet adventurism and if they supported resistance to the Soviet Union wherever there was a threat. In an indication of how much America was preoccupied with the Soviet threat, excerpts of the article were published in the popular magazines *Life* and *Reader's Digest*.[6] It seemed that even stay-at-home moms and factory workers were up to speed on the nuances of US foreign policy toward Moscow.

In Europe, Altay was the trickledown of the containment policy. He attended the founding congress and was an original member of the US-supported Committee for the Liberation of Turkestan, which started publishing a journal in 1951. The goal of the *Turk Eli* journal was to help unify Central Asian exile communities around the world in opposing Soviet communism. To that end, in addition to being directed to libraries and institutes inside the Soviet Union, the journal, which was published in Russian and in the major Turkic languages of Central Asia, was sent to the Turkic diaspora in Afghanistan, Pakistan, and Turkey.[7]

Altay was the third-ranking member of *Turk Eli*'s editorial board, in line with inclusivity rules set up by American funders. Those rules, based on population sizes of the Soviet Central Asian republics, mandated at inception that a Kazakh be the chairman and an Uzbek be the deputy chairman. It was spoon-fed democracy support to prevent domination by one group and to encourage the development of a unified opposition voice from Soviet Central Asia.

Altay, who became editor of the *Turk Eli* journal in 1953, contributed hard-hitting articles that, no doubt, angered communists in Moscow and Frunze. On the 1916 Ürkün uprising, Altay argued that the cause of the national rebellion was Russian domination over the Kyrgyz and the Kyrgyz people's fight for independence, not a class struggle between haves and have-nots as communist historians were depicting. He also took on the Soviet KGB, illustrating how KGB leadership in the republics had been imposed by Moscow.

But there weren't many readers of the journal in the diaspora, and the Soviets successfully blocked the journal from entering the country by mail or courier. So the next idea was to set up a radio station that could broadcast straight into the homes of Soviet citizens in their own languages.

The rationale behind radio broadcasts was twofold: the Soviets would have a hard time jamming the airwaves; and, second, listeners inside the Soviet Union would hear an alternate version of events happening in their own republics.

There was support for the radio station among the diaspora groups. And there was funding from the CIA, which supported a range of anti-communist programs around the world, including journals, magazines, and student associations.[8]

Radio Liberty became a pet project of the CIA-funded American Committee for the Liberation of the Peoples of Russia. Started in 1951, Amcommlib, as it came to be known, had the goal of uniting the different Soviet nationality groups in opposing Soviet communism. Altay's Committee for the Liberation of Turkestan was one of Amcommlib's "children."

As the funder of Amcommlib, the US government became parent to a dysfunctional family. The "children" constantly bickered. For starters, the non-Russian groups couldn't look past the committee's name, which they saw as humiliating by making them known as "peoples of Russia." Friction centered on the "nationality" groups' demand not just for the collapse of the Soviet Union but also for freedom from Russian domination. They believed the bigger and more organized Russian organizations in Amcommlib were only feigning interest in supporting their independence. In the event of the collapse of the Soviet Union, they believed that the Russian organizations would continue to subjugate the smaller peoples.

So the Americans had a cat fight on their hands. Name changes followed in hopes that removal of the word "Russia" might help: the American Committee for the Liberation of the Peoples of Russia became the American Committee for the Liberation of the Peoples of the USSR. Eventually, the Russian and non-Russian groups united by putting their common enemy in the name, so the third and final name was the American Committee for the Liberation from Bolshevism.[9] That agreement helped pave the way for a June 1952 conference in Starnberg, West Germany, where nine US-supported committees agreed to launch the radio station.[10]

Thus, Radio Liberty was born. With its brother organization Radio Free Europe (RFE), Radio Liberty was a tool in the US arsenal to wage a political struggle against communism. RFE focused on the East European satellite countries, while Radio Liberty targeted people inside the Soviet Union. The hope was that Soviet citizens supplied with another source of information about their country would begin to question communist propaganda. The most optimistic backers of Radio Liberty believed it would inspire Soviet citizens to push for a more democratic form of government.

On March 1, 1953, Radio Liberty's Russian-language service debuted. About two weeks later, eleven language services ran their inaugural broadcasts, which included Altay's report to Soviet Kyrgyzia on Stalin's death.

Challenges at Radio Liberty in those first years were considerable. Hiring was a particular bear. Altay's fumbling on his first broadcast was indicative of a lack of qualified broadcast journalists. Indeed, to some, the idea of a competent Soviet broadcaster was an oxymoron since there had been no independent media in the Soviet Union since 1917. Most Soviet exiles had not worked in government, culture, or the press, nor did many speak English. So, there was a lot of training, much repetition, and many retakes.

The Americans themselves were partly to blame. American administrators had set up Radio Liberty's Turkestan Department just like the journal Turk Eli, with positions apportioned not on merit but according to the predetermined formula-based population. As a Kyrgyz, Altay had the right to the No. 3 person in the office, that of broadcaster, below the Kazakh editor and Uzbek deputy editor but above the Turkmen secretary. In this sense, Radio Liberty was a development project demanding patience as much as it was a platform for waging ideological struggle in the Cold War.

An additional challenge was that Radio Liberty's signal had a hard time getting through to Soviet listeners. Antiquated transmitters were one problem. Contrary to initial expectation, Soviet jamming presented another. In Kyrgyzia employees of a secret department of the Ministry of Communications would distort Radio Liberty broadcasts by placing a noise machine in front of a microphone or by playing loud music.

The jamming was, in fact, a badge of honor for Radio Liberty. For one, it was an indication that, despite outmoded transmitters, broadcasts were reaching their target audience; second, the content was deemed "dangerous" enough for the Soviets to devote resources to blocking it.

In faraway Frunze, as early as the mid-1950s, broadcasts of Radio Liberty, or Radio Azattyk as it was known in Kyrgyz, were filling a void. Resourceful Kyrgyz with access to a transistor radio would invite trusted friends over to their apartments to listen to Altay's fifteen-minute news broadcast. Or they would gather in dachas near the mountains outside of Frunze. The most die-hard listeners would build their summer cottages on the basis of where reception of the signal was best. At twilight and later in the evenings, when atmospheric conditions improved reception, they would hear the crackle of a connection, a familiar Kyrgyz melody that inaugurated the broadcasts of the Kyrgyz Service and then the voice of Azamat Altay.[11]

The fumbling broadcaster was starting to develop a following in the mountainous republic: "Have you heard the radio show with that guy?" neighbors would ask each other sotto voce.[12]

─⁓─

Despite his improved standing in Europe, Altay was still anxious. He was a fugitive from Soviet law, having been sentenced in 1949 to twenty-five years in prison for desertion. With the Cold War in Europe in full swing, he was aware that Soviet informers were on the prowl. They were even penetrating Radio Liberty. Later in the 1950s, a Belarussian employee of Radio Liberty would be found dead in a river near Munich under suspicious circumstances.[13] It was also clear that, contrary to what Altay and others hoped, the Soviet Union would not be collapsing anytime soon, so returning home was a far-fetched idea.

Altay set his sights on America. He had gotten to know Americans working at the radio station and relished the opportunity to start a new life across the ocean, free from concerns about informers and spies. Altay had tried once before in the early 1950s to immigrate to the United States, only to be told by US consular officials that America was not accepting

Asians.[14] But at a holiday reception in Munich in 1956, he chatted with an American businessman, who became very interested in the Kyrgyz people after speaking with Altay. That evening the businessman offered to help a group of Kyrgyz move to the United States.

Altay quickly gathered the necessary information from five Kyrgyz refugees in Europe hoping to resettle in the United States. Three of the Kyrgyz, including Altay, ended up receiving visas after background checks.[15] But even when good fortune smiled, it seemed Altay couldn't escape the demons. Before he was about to depart, a Russian man in Europe, in an apparent attempt to prevent Altay from leaving, accused him of accepting money from the Soviet government. The baseless accusation had its roots in the year 1948, when Altay had purchased a winning ticket in the French lottery. The twenty-franc ticket won him one million francs or about $8,400 at the time, a tidy sum when he needed help.

After keeping some for himself to buy a car, Altay left a portion to charities in France and financed a Soviet refugee's trip to Switzerland to get medical treatment for her ailing daughter. But that didn't matter to the accuser, who was likely jealous of Altay or perhaps even working for the Soviets. Fortunately, Altay, who was a copious record keeper, had kept the receipt and was able to show he had justly collected his winnings from the lottery.

Upon his arrival in New York on September 15, 1956, Altay was met at New York International Airport by representatives of the Tolstoy Foundation, which was helping displaced persons from the Soviet Union settle in the United States. Altay handed them three dollars, the cost of his subsidized flight to America.

New York's Russian-language newspaper *Novoe Russkoye Slovo* carried news of Altay's arrival, listing his name along with other displaced persons migrating from Europe.[16] Altay called his arrival in the United States his "second birth."

6

Recovering Dignity

In the postwar years, the Soviet Union reoriented its economy away from war and set itself on a remarkable path of recovery that reshaped life across the country, including in the Muslim republics. The planned economic system was at its apex, channeling resources to heavy industry and organizing workers to carry out central commands. In the 1950s in Soviet Central Asia, communist-inspired work brigades built hospitals, bridges, water-supply systems, and electric power stations where they had never existed before.

Once considered one of the most underdeveloped Soviet republics, Kyrgyzia in the years after the war could boast of a capital city, with amenities never seen before, such as public baths, dry cleaners, and hotels. Over a span of ten years, the planned economy churned out hundreds of thousands of prefabricated housing units, one of which the Aitmatov family would move into in 1957. Consumer goods such as TVs, washing machines, and refrigerators—long in short supply—started to trickle down to shops.[1]

The modernizing city of Frunze became Chingiz Aitmatov's home when he started attending the Kyrgyz Agricultural Institute in 1948 (see figure 6.1). With Russians and other Slavs making up a majority of the city's inhabitants, Russian was spoken almost exclusively on the streets, a far cry from the villages in Talas where Aitmatov had lived for the previous decade. There was a vibrant cultural life, mostly imported from Russia, with stage and screen productions serving to educate the new "Soviet man." On free nights, Chingiz and his fellow students at the agricultural institute could choose from Russian-language movie theaters, the ballet, opera, circus, and even a puppet theater.[2]

Figure 6.1: Nagima Aitmatova with her four children in 1950 (*left to right*): Ilgiz, Lutsia, Roza, and Chingiz. Source: Central State Archives of the Kyrgyz Republic.

Fluent in Russian, Chingiz represented the leading edge of "Sovietization" in Kyrgyzia, a process that had as one of its key components the "elder brother" role of the Russian people to help guide minority nationalities. Chingiz became immersed in Russian culture and took a special liking to the Russian classics of Tolstoy and Dostoyevsky, often staying up in his dorm room until the early morning hours to finish a book.

At the same time, the literary and cultural achievements of the Kyrgyz people were printed in books, shown on the screen, and sung on stages in accessible formats for a population that was becoming increasingly literate. It was, a leading Kyrgyz politician would say years later, comparable to a renaissance, and it carried young Chingiz Aitmatov in its current.[3]

During those years in Frunze, Aitmatov started writing. His first short stories were formulaic, portraying progressive changes under communism, such as the mechanization of agriculture and the rise of a communist-inspired generation like himself. He followed the dictates

of socialist realism, which required Soviet writers to produce optimistic—and boring—works serving the cause of communism.[4] Dutiful to
the demands of the party and a believer in the promises of the October
Revolution, Aitmatov developed heroes who overcame obstacles like the
retrograde thinking of the older generation and therefore represented a
victory of the new communist culture over patriarchal feudal life.

———

But just as he was becoming indoctrinated in the communist world-
view, Chingiz's past came back to haunt him, like a tug on the shoulder
saying, "Not so fast." In 1952 the agricultural institute revoked his stipend
after a letter arrived from Sheker asking why the institute was granting
a university stipend to the "son of an enemy of the people." The public
exposure effectively closed his path to graduate school.

The letter was a rude reminder to Chingiz of his outlier status. With a
raw sense of injustice gnawing inside him, Chingiz began his last year at
the institute. One day in that fall of 1952, word spread that the *Manas* epic
was being put "on trial." Yes, the folktales of his childhood were under
attack. Karakyz-apa's sense of indignation welled up inside Chingiz as
he raced across town to grab a seat at the "trial."

———

For the Kyrgyz people, the *Manas* epic is a repository of history, recording Manas's attempts to unite the disparate Kyrgyz tribes against
invading neighbors. It celebrates qualities the Kyrgyz hold dear today:
courage, stoicism, patriotism, and love of freedom. With approximately
four hundred thousand lines, *Manas* dwarfs two acclaimed Western epics *The Iliad* and *The Odyssey* with their combined twenty-eight thousand
lines, and surpasses the hundred thousand lines of the Mahabharata, the
epic narrative of ancient India.

Initially just songs and poems strung together over thousands of
years, the epic coalesced in the fifteenth century when a famous singer
collected them into a unified story. The epic poem was not written down
until the 1850s, by which time it had traveled up and down the Kyrgyz
mountains for hundreds of years, relayed orally by bards, or *manaschi*,
as they are called.

Manaschi were among the most venerated figures in Kyrgyz nomadic society. Their stories connected generations of Kyrgyz to a common narrative of suffering and bravery. For a people without a culture of education, the *manaschi* served as mobile history books.

The Kyrgyz people liken the evolution of the story of *Manas* over the centuries to the rock towers one often finds on hikes in Kyrgyzstan—built spontaneously and piled higher with new tales and legends, all conveyed by *manaschi* in idiomatically rich and colorful Kyrgyz. In the old days, when the *manaschi* ran their own schools, parents would clamor to enroll their children, much as Irish Catholic families would hope for one of their sons to become a priest.

Combining the spiritual heritage of a Dalai Lama with the aura of a music star, *manaschi* were treated like royalty upon their arrival in villages, usually upon a horse. Dressed in a long black robe and wearing a kalpak, a *manaschi* would find a comfortable spot in the village center, likely sitting cross-legged on the ground, beneath a favored tree or against a backdrop of mountains. A local musician would often step forward to provide accompaniment on the three-stringed *komuz* while the audience settled in—herders returning from the pastures, farmers coming in from the fields, housewives finishing last chores and children of all ages. They fanned out in all directions around the *manaschi*, ready to follow the exploits of their heroes.

There was something for everyone in the performance. For those who liked hero figures, there was Manas, the historical ruler who unified the forty Kyrgyz tribes in their fight against outside invaders. Women likely gravitated toward Kanykei, a brave and independent woman of the steppe. Children reveled in the tales of Manas's warriors and their battles with the Kalmyks and Chinese. Today in Kyrgyzstan it's common to find Kyrgyz people, stores, and even political parties named after characters in the epic.

A *manaschi* of old would sometimes recite for days on end, often falling into a trance, with the cadence of his voice rising and falling with the mood of the narrative. Improvising like jazz musicians, the best *manaschis* would gesticulate to add color to eventful parts of the drama. When a *manaschi* was ready to leave for the next village, villagers offered gifts in gratitude: birds, a horse, or maybe even the hand in marriage of a daughter.

—⁓—

And now *Manas* was fighting for its rightful place in society, just like Chingiz. The trial was actually a debate about parts of the epic that Soviet ideologues claimed glorified the Kyrgyz people's feudal past. Word had it that Stalin himself had been outraged when he had read a Russian version of the epic in 1946. In the Soviet leader's drive to form a so-called Soviet man, there was little room for a "nationalistic" epic.

A minipurge ensued in Kyrgyzia, with three *Manas* scholars—Tashim Baidzhiev, Ziyash Bektenov, and Tazabek Samanchin—arrested over a period of six months in 1949 and 1950. The scholars, who had worked on the Russian translation of the epos, were charged with being anti-Soviet nationalists and given ten-year jail sentences.[5] There were larger considerations at work as well. With the Soviet Union cementing ties with communist China in an alliance against the West, the epic needed to be cleansed of references to ravaging Chinese invaders.

After traveling across town, Chingiz squeezed his way into the National Academy of Sciences building. The hall buzzed with excitement. Spectators expected the fate of the epic poem to be decided that day. Would *Manas* survive intact as the standard bearer of the Kyrgyz people or would it be manipulated or maybe even banned by Soviet ideologues, as had happened to the Kazakh and Uzbek epics in the previous year?

With his back pressed against the side of the main doorway, Chingiz craned his neck above other spectators to watch the proceedings. At six feet tall, he had grown into a handsome man. The teenage postman had matured in the years after the war, with a full head of black hair and a broad face that hinted at the European ancestry of his Tatar mother: lighter skin, rounder eyes, and a more prominent nose.

But Kyrgyz blood ran through his veins. Aitmatov cherished *Manas*'s place in the folklore of his people. He remembered nights in Sheker around the fire when Karakyz-apa told stories about Manas leading the Kyrgyz back to the Ala-Too Mountains, his son Semetei revenging the death of his father, and his grandson Seitek coming down from the mountains where he was raised in hiding by shepherds to defeat dreaded ruler Konchoro.

———

On the stage in the conference hall at the National Academy of Sciences, Aitmatov spotted ten to fifteen people sitting in chairs arranged in a line. Iskhak Razzakov, general secretary of the Kyrgyz Communist Party, occupied the center chair. To his right sat the Kazakh writer Mukhtar Auezov.

There was no more loyal friend to the Kyrgyz people than Auezov. The fifty-one-year-old bookish-looking writer with glasses and a mop of thinning hair had traveled up and down the Kyrgyz mountains in the late 1920s recording *manaschi* in an effort to compile a written version. He also supported more Central Asian autonomy from Moscow. His own views on Kazakhstan were in line with the signers of the Letter of Thirty in Soviet Kyrgyzia, except Auezov wanted reforms to support a greater Kazakh presence in government. Like his counterparts in Kyrgyzia, Auezov had suffered for his views. In the 1930s, Auezov had been forced to disassociate himself from colleagues and to renounce his own works after being branded a "nationalist," the catchall term used by paranoid communists to denote a person who promoted his native language and customs. Eventually convicted for purported anti-Soviet offenses, he served a three-year suspended sentence.

During the Great Purges, Auezov had witnessed the repression of some of the best minds in Central Asia, many of whom had worked with him on the transcription of *Manas* in the 1930s, men like Tynystanov and Russian Turkologist Evgenii Polivanov.[6] But through it all, he had managed to maintain his sanity, producing in the 1940s a multivolume work on the Kazakh poet Abai Kunanbaev that made him one of the most famous writers in Kazakhstan. Auezov would win the coveted Lenin Prize for Literature in 1959.

Now Auezov had come to Frunze to defend the epic. And as he sat on the podium, the balding Auezov was again the target of communist hardliners in Kazakhstan. In a renewed campaign against so-called nationalists, Auezov had been criticized for glorifying Kazakh folklore and distorting history.

As Auezov listened, occasionally jotting down notes, speakers took their turns at the podium criticizing the epos. Never mind that the Red Army's Asian battalions had supposedly been inspired by excerpts of *Manas* during World War II. The speakers spouted that *Manas* was alien to the party line or a propaganda tool for pan-Turkism.

After the harangues against the Kyrgyz epic, like a breakwater against the tide, Auezov rose from his seat and walked to a podium in the center of the stage. "Maybe in *Manas* there are some salutary words about bais and other nobility. But it is truly a priceless treasure of an entire people," the Kazakh writer said. "To tear it from the life of the Kyrgyz people is like cutting off the tongue of all Kyrgyz."

Although no verdict was pronounced in the hall that day, Kyrgyz spectators applauded as if Manas had been pulled from the guillotine. They cheered, teared up, and hugged one another. "*Süyünchü, süyünchü*"— good news!—they cried. "God bless Mukhtar's mother and the whole Kazakh people."[7]

For twenty-three-year-old Chingiz Aitmatov, Auezov's performance was inspirational. It was the first time he had witnessed somebody stand up to injustice in public. Aitmatov would long recall how Auezov had risked his own career and security by coming to Frunze, how the slight academic with the high forehead and receding hairline had battled heartless Soviet ideology with nothing but his own words and ideas.

Like Karakyz-apa's stories at the hearth, Auezov's defense of *Manas* fed a contrarian spirit inside the aspiring Kyrgyz writer.

—◦◦◦—

Several months after Auezov's brave stand in Frunze, Joseph Stalin died. For a minute on March 5, 1953, life stopped across the wide expanse of the Soviet Union. While a funeral dirge played on the radio, millions of Soviet citizens—from the sands of the Central Asian deserts to the frigid waters of the Arctic Ocean and from the cobblestone streets of the Baltic republics to the far border with China—came to a halt on street corners, suspended their work in the fields and stood at their factory positions. The greatest, most dominating, and despotic leader the Soviet Union had known was dead.

Chingiz Aitmatov was among the crowds in Frunze who turned out for the procession honoring Stalin a few days later. He may well have shed tears for the man who had directed the Soviet victory over the Germans, but it's likely his stomach churned from the inexplicable cruelty that had stolen his father and three uncles and branded his family an enemy of the people.

Aitmatov was not an anomaly in his mixed response to Stalin's death. Like many citizens growing up in the twisted reality of the Soviet Union, contradictions had become a part of everyday life. There was one's public persona—formed in large part by living day-to-day life in accordance with the demands of the party—and one's inner life of thoughts and feelings. Chingiz Aitmatov was learning to balance the two sides. Outwardly he was an earnest supporter of the state; inwardly he burned with a fire that he knew could only be expressed through writing.

With the door blocked to graduate studies, in the fall of 1953 Chingiz got a job as a veterinarian. He moved to an experimental farm outside Frunze with his wife, Kerez Shamshibaeva, a medical doctor, whom he had married in 1951, and soon thereafter sent for his mother and siblings in Talas (see figure 6.2). Seven people representing three generations, including Chingiz's infant son Sanjar, squeezed into two rooms at the farm. Living in Frunze, his sisters could go to university, and Nagima could get needed medical care for asthma and arthritis.

His rejection at the institute had strengthened Chingiz's resolve to be a writer.[8] He spent his days inspecting cows and bulls, but he devoted his free time to developing characters and plotlines that spoke more subtly about the onward march of communism. In an acknowledgment of his literary prowess and work as a scientist, Aitmatov was accepted into the Soviet Writers Union. Shortly thereafter, as a promising young writer from an ethnic minority, he was selected to study for two years in Moscow at the prestigious Gorky Institute of Literature, the training ground for the Soviet Union's up-and-coming writers and poets. It was a huge step forward for the son of an "enemy of the people."

In Moscow, Aitmatov soaked up the intellectual ferment, attending lectures, querying professors, and discussing the latest books with his

Figure 6.2: Chingiz Aitmatov (*right*) working as a veterinarian at an experimental farm outside Frunze in 1954. Source: Central State Archives of the Kyrgyz Republic.

fellow classmates. Amid the hustle and bustle of Moscow, he became convinced that he should focus his writing on village life in Kyrgyzia during the Great Patriotic War, as the Soviets called World War II—that crucible of privation and sacrifice through which he himself had passed.

"If I hadn't returned to my village, to those people whom I knew as a boy, to the image of my childhood motherland, I wouldn't have become a writer," Aitmatov would write in 1978. "I would be an expert in agriculture and animal husbandry."[9]

Aitmatov's decision to mine Sheker for story lines became the platform for his realist approach to writing. He wrote about the lives of people he had known during the war, careful, of course, to place them in the proper Soviet context. His social nature and curiosity led him to seek out memorable villagers from his youth and build characters based on them.

That was the case with Aitmatov's first novella, *Face to Face*, published in 1957 while he was still a student at the Gorky Institute. True to Aitmatov's writing creed, the novella was based on a true story of a deserter from the Red Army named Ismail who had actually survived in the mountains outside Sheker before being apprehended. In Aitmatov's rendering, Ismail is an odious character who grows more inhuman the longer he hides in the hills. In the novella's most memorable scene, a ravenous Ismail steals a neighbor's cow, cuts it open, and gorges on raw meat.

But critics in Kyrgyzia weren't interested in real-life stories, and they pelted the novella with criticism. How could an upstart author embarrass his home republic by shedding light on a deserter? Why show a renegade as a tragic figure when so many heroes died in the war, they asked? Yet in Moscow, where new trends in the arts were more welcomed in the period of relaxation following Stalin's death, Aitmatov's novella was well received. The riddle of Soviet publishing was that progressive writers from the republics often had a better chance of being recognized in Moscow than in their home republics. This was especially true in Kyrgyzia, where, after successive purges of the republic's elite, local party leaders and officials in the Kyrgyz Writers Union hewed closely to orthodox policy positions and lashed out at any deviations, such as blazing new trails in literature.

Even some party bureaucrats in the Soviet Writers Union were inclined to see *Face to Face* as groundbreaking—the first story ever about a Soviet deserter. And yet it covered its bases by upholding Soviet mores. Indeed, in *Face to Face*, Aitmatov gave socialist realism its due: while Ismail is debased, his wife turns him in and thus represents the upstanding Soviet citizen. But with his decision to focus much of the narrative on a deserter, Aitmatov underscored the age-old plight of the individual against the group—the struggle of man to be free—a far different angle than socialist realism.

In *Face to Face*, that individual was an unsympathetic degenerate, unworthy of much attention, but in his subsequent works Aitmatov's heroes would become more admirable. And as his heroes became more likeable, the system they were opposing became less so.

Success came at a price. The attacks against him in Kyrgyzia so debilitated Chingiz that he broke down physically. During much of the summer of 1957, he was confined to bed at the family apartment in Frunze, suffering from exhaustion with a rash spreading on his body. That's when, finally—after twenty years of no news—the family received a glimmer of hope about Törökul Aitmatov's fate.

Nagima Aitmatova had been waiting for news of her husband's whereabouts since 1939, the year she had found out that Törökul had been exiled to "far camps" without permission to communicate. That ten-year sentence had expired in 1949, with no updates about her husband. Perhaps, Nagima thought, Törökul had remarried in Siberia and even started a new family. She didn't begrudge him that.

"Just let him be alive," she would tell her children.

But as another ten years of waiting came to an end, Nagima's indomitable hope began to falter. The family had long ago stopped listening expectantly to footsteps along the street and knocks on the door. Her letter of January 1956 to the prosecutor general of Kyrgyzia had been met by stalling: her husband's case was being reviewed, she was told.

With his mother flagging, Chingiz had stepped in. After news of General Secretary Nikita Khrushchev's secret speech in February 1956 leaked out, he sensed a shift in Soviet society that might shed light on his father's fate. In the speech, Khrushchev had denounced Stalin for liquidating tens of thousands of honest communist and military leaders, people just like Törökul. The Aitmatov family's hopes rose even higher when Khrushchev closed down most labor camps, resulting in the release of millions of political prisoners.[10]

Pinning his hopes on the Soviet system being more forthcoming than Kyrgyz authorities, Chingiz appealed to the Office of the Military Prosecutor in Moscow in July 1956 for information about his father. "We don't know if he's alive or not, when he was sentenced and for what, and we don't know if he was really guilty," Chingiz wrote. "It's important for us to know the truth, to recover the spotless honor of our father and our family before the people."[11]

That letter produced a response in August 1957. In her arthritic hands—finally, after numerous letters and inquiries—Nagima Aitmatov gripped an official summons to NKVD headquarters to learn Törökul's fate. Her cheeks reddened, her green eyes sparkled a bit more, and she moved better around the family's apartment in Frunze. But bedridden Chingiz was in no condition to accompany his mother, so he urged his youngest sister, twenty-year-old Roza, to go with Nagima to NKVD headquarters.

Mother and daughter set off from the family's home on the outskirts of Frunze. On the bus Nagima talked excitedly, like a giddy schoolgirl.

Maybe she would even meet Törökul, she ventured to Roza. The family knew of other families whose loved ones had made it home after Khrushchev's announcement. So, why not Törökul?

While Roza waited below, Nagima climbed the stairs of the NKVD headquarters. Her lined face and pinched expression were evidence of how markedly she had aged over the previous twenty years. Racked by asthma and arthritis in her joints, she was painfully thin, a shell of the soft-skinned, blond-haired woman who had married Törökul decades earlier.

Nagima emerged a while later, ashen-faced. Holding back her own tears, Roza embraced her mother. In place of the invitation, Nagima held a piece of paper informing the family of Törökul's posthumous rehabilitation. Like millions of others, Törökul had been exonerated. There was no criminal case against him; he had committed no crime. But he was gone forever. A few days later, the family would receive Törökul's official death certificate:

Date of death: November 5, 1938.
Reason of death: unknown.
Place of death: unknown.

Nagima and Roza gathered themselves before heading home. There were unanswered questions, but they had little confidence they would ever know the truth. After all, it had taken the NKVD twenty years to acknowledge Törökul's death.

"We must subjugate ourselves to fate," Nagima said. "We can change nothing." They agreed not to cry when they returned home. "We don't want to disappoint Chingiz and have him collapse completely," Nagima said.[12]

—~~~—

Recovered from exhaustion, Chingiz returned to Moscow in the fall of 1957 for his second and final year at the Gorky Institute. It was a heady time, with Khrushchev's Thaw allowing for more freedom of expression in the literary field. Aitmatov set about writing his second novella, a love story that had been germinating in his head for months.

Jamilya, the novella's eponymous hero, is an unconventional young woman. Forced to marry a young man who is drafted into the military, Jamilya lives with her in-laws, as was the tradition. But in her mannerisms and character, she is a free spirit who laughs and plays practical jokes, seemingly unaware of her magnetic beauty. She is spry and quick-witted. But in the same way that Aitmatov had courted scandal with an army deserter, he flouted convention by having Jamilya run off with another man, thus deserting her husband.

The story is about a young woman's pursuit of freedom in the face of traditional conventions that restrain her, and how that pursuit liberates not just Jamilya but also those around her. In one of the novella's memorable scenes, Jamilya beckons Daniyar, the melancholy wounded veteran whom she often ridicules, to sing as they return from a day's work. The prompt is likely just more jesting from Jamilya.

But Daniyar's soulful renditions of Kyrgyz melodies speak to Jamilya's sadness about her unhappy marriage. She gazes at Daniyar, transfixed and tempered. As Seit, Jamilya's young brother-in-law, watches the love affair between Jamilya and Daniyar blossom, he is inspired to follow his own dream. Making an unusual choice for a village boy, he leaves home to study art at a university in Frunze.

At a time when Soviet literature was emphasizing the impersonal collective, *Jamilya* resounded with the importance of the individual's quest for personal liberty, creative expression, and freethinking. It's an uplifting story of the power of love and how risk taking is an essential part of creativity.

But that was all too much for staid Kyrgyzia. The republic's top literary journal refused to publish the novella, claiming, "Kyrgyz women do not behave that way."[13] At a Communist Party meeting, a member of the older generation of Kyrgyzia's writers tore into Aitmatov for failing to follow the dictates of socialist realism. "Each instance of divorce," the elderly writer said, "is a problem of huge importance that must be discussed by the Communist Party. The party is the bulwark protecting the unity of each family."[14]

Did Aitmatov not understand that divorce was like a scarlet letter, and that it was a writer's duty to depict divorce-seeking couples negatively, the writer wondered aloud? In the communist view, Jamilya was a betrayer not just of a man but of the party too. Using communist jargon, the writer lectured Aitmatov on proper communist etiquette that evidently extended to people's personal affairs.

To save time, Aitmatov had written *Jamilya* simultaneously in two languages, first a page in Kyrgyz and then he would translate that page immediately into Russian before continuing. This way, he reasoned, he could get the Russian version out in Moscow and maybe blunt orthodox critics at home.

He wasn't able to avoid attacks in Frunze, but the Russian version was a smashing success and eventually gained the young Kyrgyz writer international acclaim. The story was published in the October 1958 edition of the literary journal *Novy Mir*, whose editor Alexander Tvardovski was taking advantage of the Thaw to publish daring prose, including works by Alexander Solzhenitsyn.[15]

But the real midwife of *Jamilya* was Mukhtar Auezov, the man whom Aitmatov had admired from afar in 1952 at the *Manas* trial. Connected like falling dominos, a series of serendipitous events in Moscow propelled Aitmatov to fame: a crowded literary event, at which Aitmatov gives up his chair to Auezov; a visit with the venerated Kazakh writer where Aitmatov gives him a copy of *Jamilya*; Auezov's introduction of Aitmatov to the French writer Louis Aragon, who is captivated by *Jamilya* and writes a review after translating the novella into French.[16]

In Aragon's review, which ran in *L'Humanité*, the newspaper of the French Communist Party, he introduced French readers to Kyrgyzia—a country he described as "wedged between Tajikistan, China and Kazakhstan." Like a tour guide to an unfamiliar land, Aragon used details from Aitmatov's novella to educate French readers about fragrant flowers in Talas, a one-track railway running along the river and carts laden with wheat clattering along the steppe. It was likely one of the first descriptions of Kyrgyzia in a Western publication.

Aragon praised the fifty-two-page novella. "There is not an excess word nor a phrase that doesn't touch the soul," he wrote. He then penned the words that would carry Aitmatov's name past the petty recriminations of conservative communists in Frunze and far beyond the borders of Kyrgyzia. "Somehow, somewhere in Central Asia, at the beginning of the second half of the 20th century, a young man could write a story that, I swear to you, is the most beautiful love story in the world."[17]

7

The Sting of Rejection

Nearing forty years old, Azamat Altay started to despair about his prospects for marrying. During his time in Germany, he had dated women, but those relationships had never lasted. A failed date with a woman named Olga was a bitter reminder that he would never find a match in Germany.

At a Munich restaurant one evening, as Altay secured an empty table, Olga walked past a group of German men who had evidently noticed her enter with the Asian-looking Altay. The men addressed her loud enough for other patrons to hear. When she joined Altay at the table, she was distraught. "It's good you don't speak German," a tearful Olga said. "They asked me where a pure-blooded Aryan woman drags out this Mongol from."

The pejorative "Mongol" was loaded with invective. The insult had roots in fascist views of racial superiority, but also in the grim memories of the battle for Berlin and the ensuring Soviet occupation. According to researchers, at least 110,000 German women, from young girls to grandmothers, were raped between late summer and early autumn 1945. Germans pointed the finger at Soviet soldiers, who, hardened after years of fighting and inebriated with victory and alcohol, treated the woman as war spoils. Some of the most horrific abuse involved so-called Mongol-looking Soviet soldiers.[1]

"Their words aren't worth your tears," Altay tried to comfort Olga. "Go find a pure-blood. Maybe one day I will find myself a non-pure blood."

Such unpleasant incidents were one of the reasons why Altay had wanted a new start in the United States. But he didn't have much luck meeting possible matches in New York, so in 1958, on the way back from the hajj pilgrimage in Saudi Arabia, he stopped in Turkey, where friends from his postwar days had relocated. They assured Altay that he had a better chance of finding a Muslim wife in Istanbul, a melting pot of Turkic peoples cast adrift by World War II. Altay could mingle with Kyrgyz, Kazakhs, and Tatars, and choose from among his friends' unmarried sisters and sisters-in-law.

But after meeting fifteen "candidates" in three days, Altay didn't find a fit. He resigned himself to returning to New York a bachelor. But a Kazakh friend proposed a last meeting. He brought two sisters to meet Altay, who by this time was fed up with conversation and niceties. The two friends hit on a quick way to end the matchmaking session. If Altay liked the woman sitting nearest him, he would answer yes to his Kazakh friend's question "Did you put the book back correctly?"

That "book" became his wife, Saniye, and she joined Altay in New York in 1959 (see figure 7.1). It's not surprising Altay took a liking to Saniye, with her soft features and bright smile. She was an antidote to the stubborn, brittle sides of his personality. Raised in a Tatar family from Russia's Ural Mountains region, by the time she met Altay, the thirty-seven-year-old Saniye, too, had seen her share of strife. Like Altay, the winds of history had scattered her family around the globe, forcing them to flee chaos in the Soviet Union in the 1920s and take refuge in China and Japan before arriving in Turkey.

Fortunately, Saniye spoke English, which boded well for an easier transition in America. The couple moved into an apartment on Linden Avenue in Brooklyn and started a life together. Over the coming decades, they would occupy traditional roles in their relationship: Altay as the breadwinner and Saniye as homemaker.

Partnering with Saniye spurred Altay to connect with the exile Tatar community in New York. He joined the American-Tatar Association. With the Kyrgyz and Tatars sharing a similar history, language and religion, there was a natural kinship. Members of the tiny Kyrgyz diaspora in New York celebrated holidays at the association's house in College Point, Queens. For the newlywed couple who would never have children, the tight-knit Tatar community became a center of social life; they attended picnics and celebrations of rites of passage, such as birthdays, weddings,

Figure 7.1: Azamat Altay and his wife Saniye in New York in 1959, around the time of their marriage. Source: Photo courtesy of Gulnara Turganbaeva.

and funerals. Despite being a Kyrgyz, Altay would eventually be elected president of the American-Tatar Association and give presentations on famous figures in Tatar history at the association's meetings.

At the same time, Altay kept in touch with his fellow Kyrgyz, particularly the ones who had come over with him in 1956 and also settled in New York. He often visited Jorobek Ashur, an illiterate man from southern Kyrgyzstan who lived with his German wife and four children in Brooklyn. Here was a man, cast by the winds of fate into Western societies, who couldn't even read and write his own language, let alone master new languages. When a letter arrived from Soviet Kyrgyzia, Ashur would rely on Altay to read it to him and then write a response back.

Altay became quite attached to Ashur's four children, all of whom had Kyrgyz names that Altay himself had given them. He would teach them Kyrgyz phrases when he visited on the weekends. Jorobek's son Kurmanbek especially enjoyed learning Kyrgyz words. He would ask questions and talk of visiting his father's birthplace in southern Kyrgyzia. When the childless Altay remarked that he had no children to bury him, Kurmanbek piped up: "What about me?"

If Altay was integrating into American society, Ashur remained marginal, able to work only as a doorman and limited to cursory conversations with his quickly Americanizing children because they didn't share a common language.

Altay's own English improved with the passing of years, although he would always retain a strong accent.[2] The major problem he faced in assimilation was not culture shock or finding work but his unwieldy name. Americans just couldn't seem to get their mouths around his nine-syllable name, Kudaibergen Kojomberdiev. A run-in with the police in the early 1960s was the "final straw."

After he was stopped for speeding in New York, Altay handed his license to the police officer. But the policeman, evidently frustrated at being unable to pronounce Altay's full birth name, assessed him a higher-than-usual fine, based, the policeman said, on the number of letters in Altay's name. That was twenty-four letters, so it must have been a whopper of a fine.

Altay was indignant. He writes in his memoir that he when he protested the amount of the fine in court, the judge actually increased the amount he had to pay in hopes that Altay would never again appear in court with such a long name.

So, in 1961 in anticipation of receiving American citizenship, Altay, a man who had used numerous pseudonyms in his writing and reporting, changed his name from Kudaibergen Kojomberdiev to Azamat Altay. He chose his new name after studied consideration. The word "Azamat" is a compliment in Kyrgyz, with the connotation of "praiseworthy." "Altay" indicates the ancient homeland of the Kyrgyz people in the Altai Mountains in Siberia. As a result, Altay went from being known as the "God given son of Kojomberdi" to "the praiseworthy son of the Altai Mountains." And Americans got a mercifully shorter name, the new one nine syllables shorter than his birth name. Azamat Altay faced no problems in gaining US citizenship, collecting a new passport with his new name inscribed in November 1961.

———

The early 1960s was a tense time in superpower relations. On the world stage, Khrushchev blustered and threatened. "Your grandchildren will live under Communism," he had famously said in 1957 to millions of American viewers while being interviewed on the CBS news program *Face the Nation*.[3]

While the boisterous Khrushchev was given to exaggeration, the US government had reason to be worried. Not only was the planned economy raising the standard of living across the Soviet Union, including in remote places like Kyrgyzia; it was also besting the US in military and space competition. The Soviets had tested a nuclear weapon in 1949, and they surged ahead in the space race in 1957 with the launch of Sputnik, the world's first space satellite. In 1961 the Soviet cosmonaut Yuri Gagarin became the first human to journey into outer space.

Then in August 1961, a crisis in Berlin set the world on edge. In an overnight operation supported by the Soviet Union, communist East Germany erected a barrier to stop its citizens from fleeing to the West. Since 1945, more than three million East Germans had escaped the Soviet-occupied zone, causing deep concern in Moscow about the long-term viability of their communist German counterpart.[4] The blitzkrieg-type operation during the night of August 13 had been intended to close down a popular escape route.

For several weeks afterward, the world watched anxiously as the superpowers trained firepower on one another. American M48 Patton and Soviet T-54 tanks faced each other—like boxers starring each other down. But work continued, and over the course of several weeks temporary barbed wire gave way to a 110-mile cement and brick structure that came to be known as the Berlin Wall, the most visible symbol of the world's division into two rival camps.

Churchill's figurative Iron Curtain had become a concrete barrier walling in East Germans, like animals in a zoo.

———

Altay's name change added to his mystique. He had already long been considered a top enemy of the Soviet Union, "one of the ringleaders of anti-communist activity" in Central Asia, according to the Soviet "black list." Soviet authorities tacked Azamat Altay onto the list of pseudonyms and noms de guerre he had used over the years: Kadyr Asanov, Kurman-bekov Abdy, Kudaibergen Koshoi, and Kudaibergen Kyrgyz.[5]

Because of Altay's high profile, the KGB knew it would score a propaganda coup if Altay—one of the founding members of Radio Liberty's Turkestan Service and now an American citizen—could be convinced to return to the Soviet Union. Soviet spies had done their homework—keeping up with his move to the United States and his name change—and set about luring him back home. Aware of his homesickness, the KGB exploited his weak point: lack of communication with his father.

Or, rather, the KGB continued to exploit his weak point.

Unbeknownst to Altay, the KGB had made contact with him in 1958 in Saudi Arabia when he was on the hajj pilgrimage. The approach was made through a Muslim preacher from southern Kyrgyzia named Muslim Jeyenbekov who was visiting Mecca as part of a delegation from the Soviet Union. The preacher greeted Altay warmly, and the two men talked for a long time about Islam in Soviet Kyrgyzia.[6]

After visiting Altay's father upon his return to Kyrgyzia, Jeyenbekov wrote Altay that his father had slaughtered a lamb in gratitude for the good news that his son was alive and well in America. Altay and the preacher corresponded for several years, with the preacher addressing Altay with the honorific "haji" and calling him "my eternal friend who I discovered in Mecca." The wily preacher made sure to congratulate Altay on his marriage, sent him books for his personal library, and hinted at Altay's possible return.[7]

A second approach came later in the late 1960s from a high-ranking official in Altay's village of Korumduu. In a letter dated September 25, 1969, the chairman of the village's collective farm updated Altay on village happenings, making sure to name Altay's relatives and inform him of how their children were doing. Then, striking an empathetic tone, the chairman dangled his bait, writing that not all Soviet POWs from World War II were guilty of treason. He closed out with an intriguingly honest appeal to Altay to return home: "It's better to live like a slave in your homeland than like a sultan in a foreign country."

Neither the preacher's well-crafted approach nor the collective chairman's sentimental appeal worked. Decades of surviving on his own had hardened Altay, and he was clearheaded about the fate that awaited him should he return to the Soviet Union. "I didn't stay here to be a sultan," Altay replied to the chairman. "I cannot say anything about returning home. Children of the same parents are different. I found my own way."[8]

———

The KGB operations against Altay were part of a sprawling espionage and intelligence network that worked across the world. In New York, Soviet efforts to advance communism and US attempts to blunt it met head on. Under the cover of both their consulate and the UN mission, the Soviets engaged the United States in a soft power struggle.

New York City had long been a center of espionage and counter-espionage. After World War II, the city roiled with the influx of tens of thousands of Soviet refugees, including Altay himself. Virtually every minority group from the Soviet Union—be they Russians, Ukrainians, Armenians or from the Baltic republics or Central Asia—had a beachhead in the New York metropolitan area from which they pushed an anti-Soviet agenda.

Soviet activity in the intellectual Cold War in New York emanated from the Four Continents' Bookstore (FCB) at 822 Broadway Avenue. Allegedly operating independently as a communist-registered organization in the United States, the FCB was, in reality, an appendage of Soviet intelligence, receiving operating orders from the Soviet embassy and shipments of books from the Soviet Union. As the long arm of Soviet propaganda in the United States, FCB sold Soviet literature, language, and scientific material in North America. The works of Marx, Engels, and Lenin were on sale, as well as the Moscow daily newspapers *Izvestiya* and *Pravda*.[9]

On the US side, the CIA countered with its own book program. In what one employee later described as "a Marshall Plan for the mind," the CIA, in cooperation with Radio Liberty, established a wholly owned CIA company that masqueraded as a private publishing house.[10] Operating out of offices on Park Avenue South in Manhattan, the Bedford Publishing House printed Russian-language translations of books on politics, economics, philosophy, art, and technology. These were then given at no charge to Soviet travelers to the West or provided to Westerners to distribute while visiting the Soviet Union.

Soviet citizens, it turned out, were hungry for Western reading material, especially books banned in the Soviet Union. They gobbled up medical texts, novels by Joyce and Nabokov, as well as art museum catalogs and Parisian fashion magazines. The program worked like a personalized book club, with files kept on recipients' reading tastes.[11] Papers in Altay's archives indicate that on occasion he would provide lists of books by Kyrgyz authors, including Aitmatov's novels, to be supplied to visitors from the Soviet Union.

Members of the Moscow Philharmonic reportedly slipped book pages in between music sheets to conceal them on their way back to Moscow. A woman flying from London to Moscow hid a miniaturized edition of Solzhenitsyn's *Gulag Archipelago* in her infant son's diaper. All told, from 1956 to 1970, the book program, which at its height had offices in London, Paris, Munich, and Rome, reportedly delivered up to one million books to the Soviet Union.

The "soft" Cold War and targeting by the KGB notwithstanding, day-to-day life in New York was rather mundane for Altay. He would commute to Manhattan and then change subway lines to head up to Columbia University, where he worked at Butler Library (see figure 7.2). Altay had started working in the Slavic Acquisitions Department in September 1963 after seven years at the New York Public Library.

Positions at both libraries were technical in nature—locating and ordering books and organizing and updating card catalogs—and thus not very intellectually challenging. But the library jobs suited him because they allowed him to read the latest publications from Soviet Central Asia and didn't require him to have a fluent grasp of English.

The working environment in the Slavic Acquisitions Departments resembled New York City's diverse émigré community. There were Russians who had fled after the revolution, a Belorussian, a Pole, and a Slovak. The group was collegial, with jokes about the Russians as the "elder brothers" and the other nationalities, including the lone Kyrgyz, as the "younger brothers."

Altay earned a reputation as a hardworking, reliable employee, but he chafed at working with some of the women in the office. His short

Figure 7.2: Azamat Altay at Columbia University's Butler Library in the 1960s or 1970s. Source: Photo courtesy of Gulnara Turganbaeva.

temper got him in trouble, just as it had at New York Public Library, where he had clashed with his boss. As befit his upbringing in a traditional society, Altay believed that a woman's place was at home while a man should earn a living outside the house. Having little experience working with women in professional environments, he had run-ins with female bosses and coworkers. With his broad shoulders and stocky torso, he was a physically strong specimen and could be quite intimidating when his temper flared during disagreements. By his own admission, he cost himself a promotion at Columbia for losing his cool after a female boss proposed that he cull the Slavic collections for superfluous books. "Even a cleaning lady wouldn't throw out books," Altay had fired back. Altay's retort was as much a cultural difference as it was a question of temper. Where he came from books were precious, so precious that he had buried some for safekeeping during the purges. They were not to be thrown away.

In other ways, Altay's hard-charging attitude paid dividends. Believing that only a lazy person couldn't find work in America, he had multiple sources of income. In addition to his work as a Turkic-language specialist at Butler Library, he wrote a weekly column for Radio Liberty called "Report from America." His reporting allowed him to keep his hand in journalism and his name circulating at Radio Liberty; sometimes his reports were picked up by dozens of language services.

Altay's most fulfilling work, though, was with Edward Allworth, a brilliant scholar of Turkic history who arrived at Columbia University in the early 1960s. For Altay, Allworth was an American version of Alexandre Bennigsen, Altay's longtime friend in Europe. Allworth, who himself had parachuted behind German lines on D-Day and carried through with the 101st Airborne Division to the Allied victory a year later, became the same sort of combination of friend and mentor to the transplanted Altay that Bennigsen had been. Allworth was an inveterate anticommunist and a consummate scholar of Central Asia, with a knowledge of numerous Central Asian languages. Like Altay, he was a formal man, wearing a suit and tie to class every day, and self-effacing, declining to speak much about his wartime service or his own achievements.[12]

In the early 1960s, Altay and Allworth, men joined together by wartime service in occupied France and similar dispositions, began a productive fifteen-year working relationship. Allworth, then an associate professor of Turco-Soviet Studies, enlisted Altay to research Turkic-language holdings in the United States for a bibliographic reference book. Along with his colleagues, each of whom possessed different Turkic- or Persian-language skills, Altay scoured libraries across the country, registering their Turkic-language books and manuscripts. The findings of the researchers were then compiled by Allworth in a four-hundred-page book that, when it was published in 1971, was the most comprehensive register of its kind.

Altay's research work with Allworth, who later became director of the Program on Soviet Nationality Problems, contributed to Columbia University's reputation in the 1970s and 1980s as the leading institution in the United States for the study of nationalities in the Soviet Union. With the help of Altay and others siphoning through Soviet Central Asian publications and literature, graduate students completed pioneering research into Moscow's relations with the Central Asian republics.

While his actual work in Butler Library was rather rote, Altay relished being around books, particularly Columbia's extensive holdings of books in Kyrgyz. That collection included original versions of the *Manas* epic, not the expurgated versions in circulation in the Soviet Union. Altay took pride in the fact that Columbia University had become a sort of holding pen for the denigrated epic, as well as for books banned in the Soviet Union. He remembered how, as a teenager spooked by the communist government's campaign against Kasym Tynystanov in the 1930s, he had hidden his own copies of Tynystanov's books in a metal box which he had then buried in the ground near his house. At Columbia, however, Tynystanov's books stood proudly on the shelves, and Altay taught himself the Arabic alphabet so he could read the author's early works.

———

By the mid-1960s, a sense of deep loss and melancholy stirred Altay's soul. He had been away from Kyrgyzia for more than two decades, long enough for a new generation to grow up. As he neared his fifties, he wondered if he would always be an outcast from his own society, if he would ever embrace his father again.

While helping graduate students and working in the library provided consolation that he was keeping the Kyrgyz culture alive, he pined for meetings with actual people. Only Kyrgyz could talk about the mountains and lakes, discuss common acquaintances and replenish his stagnant memories.

Thus, he had been thrilled in 1959 when his boss at New York Public Library asked him to host Mukhtar Auezov, who was traveling in the United States as a member of a delegation of Soviet writers. Altay knew Auezov's background—his support for an independent Turkestan in the early 1920s, his defense of the *Manas* epic in 1952, and the fact that he had recently won the Soviet Union's highest literary prize.

Normally, Soviet delegations traveling in the West—and especially in the United States—were required to stick to regimented schedules so as to minimize unsanctioned contact with foreigners. But as a scholar of the Central Asian epics, Auezov knew the New York Public Library had a superb collection of Turkic-language eposes that were unavailable in the Soviet Union, so he asked the US State Department to set up a personal visit for him to the library.

Dressed in a coat and tie for the special occasion, Altay made a detour on his way to the library to buy the Kazakh author's latest book *The Path of Abay*, for which he had just been awarded the Lenin Prize, thus becoming the first Central Asian to receive the award. Altay hoped the famous Kazakh author would sign a copy of his book.

Altay stopped in at the Four Corners Bookstore. Yes, the bookstore that was the focal point of KGB operations in the United States carried a book by a so-called Kazakh nationalist writer. The bookstore might not have had such a book in stock ten years earlier, but with the Thaw under way and de-Stalinization working in Auezov's favor, Altay was in luck.

Recognizing a face from Central Asia upon his arrival at Butler Library, Auezov greeted Altay in Kazakh.

"So, you are from the regions of Kyrgyzia?" asked Auezov.

"From Issyk Kul," Altay replied in Kyrgyz.

"From what tribe?"

"From the Bugu tribe," Altay answered.

"My friend, you are from one of the most famous Kyrgyz tribes," Auezov said.

It was just the sort of conversation opener Altay longed for. Immediate connection. The two men bantered back and forth, with Auezov speaking Kazakh and Altay replying in Kyrgyz. The two men then looked over the books Altay had collected for Auezov's visit, including the library's copy of a Turkic epic poem that Altay had located. Auezov politely declined Altay's invitation to dinner, replying diplomatically that the delegation had little free time in its schedule.

Although his meeting with Altay was short, it made an impression on Auezov. On a visit to Kyrgyzia in 1960, he would tell a group of young writers that, much to his surprise, he had met a Kyrgyz man in New York, a "young, educated Kyrgyz of yours from the south shore of Issyk Kul."

"He invited me to his house," Auezov told the writers, "but they didn't let me go."[13]

For Beksultan Jakiev, an aspiring writer in the audience, Auezov's tale of a Kyrgyz in America was spellbinding. How could one of his countrymen have survived to make it to the land of the enemy and then actually host Auezov at his place of work? It was as if the Kazakh writer had told the gathering that Altay was making a life for himself on the moon. The story left a deep imprint on Jakiev, as did the fact that he and Altay hailed from the same collective farm near Lake Issyk Kul.

—⁓—

Expo 67 was a truly international event, gathering sixty-two nations in Montreal around the theme "Man and His World" and thus providing an accessible platform for Altay to meet his fellow Kyrgyz among the Soviet delegation. From April to October 1967, fifty million visitors entered the fairgrounds, which were built on reclaimed land and newly created islands in the St. Lawrence River. Most visitors gravitated to the eye-catching pavilions of the Soviet Union and the United States, which vied for attention in a subtle version of the Cold War.

The Soviet pavilion, with walls of glass and a gold-colored ski-jump roof, was a big draw. Across a narrow channel of water stood the US pavilion, which was modeled after a geodesic sphere and seemed to sparkle and float above the park grounds like a silvery bubble. Inside their respective pavilions, both nations showed off their space prowess, with the Soviets exhibiting a replica of Yuri Gagarin's space capsule and the Americans showcasing technology that would eventually help carry astronauts to the moon.[14]

Altay arrived in Montreal as Radio Liberty's correspondent to cover "Days of Kyrgyzia," one of many national festivals in the Soviet pavilion featuring painters, dancers, and writers from the Soviet republics.

While Altay was excited to meet some of the most famous cultural figures of Soviet Kyrgyzia, he was particularly keen to meet Bübüs-aira Beishenalieva, the republic's prima ballerina. Beishenalieva was, perhaps, Kyrgyzia's greatest cultural treasure, a gifted dancer whose improbable rise from a Kyrgyz village to Leningrad's Marinsky Theater seemed to confirm communism's promise of civilizing the masses. For this reason, she was an ideal person for the Soviets to showcase at Expo 67.

Altay first met a group of Kyrgyz writers and artists. The head of the Kyrgyz delegation Beishenbay Murataliev, a high-ranking member of the Kyrgyz Communist Party's Central Committee, gave Altay a warm welcome, remarking in front of the group that Altay had come from the United States to celebrate the republic's national festival. Another man asked in a sympathetic way about Altay's captivity as a prisoner of war. There were innocuous questions about the number of Kyrgyz living in America and what they did for jobs. The two sides, on opposite sides of the Cold War divide, were sniffing each other out.

Altay recognized Kyrgyzia's most famous landscape painter, the mustachioed Gapar Aitiev, with whom he had worked at a youth newspaper before the war.

"Gapar-aga," Altay addressed Aitiev with the honorific for older Kyrgyz. "I know you from the old days when you were editor of the *Young Lenin* newspaper."

Aitiev's answer sliced Altay like a knife. "You live among the skyscrapers of New York," the painter said. "You betrayed your people."

The others in the room went silent.

Altay protested: "Gapar-aga, that was my fate. I had to live in New York."

"Soon your New York will be smothered," Aitiev retorted.

Altay lost his cool. Discarding the Soviet name of the republic's capital, Frunze, he fired back using the Kyrgyz name: "Gapar, I would never wish that Bishkek would be smothered, but I do wish that the Moscow you pray to will crumble."

"Get out of here, you CIA agent," Aitiev screamed.

Murataliev, an even-tempered, judicious man, reprimanded Aitiev for instigating the argument. Altay exited the room and waited for a bus to take him back to the pavilion, tears welling in his eyes. Aitiev emerged onto the street and, evidently trying to make amends, straightened Altay's crooked tie.

Altay set his sights on meeting Beishenalieva. He felt he knew her life story already: how she had grown up in a village in northern Kyrgyzia and then been trained in Leningrad by the legendary Russian ballerina Galina Ulanova. Back in New York, he had even persuaded a student at Columbia University to write her dissertation on Kyrgyzia's star ballerina and then helped by snipping articles and photos from Kyrgyz newspapers and magazines.

Upon being introduced to Altay, Beishenalieva continued to stand. Though she spoke Kyrgyz fluently, she addressed Altay in Russian. Both were bad omens.

"Here's a gift from the Soviet Union," Beishenalieva said stiffly, handing Altay a packet of cigarettes.

After thanking her, Altay explained how he had ended up living outside the Soviet Union.

"You aren't worth a cent if you live in a foreign country," Beishenalieva rudely interjected.

Gathering himself from another emotional blow, Altay said, "Bübüsaira, I know you have a son. I pray to God that he knows nothing of the things I have had to live through."

Altay returned the pack of cigarettes to Beishenalieva and left the room.[15]

―――――

Altay retreated to a bar. While the encounter with Aitiev was bruising, Beishenalieva's rejection exploded like a bomb over his head. The Bübüsaira he had imagined—elegant, beautiful, and understanding—was actually mean-spirited and full of rancor. The wounds ran deep, and they would take a long time to heal.

Altay learned later that delegation head Murataliev had reprimanded the Kyrgyz participants for their rude behavior, warning them that those who didn't know how to behave in a civil way would hurt their chances of traveling abroad in the future. By their caustic comments, they had damaged Kyrgyzia's reputation, the party official said. It was a valiant gesture from a humane man, but the damage had already been done.

8

Balancing Acts

In the high-ceilinged Moscow reception hall, the Soviet Union's cultural elite applauded as Chingiz Aitmatov was awarded the 1963 Lenin Prize for Literature. Members of the audience snapped photos as the thirty-four-year-old Aitmatov, dressed in a dark suit with a light-colored tie, embraced white-haired officials, and dignitaries on the stage. In remarks to the audience, after paying tribute to the Russian people and to Russian literature for helping to form him as a writer, he addressed the Kyrgyz people, the wellspring of his stories.

"The fact that today a Kyrgyz writer is receiving the country's highest award for literary achievement is the achievement of the entire Kyrgyz people," he said in a high-pitched voice. "This is its maturity."[1]

Aitmatov was the second writer from Central Asia—after Mukhtar Auezov in 1959—to win the prestigious Lenin Prize, the Soviet Union's most prestigious literary award. With his realist portrayals of Kyrgyz life after the war, Aitmatov had struck a chord in Soviet society, a chord that, to be sure, tacked along the socialist realism line but not to excess. Local newspapers in Kyrgyzia covered the awards ceremony with columns of print. The government of Soviet Kyrgyzia printed a booklet urging librarians in the republic to use Aitmatov's works to educate the public on the "high moral qualities of the Soviet man." A humble native son had risen to the heights of literary stardom (see figure 8.1).

Back in Frunze, members of the Aitmatov family cheered the monumental event for a different reason. The Lenin Prize confirmed the family's return to the ranks of respected members of society. No longer would Chingiz or his siblings have to endure cold shoulders or looks of

Figure 8.1: Chingiz Aimatov signing copies of *Jamilya* at a book fair in Frunze in 1963.
Source: Central State Archives of the Kyrgyz Republic.

disdain from party hacks or opportunistic bureaucrats intent on denying
them rightfully earned opportunities.

Upon his return from the awards ceremony in Moscow, Chingiz went
straight from the airport to the hospital, where Nagima was resting after
taking ill a few days before the ceremony. To keep her company, she had
posted a photo of the late Törökul with young Chingiz in her room. Raising herself unsteadily from her bed, Nagima collapsed into Chingiz's
arms and burst into tears. The fear that had gripped her for decades—
ever since Törökul had spoken of his impending arrest in 1937—was
finally starting to ebb.

⸺

Not long after he saw his mother, Chingiz shared his good news with
Bübüsaira Beishenalieva—the prima ballerina who would treat Azamat
Altay so coldly in Montreal in 1967. Beishenalieva was Aitmatov's mis-
tress—and his soul mate—and their relationship would give him the
happiest days of his life.

Aitmatov and Beishenalieva had met in Leningrad in July 1959. Their
rendezvous came during a tour of the cruiser *Aurora*, the ship that had

Figure 8.2: Chingiz Aitmatov and Bübüsaira Beishenalieva aboard the cruiser *Aurora* in Leningrad in July 1959. To the right of Aitmatov is Turdukan Usubaliev, who would rise to become the leader of the Communist Party of Soviet Kyrgyzia for twenty-five years. Source: Central State Archives of the Kyrgyz Republic.

launched the 1917 revolution (see figure 8.2). Beishenalieva was in Leningrad for the filming of a Kyrgyz ballet at Leningrad Film Studios; Aitmatov was a member of a high-level Kyrgyz delegation visiting with sailors from Kyrgyzia serving in the Soviet Baltic Fleet. Aitmatov was captivated by Beishenalieva's sparkling eyes, dancer's figure and black hair blowing in the breeze. It was as if, Aitmatov would recall years later, "our feelings suddenly ignited and burst into flames."[2]

Amid fulfilling their official duties, the two managed to spend much of the next week together, their romance heightened by Leningrad's famed White Nights. They strolled along canals, conversed on park benches and visited the museums of the Venice of the North, as Leningrad was known because of its design by Italian architects during the eighteenth century. They continued their courtship in Moscow when Aitmatov came up with a ruse to prolong his trip.

—⁓—

Beishenalieva was attractive, independent, and untraditional. She combined beauty, soft skin and a bright smile, with physical strength, and arm and leg muscles toned through years of ballet training. But she was not fixated on physical conditioning; she followed no particular diet and smoked cigarettes. She was stylish, with a taste for imported clothes, and self-sufficient: at home, she cleaned the house and fixed her own clogged pipes. Married at eighteen, a mother at nineteen, and divorced shortly thereafter, she lived alone with her son, unusual in Soviet society at the time.

Unconventional as she might have been, Beishenalieva was indebted to the Soviet system for transforming her from a provincial village girl who couldn't speak Russian into a multilingual ballerina who traveled the world. She was a loyal citizen and did the system's bidding, including ostracizing "traitors" like Altay.

Recruiters from the storied Leningrad State Choreographic Institute, the feeder school for Leningrad's Marinsky Ballet, had discovered Beishenalieva when they were touring Kyrgyzia in search of aspiring dancers. The recruitment was part of the Soviet Union's cultural policy to extend the arts of Russia throughout the Soviet republics. Deemed to possess the physical characteristics for future success in ballet, ten-year-old Beishenalieva left her home village in 1936 to study in Leningrad.

As part of a vanguard group of twenty-four ballet students from Kyrgyzia, she learned French, studied the piano, and trained in ballet. "We didn't know," she would say later of those early years in Leningrad. "We just believed."

After excelling in Leningrad under the tutelage of renowned ballet instructor Agrippina Vaganova, Beishenalieva became the lead dancer for the Kyrgyz Ballet troupe in the late 1940s and shortly thereafter started teaching ballet at the Frunze Choreographic School.[3] She performed throughout the Soviet Union and toured Eastern Europe, even dancing with Soviet General Secretary Khrushchev in 1958 at a festival in Moscow celebrating Kyrgyz culture.

Nothing evidenced Beishenalieva's transition from Kyrgyz village girl to Soviet ballerina more than a visit to her home village of Vorontsovka, nestled in the foothills of the Ala Too Mountains. In the 1960s and early 1970s, few residents of Vorontsovka had ever heard of, let alone seen, ballet. So when village elders asked Beishenalieva to demonstrate her skills, she took off her coat and, there in front of the *aksakals*—respected elders, or "white beards"—did thirty-four fouettés. While village women turned away from the unfamiliar spectacle, the *aksakals* nodded their heads in approval as Beishenalieva spun around and around. "Now we can rest assured that we have seen ballet performed," they said.[4]

During their first days together in Leningrad, Aitmatov gave Beishenalieva a signed copy of *Jamilya*. "I dedicate this modest story to my most favorite and dear person in the world," Aitmatov wrote in the front pages as if they had been together for years, not days. Under his signature and the date August 2, 1959, he added, "I hope we always remember this day, this happy day in our lives."

Aitmatov's gift of *Jamilya* to the independent-minded Beishenalieva was only fitting, a romantic gesture to his heroine come-to-life. Some even surmise the writer had Beishenalieva in mind when he wrote *Jamilya* in his dorm room in Moscow.

He may well have.

When he was a student at the Agricultural Institute in Frunze in the early 1950s, Aitmatov would watch Beishenalieva perform at the Kyrgyz Opera and Ballet Theater. Crudely put, he was a Beishenalieva groupie. He especially enjoyed seeing her in *Swan Lake*. After the performance was over, Aitmatov would follow her home in the dark, allowing a respectful distance so as not to cause alarm. Aware that someone was following her, an unperturbed Beishenalieva would ask, without turning around, "What do you need, young man?" Too shy to answer, Aitmatov would peel off and return to his dorm while Beishenalieva would continue on her way.[5]

Eighteen years after the end of World War II, *Mother's Field* was published in Kyrgyz and Russian in 1963. True to Aitmatov's innovator role in Soviet literature, the short story takes an unfamiliar tack by emphasizing war's destructive nature. The story's protagonist, a Kyrgyz woman named Tolgonai, mourns the loss of the male members of her family during the war. Tolgonai is yet another strong female heroine in Aitmatov's works, following Seide in *Face to Face* and Jamilya.[6]

During the course of the war, Tolgonai's eldest son and husband are killed during the Battle of Moscow, her second son dies targeting a German ammunition depot, and she never hears again from her third son, who sneaks away from home as an underage volunteer and joins an airborne division. Tolganai's misfortune is that the Red Army had no policy about recalling family members from the front lines if they were the only males left in the family. She is alone at the end of the war, with only her widowed daughter-in-law as company.

Juxtaposing harvests in the village to tragic losses of war, Aitmatov underscores man's connection with nature's cycles of bounty and scarcity. But his craftsmanship is most evident in the way he calls on Kyrgyz folklore. On the surface, the story is about sacrifice in the war against the Germans. But the story changes to a plea to stop war when interpreted through the prism of the touching dialogue between an elderly Tolganai and Mother Earth, who is an embodiment of the Kyrgyz goddess of human and earthly fertility. In a harvested field, silent with the approach of fall, Tolganai commiserates with Mother Earth, a patient listener and her constant companion through lonely decades.

"Tell me, Mother Earth, tell me the truth," a weary Tolganai asks. "Can people live without war?"

"The answer doesn't depend on me," Mother Earth responds. "It depends on you, on people, on your will and reason."[7]

Aitmatov's antiwar theme raised the ire of Soviet critics for whom *Mother's Field* departed too abruptly from the tenets of socialist realism. Indeed, by shedding light on another side of war, Aitmatov bucked the demand that writers promote the party's policy on issues of the day—that the Great Patriotic War, as the Soviets named World War II, was good because the Soviet Union had won. Aitmatov's contrary view showed war to be the cause of profound loss. Tolgonai captures this dichotomy when she remarks upon hearing the war is over, "Victory, how many losses did we have to take for you?"[8]

With the publication of *Mother's Field*, Aitmatov, though just in his midthirties, showed hints of the preternatural wisdom that would come to define his writing. He provided an insightful definition of happiness when Tolganai tells her husband Suvankul that happiness "doesn't happen all of a sudden, like a rainstorm in the summer falling on your head, but comes to a man by degrees, depending on how he relates to life, to those around him. One thing adds to another, and from little pieces, we get what we call happiness."[9]

The same sensitive and spiritual voice ushers forth from Aitmatov's epigraph to *Mother's Field*:

> Father, I don't know where you are buried. I dedicate this book to you, Törökul Aitmatov.
> Mother, you raised all four of us. I dedicate this book to you, Nagima Aitmatova.[10]

By addressing his father's disappearance and his mother's suffering, Aitmatov indirectly, yet skillfully condemns Stalin's purges as a form of war.

During the 1960s, the paradox of Aitmatov was taking shape. He was a fluent Russian speaker from humble origins who had become a productive member of communist society, eventually joining the Communist Party in 1959. Like Beishenalieva, he was a Soviet-made man. These criteria enabled him to profit from the Soviet nationalities policy, which promoted loyal artists and writers from the constituent republics. He gained access to the perks of the system: entry to guest houses, a chauffeur, and audiences with political leaders.

At the same time, though, he was cultivating the skill to write freely but in a screened way. It was as if he were creating a code that only he and discerning readers could understand.

Aitmatov's everyday existence was a careful balancing of thoughts, words, and actions to preserve the space to write. Haunted by the disappearance of his father, he avoided directly challenging Soviet authority. His personality—he was not quick to judge nor impulsive—helped him maintain an even keel between staying true to his conscience and being obedient to the party.

Aitmatov's balancing act was challenged when Khrushchev fell from power in 1964. Buckling under a tightening of the literary space, leading writers in Moscow admitted to "errors" and promised to abide by the party's dictates. Two years later the trial of two writers sent a shudder through the Soviet writing establishment. Andrei Sinyavsky and Yuli Daniel were put on trial for sending manuscripts outside the Soviet Union, including Sinyavsky's damning portrayal of socialist realism. The

Soviet court sentenced the two men, who defended themselves valiantly at a trial that was widely covered in the West, to seven and five years of hard labor, respectively.

With the exception of hardened dissidents like Alexander Solzhenitsyn and poet Joseph Brodsky, most of the Soviet literary elite recalibrated. Aitmatov himself tacked to the conservative side. He published a letter in *Komsomolskaya Pravda* which criticized up-and-coming Russian writers, including Yevgeni Yevtushenko, for their rejection of socialist realism. Aitmatov wrote that they provided no positive models to Soviet readers. Aitmatov appeared to do this for political reasons, but he also believed that the young writers had violated one of his personal tenets about writing—that literature should serve a moral purpose, as a kind of guiding light. Aitmatov's pro-establishment stance likely helped him gain support among conservatives in the Soviet Writers Union and bought him some breathing room in claustrophobic Kyrgyzia, where local orthodox communists were ascendant.[11]

Their flag bearer was Communist Party head Turdakun Usubaliev, who had come to power in 1961 and would rule the republic for the following twenty-four years. Usubaliev's regime was marked by fealty to Moscow and a policy of Russification; Kyrgyz authorities clamped down on any vestiges of pro-Kyrgyz sentiment left over from the series of "thaws" under Khrushchev, and Usubaliev would famously declare that tribalism no longer existed in Kyrgyzia.

Aitmatov and Usubaliev would butt heads over the ensuing decades, precisely because, while Usubaliev ruled locally, he couldn't control Aitmatov, who had significant influence in Moscow. Those connections would help Aitmatov publish his works in Moscow in Russian, even before they came out in Kyrgyz, thus enabling him to leapfrog the Kyrgyz Communist Party.

In the mid- to late 1960s, a resentful party leadership tried to corral Aitmatov and other progressive writers from Kyrgyzia by calling on writers to popularize "approved character traits and standards of behavior" of the new Soviet man. Works of literature, the party instructed, should have the Soviet people as their main hero and emphasize the "vitality and greatness" of socialist society.[12] But with his strong and independent characters, Aitmatov had long ago left behind that recipe for stilted literature.

It was the riddle of Aitmatov. Criticized in Kyrgyzia for not being sufficiently loyal to socialist realism, he could be critical of certain Soviet writers for straying too far from socialist realism norms. The distance between the two positions would seem unbridgeable, but Aitmatov straddled two horses: on the surface his moral purpose meshed with Soviet platitudes about the role of literature, but his spirited and often conflicted characters transcended the wooden characters featured in works of socialist realism.

Chingiz Aitmatov was mastering skillful writing, employing Kyrgyz myths and legends to hide subversive messages. Milder and less caustic than the outspoken dissidents, Aitmatov was outwardly loyal to the party, making strategic retreats and concessions when necessary. But inwardly he was subversive; taboo and not taboo at the same time.

In the process, his writing became a magnet for closet freedom seekers in remote Kyrgyzia, where there was little access to the *tamizdat* or *samizdat* works of Soviet dissidents.[13] They detected code words and deciphered concealed meaning in seemingly standard plotlines. Inside the Kyrgyz Writers Union, a group of progressive young writers, at risk to their own careers, rallied to defend Aitmatov from charges of "perversion of national values" and "idealization of immorality." Among them was Beksultan Jakiev, the young writer who had been enthralled by Mukhtar Auezov's account of meeting Altay in New York.[14]

In the midst of Aitmatov's political balancing act, there was the escape to his relationship with Beishenalieva. With hectic travel schedules and family obligations pulling them in opposite directions, time together was treasured. They snatched the gift afforded them when, with both serving as deputies to the Soviet parliament, they traveled to Moscow two times a year.

One time, they returned to Frunze on the Moscow–Alma Ata train on its journey across broad expanses of the Soviet Union. In a compartment to themselves, they were freed from the pressures of politics, professional responsibilities, and family. No knocks on the door, no phone calls, no requests. For three days, they kept each other company, discussing—and occasionally sparring—about literature and art, with one conversation building on another.

They would look out the window, at the green plains of Russia and then the steppes of Kazakhstan. When they disembarked at a stop in Aralsk, which then bordered the Aral Sea, they were greeted by a fresh sea breeze.[15] Locked away in their own world, they continued on their way through the steppe towns of Kyzyl Orda and Chimkent before arriving in Alma Ata.

"There are days which you would never trade for a whole century," Beishenalieva told Aitmatov during the trip.[16]

The effusive comment was unusual for Beishenalieva, who was typically restrained in her emotions. Trained to perform in front of demanding audiences, she carried herself with a studied distance, borne of self-confidence from her ascent to the highest ranks of her profession.

Three years Aitmatov's senior, Beishenalieva was the doubting partner in their relationship, questioning romance, and skeptical about marriage, which she had tried several times. "The ordinariness of daily life kills great sentiments," she would say.[17]

Aitmatov, meanwhile, was the romantic who needed reassurance.

"I sometimes begin to doubt the sincerity of your words about your love for me," Aitmatov wrote to her in the early 1960s. "My situation is exit-less, and I am doomed that I cannot turn away and leave you for a single step."[18]

For a man who had lost his father tragically, the relationship with Beishenalieva seemed to feed a deep-seated longing. Aitmatov would later say that they were destined for each other; she was his muse, "the most priceless gift of fate" he had ever received.

As if propelled forward by his romance with Beishenalieva, Aitmatov infused his writing in the 1960s with spirited and independent characters. Their lives of action, regret, and tragedy belied communist dictums of rosy progress and theory-driven human development.

Tanabai, the fallen hero of Aitmatov's novella *Farewell, Gulsary*, published in Moscow in 1966, is a case in point. His rash behavior at the start of collectivization sets the tone for a life of disappointment and sadness. In his eagerness to support collectivization, the simple-minded herdsman brands his moderately prosperous brother a kulak, causing him to be exiled to Siberia. In this way, Tanabai is a foil for the failure of collectivization.

Aitmatov builds the story around an elderly Tanabai recalling his life as he kneels beside his faithful horse Gulsary, who is expiring on the roadside. More than in his previous works, Aitmatov, a trained veterinarian, brings to the fore the connection between man and nature. It is embodied in the relationship between the beaten Tanabai and broken down Gulsary, and again in a folktalke that becomes the cover for a cleverly concealed narrative line.

The folktale tells the story of an overly eager hunter named Karagul who, after hunting down a herd of goats, traps the mother goat and her mate on a cliff. Dismissing the mother goat's warning to spare her mate, Karagul shoots the male goat. In the ensuing chase for the mother goat, Karagul himself ends up at an impassable spot, unable to climb down. The mother goat curses him for killing off her herd and then leaves him for his father to find days later. Unable to rescue Karagul, who himself realizes there is no way out of his predicament, the father is forced to shoot his son.

While Aitmatov's first story line ends in expected fashion—with Tanabai contemplating a return to the Communist Party—the narrative suggests a darker turn. The father, by teaching his son how to hunt, represents the good intentions of the party. In contrast, Karagul, like the party's harebrained schemes of collectivization, has gone awry, with hubris and arrogance leading him to nearly exterminate a heard of goats, a tragic mistake which rebounds on him.

Aitmatov's warning to his fellow Soviet citizens is clear: heed your relationships with people, and don't subjugate yourself to slogans and ideas. Thus, the second story line appears to squash any optimism surrounding Tanabai coming back to the party. Tanabai cannot undo the grievous sins of the past, like his uncivilized treatment of his brother. A victim of his own reckless impulsiveness, he is only waiting to pass on, like his old horse next to him.

With the novel, Aitmatov skirted the borders of what was deemed acceptable in Soviet letters. Nevertheless, perhaps because of his crafty writing and standing in Soviet society, officially approved reviews of *Farewell, Gulsary* praised the novella for being in the finest traditions of socialist realism, noting that Aitmatov had described a typical Soviet worker who helped the country overcome hardships in the postwar period. They also noted how the novella ended on a positive note, with Tanabai contemplating rejoining the party.

But in Soviet Kyrgyzia, Aitmatov was blasted for his allegedly irresponsible treatment of reality. Party officials were livid, in particular, about his depiction of corruption in the republic. A venerated Kyrgyz writer—intent on knocking Aitmatov down a notch—attributed Aitmatov's popularity to critics outside Kyrgyzia who were captivated by the exoticism in his prose, a veiled reference to the myths and folklore Aitmatov used.

Because he had influential patrons in Moscow, like editor Alexander Tvardovski, and the political cover of serving as a deputy to the Supreme Soviet, Aitmatov was able to dodge his critics at home.

He couldn't, however, dodge his personal angst.

―⁓―

Aitmatov wrote *Farewell, Gulsary* when he was having his affair with Beishenalieva, and he writes himself into the story, or at least his emotional turmoil. In the novella, the hapless shepherd Tanabai takes up with a young widow, leaving his wife and children alone in the family yurt. One night, a fierce thunderstorm rouses him from sleep at the widow's house. Without time to grab his hat or coat, he mounts Gulsary and races to check on his herd of horses as lighting cracks overhead and rain pours down.

Pushing the horse faster and faster through the storm, he arrives to discover that his fellow shepherds have secured the herd. He finds his wife corralling the horses with the aid of a young village boy. She knows where Tanabai has been. Soaking wet along with his limping horse, he is a sad sight.

"You didn't even have time to dress right," his wife upbraids him. "At least you got your pants and boots on."

Tanabai is silent.

"Aren't you ashamed?" she asks him. "You're not young anymore. Your children are growing up, and you . . . How do you think you look to people now?"

After his wife and the boy leave, the storm clears. Smoke from a train rises in the far distance. Tanabai dismounts from his horse, walks a few steps, then throws himself to the ground. Aitmatov describes the scene from the point of view of the horse.

"Gulsary had never seen his master in such a state. He lay face down on the ground with his shoulders shaking. He cried out of shame and sadness. He knew he had wasted the happiness which had been given to him one last time in life."[19]

At the time he wrote *Farewell, Gulsary*, Chingiz Aitmatov was leading a double life. He was living at home with his wife, Kerez, and two young sons, the youngest of whom, Askar, had been born in 1959. But he pined for Beishenalieva. They had managed to arrange for apartments in the same building, but that in itself was a form of torture. In the mornings Aitmatov would call on the phone, asking her if she had woken up yet. Then if they were passing in the hallway on their way to work, they might greet each other quickly. At night Aitmatov would glance out his window to check if she had returned home. Once she turned on the light in her apartment, he would call her to say good night.

Forced to keep their relationship as low profile as possible, they limited their rendezvous and used go-betweens and letters to communicate. The letters came mostly from Aitmatov, with Beishenalieva begging off by saying she was embarrassed by her grammar mistakes. The letters became an outlet for frustration. "However difficult it may be for me," Aitmatov wrote early on in their relationship, "I am nevertheless thankful to fate that she has sent me love for you."[20]

Aitmatov's wife Kerez was understandably disturbed by the affair. She was sharing a household and a family with a man whose heart was with another woman. From time to time, Kerez would call Beishenalieva and berate her for interfering with her family's life.

The Kyrgyz Communist Party got involved as well, summoning Aitmatov to the Central Committee. After leading party officials forbade him, a married party member, to meet with Beishenalieva, Aitmatov refused to be compromised: "I love this woman. If you want to know the truth, she is for me an inspiration in my work, and you can't prevent me from seeing her."[21]

While Aitmatov wanted to get married, Beishenalieva refused. She feared the fallout for his career and was afraid that his children would become distanced from their father. Whenever he would bring up the topic, she would turn away or change the conversation.[22]

—∾∾—

In times of hardship—sickness, drought, natural disasters, and war—the Kyrgyz people for centuries had appealed to the spirit gods around them and drawn strength from their warrior hero Manas. Part of the reason the Kyrgyz so revered Mukhtar Auezov was that his brave stand in support of the national epos had helped to ensure *Manas*'s prized place in keeping history alive for new generations of Kyrgyz. Indeed, *manaschi* had continued harrumphing and gesticulating, except by the 1960s the audiences were schoolchildren, workers on collective farms, and party clerks settled in villages, instead of nomadic families in the mountains.

Aitmatov, too, found refuge in the age-old epic, particularly in the poem's link to the spiritual heritage of his ancestors. Listening to the poem somehow attenuated the stresses of contemporary life, the cares and concerns that surrounded his controversial writing and his discombobulated personal life.

The man who delivered consolation was his neighbor from the first floor of his building in Frunze, celebrated *manaschi* Sayakbai Karalaev. One day in the mid-1960s Karalaev asked Aitmatov, who had access to a car, to accompany him to a village outside Frunze.

Karalaev was the last of the legendary manaschi, a link to the storytellers who had traveled by horse from village to village, lived in yurts and subsisted on donations from friendly patrons, a bit like wandering mendicants. With the onset of urban living and the arrival of TV and radio, *manaschi* would become less of a fixture in Kyrgyz society.

Like many of his predecessors, Karalaev had found his calling through a dream. Around the turn of the twentieth century, while tending sheep as a young boy on the southern shore of Lake Issyk Kul, the story goes that he fell asleep under a tree. As Karalaev himself recounted it, the sound of hooves awakened him; a horseman wielding a shimmering sword cast the gift of oratory into the young boy's mouth.[23] From that day on, Karalaev started reciting Manas.

The young Manaschi became famous in 1916 when he refused conscription into the reserve forces of the Imperial Russian Army. His arrest emboldened his Kyrgyz compatriots around the lake in their revolt against Tsarist troops in the Ürkün uprising. Karalaev ended up fleeing across the mountains to China like so many other Kyrgyz. A few years later, he became a communist and joined the fight against White Russian forces in Siberia during the Russian Civil War. When camped around a fire, he would entertain his fellow Bolshevik troops with his recitations, even though they didn't understand a word he was saying.

By the time Aitmatov and Karalaev arrived at the collective farm, workers and residents had started to gather in the courtyard next to the collective farm's office building. There were too many people for the common hall in the building, so people found places under the open sky. Village elders got the best places, sitting on benches and chairs in the front. Younger women, their heads covered in colorful kerchiefs, and children came next. Eager for a better view, some kids scampered up trees and sat expectantly like birds on a limb. Men returning from the fields took seats in the cabins of tractors and other pieces of heavy machinery parked on the edges of the gathering crowd. Stragglers rode in on horses and donkeys, staying put in their saddles. One boy made a seat out of his prostrate camel, finding a comfortable space between the two humps.

Creating his own mobile stage, the stocky, mustachioed Karalaev climbed onto a horse, his long, black robe falling on either side of the saddle and his head framed by the ubiquitous conical kalpak. Once he started his recounting, the audience fell silent, as if cast into a spell. Pulling on the horse's reigns, Karalaev turned to face different parts of the audience surrounding him, like a clock making its rounds through the hours. He made gestures, posed and cackled, switching roles like a master actor—from arrogant tsar to devious bandit, fierce warrior to grieving wife.

All of a sudden, dark clouds appeared above. Thunder sounded, lightning cracked, and rain poured down in buckets in what Aitmatov later described as a "heavenly flood." Aitmatov rose from his stool and, covering his head with his hands, retreated into the collective farm office, expecting masses of people to do the same in search of cover. Was Sayakbai okay, he wondered? Had he fallen off his horse?

But there was no movement. Not a person stirred.

Aitmatov exited the office, and there in front of him, under pouring rain, the drenched audience sat motionless. Even the boys in the trees remained in place, listening to Karalaev in the saddle, holding the reigns and gesticulating even more energetically, as if the lighting strikes had energized him. His words slipped into a cadence with thunder and rain. In a duet of man's words with nature's powers, Karalaev sang of defeat and victory, compassion and anguish, loss and triumph, love and separation.[24]

PART THREE

9

American Rendezvous

Postmarked May 2, 1973, in Frunze, Soviet Kyrgyzia, the letter made its way to New York under skies buzzing with anticipation. In the most visible sign of warming relations between the United States and Soviet Union, space programs from the two countries were practicing for a historic space linkup in 1975.

As if to reflect the period of relaxation, or détente, that had come to US-USSR relations, Chingiz Aitmatov struck a jocular tone in his letter to his American interlocutor. "You are my only female letter-writing acquaintance, so we have to meet," he wrote Mirra Ginsburg, the translator of his latest novel *The White Ship*. "Call me Chingiz Aitmatovich," he added, discarding his usual patronymic for no apparent reason.[1]

During several years of correspondence related to Ginsburg's translation of Aitmatov's novel, the two had developed a comfortable, even playful rapport through letters. But Aitmatov's buoyant tone in the May letter was just a mask, and the correspondence with Ginsburg in America a distraction during the most difficult period of his life.

In August 1971, Nagima Aitmatova had succumbed. Chingiz had been at her bedside, watching her weary body give way. As her breathing became more labored, he couldn't help recalling his mother's defining moment—leading four children off the train in search of a safe haven in the darkest days of the Great Purges.

As the eldest child, he had sensed his mother's tragedies more acutely than his siblings—the upheaval when the family left Moscow and her dislocation in rural Kyrgyzia. She had lost her husband and the educated milieu of Moscow in one fell swoop. As an adult, Chingiz had done all he could to alleviate Nagima's sufferings, moving her as soon as possible to Frunze and making sure she had access to the best health care in the city. Over the previous decades, he had cared for her, comforted her and cradled her as she had grown weak with asthma and arthritis.

Nagima had persevered, raising four children to become, respectively, a writer, geologist, physicist, and teacher, all with families of their own. While she would go to her grave not knowing the true fate of her husband, Nagima's last words were ones of gratitude. "I am thankful to all of you," she had said to her children.

The family buried her in a cemetery in Frunze. They had the grave marker inscribed with Nagima and Törökul's names because they figured that, since they would likely never know the true fate of their father, they might as well comfort themselves by imagining him buried next to his devoted wife.

To compound Aitmatov's troubles, just a few months before Nagima's death, he had learned that Bübüsaira Beishenalieva had been diagnosed with incurable breast cancer. Beishenalieva had long neglected pain in her armpit, foregoing her annual checkups until she could no longer lift her arm. Now, her lithe dancer's figure was wasting away in a hospital down the street from Aitmatov's office in Frunze.

Aitmatov's malaise had found expression several years earlier when he had penned *The White Ship*. Soviet socialism was at its apex. There was a collective sense across the country that the Soviet government had delivered on postwar reconstruction and provided the foundation for the next generation to live better than its parents. Looking beyond material progress, however, in *The White Ship* Aitmatov told a story of moral decay. The protagonist is an unnamed boy whose parents have abandoned him. In a logging camp in the mountains above Lake Issyk Kul, he must endure the wrath of a cruel uncle, who seethes over his wife's supposed inability to bear him a child. The uncle beats his wife, castigates her simple parents, and tramples the beautiful nature that surrounds the camp.

In the book's signature moment, the uncle intimidates his meek father-in-law into shooting an antlered mother deer, which holds a special place in Kyrgyz mythology. Distraught over the death of the deer and his uncle's evil dominance, the boy drowns himself at the end of the story. Aitmatov named the uncle Orozkul, which means "slave of Allah" in various Turkic languages. It's a curious name for such a deprived character who sows unhappiness in the lives of the people around him. The name itself has led some scholars to search for a deeper meaning behind the name, given Aitmatov's ability to write in screened ways.

In their opinion, Aitmatov's point, couched indirectly as was his style, was that Orozkul, through his drinking, beating of his wife, and destruction of nature, had lost connection with his national traditions. By juxtaposing Orozkul to people in the novel who were more in tune with their surroundings, Aitmatov delivered a veiled warning about the consequences of man's willful disregard for nature and his fellow man: if products of the Soviet system, like the warped and limited Orozkul, were allowed to dominate, the world would be out of balance, tilted toward cruelty and violence.

That was a message Soviet conservatives didn't care to hear, and likely didn't hear because of Aitmatov's use of Aesopian language.[2]

Before publication, Soviet censors required Aitmatov to add an epilogue introducing a force for good to offset the novel's tragic ending. After publication, some critics were still dissatisfied, calling on Aitmatov to write literature in which good triumphs evil, with endings that showed the Communist Party triumphing over dark forces—in essence, to be a better communist writer.

It was the line of conservative party officials who were ascendant after the Daniel and Sinyavsky trial. They had engineered the dismissal of dissident writer Alexander Solzhenitsyn from the Soviet Writers Union in 1969 and forced *Novy Mir* publisher Alexander Tvardovski to resign his position at the journal just a month after he published the first installment of *The White Ship* in January 1970.[3]

The personal attacks forced Aitmatov to take the unusual step of defending his book in the Soviet press. In Soviet fashion, he fought back indirectly, latching onto 1970, the year of Lenin's centenary. He climbed aboard a campaign waged by liberals in the Soviet government to emphasize Lenin's more open-minded and patient approach to governing as opposed to Stalin's bloody legacy.

That campaign had visible manifestations—like the giant illuminated portrait of Lenin, supported by cables from a blimp, that hung suspended over Moscow—and literal firepower. Literary works, scholarly studies, and memoirs connected to Lenin were published over the course of the year. Aitmatov added to the paeans, praising Lenin in an article in *Literaturnaya Gazeta* in April 1970.

The adept Aitmatov used the propaganda piece as a cover to legitimize the plotline of *The White Ship*. He extolled Lenin for his tolerance of other nationalities, calling the Soviet leader "a symbol of the rebirth of oppressed peoples" and praising the creation of a Soviet multinational government. Addressing those who criticized *The White Ship* for introducing tragic endings, Aitmatov wrote that socialist realism allowed for many different styles and national traditions, including tragic endings.

The efforts of Aitmatov and others notwithstanding, attacks against liberals and dissidents deepened. Aitmatov donned an additional layer of protection in 1973, this one far more distasteful. At a time when the Soviet government was incensed over Andrei Sakharov's encouragement of Western nations to pressure Moscow into reforms, Aitmatov joined a KGB-engineered campaign against the dissident nuclear physicist.[4]

Aitmatov's signature was the first to appear in an alphabetical list of thirty-one Soviet writers who signed their names below a letter published in *Pravda* on August 31, 1973. The letter, which also mentioned Solzhenitsyn, denounced Sakharov for what was described as behavior "smearing the honor and dignity of Soviet scholars" and for calling on the West to continue the Cold War.[5]

Like many others in the intellectual elite, Aitmatov was likely pressured to sign.[6] His signature was the clearest indicator of the difference between him and the dissident scientist he had impugned. From deep within the scientific machinery designed to propel Soviet military might, Sakharov had evolved into a bold figure of dissent inside the Soviet Union. He was prepared to sacrifice all in support of human rights. For his defiance of the Soviet system he would endure internal exile without a telephone, under constant surveillance, and largely cut off from social contact.

The contrast with Aitmatov at the time was striking: two men on opposite sides of the barricades, one facing a hostile world and the other melting into it. But as Sakharov himself said so often, "the truth is never simple." And the similarities between the two men are worth mentioning. From a privileged place inside the system, they both came to revere the dignity of the individual and the attendant beliefs in openness, justice and human rights that shape a normal life. Sakharov worked directly; Aitmatov preferred an indirect approach that involved compromise.

In the trade-off of surviving as a progressive writer in the Soviet Union, Chingiz Aitmatov had sold a bit of himself. Aitmatov would later regret his action, but at the time his signature was the best guarantee for freedom to write.

For Soviet readers, *The White Ship* was a bleak statement about life in Soviet Central Asia. However, in New York, Ginsburg, a noted translator of Russian-language folk tales for the US market, sensed the novel had commercial potential—not for its political messages as much as for its use of ancient legends and folktales. If marketed correctly, the book could appeal to American sensibilities, she believed.

Ginsburg was right; she sold a translation of the book to Crown Publishing in New York in 1971, offering it as a fairy tale. Targeting American children aged eleven to thirteen, Crown's marketing materials emphasized a universal subtheme of Aitmatov's Soviet novel: should old legends and traditions be preserved?

During two years of translation and editing *The White Ship*, Ginsburg became convinced the story would succeed commercially in the United States. "My own feeling," she wrote in 1971 to her editor at Crown, "is that the book is beautiful, that its beauty will be seen, and that it will live."[7]

Ginsburg's intuition paid off. Her translation of the novel—Aitmatov's first novel to be translated for the American market—enjoyed a successful debut. It was named one of the top hundred children's books of 1972 by *Kirkus Reviews* and would become a nominee for the prestigious Mildred Batchelder Award for best children's books.

—⁓—

Communicating with Aitmatov had piqued Ginsburg's interest. A free-spirited woman with a Bohemian streak, she was curious about how an outwardly loyal Communist Party member was able to write such trenchant prose. Who was this subtle contrarian who was no dissident himself? She turned to the Kyrgyz she knew best in New York City for answers.

Mirra Ginsburg had called on Azamat Altay's expertise before—whenever she needed insights during her translation of folktales from Central Asia. So, when she queried Altay about Aitmatov and *The White Ship*, he was happy to oblige. Her questions arrived in letters, and his responses were returned in manila envelopes, filled with reviews of *The White Ship* and reports on the political situation in Kyrgyzia. Altay also conveyed to Ginsburg something priceless: his experiences growing up in the world Aitmatov was describing in *The White Ship*. There was the lake, the types of trees in the mountains, and why it was important for a Kyrgyz boy to know seven generations of ancestors.

The two kept each other up to date on the latest news about Aitmatov and wondered whether one day they might be able to meet the man they had learned so much about. They started to look for opportunities during détente.

—⁓—

By the early 1970s, Azamat Altay had built an "American" life in Queens, New York. He had bought a new Ford car in 1967, and, after many years of living in a high-rise apartment, he and Saniye had purchased a house in 1972 for $68,000. The three-story, redbrick townhouse fronted on Parsons Boulevard in Flushing, Queens, a residential neighborhood on the verge of becoming one of the most ethnically diverse places in America.

It was a leafy suburban neighborhood where church bells were heard on Sundays and children ran along sidewalks. A short walk up the street was the Holy Redeemer Catholic School and St. Anne's Parish. But appearances were deceiving: within just a few miles of Altay's home, immigrants from India, Pakistan, and Taiwan were adding variety to traditionally Irish and Italian neighborhoods. In the coming years, mosques and Hindu temples would rise alongside churches and synagogues.[8] As an immigrant himself, Altay fit right in.

Altay worked three jobs in those days, putting in eight hours a day at Columbia University's Butler Library, working as a correspondent for Radio Liberty, and, starting in 1973, translating parts of the Bible into Kyrgyz.

In whatever spare time remained, he fulfilled requests from people like Ginsburg who wanted information on Central Asia. When there was a free moment, he tended his garden, growing peaches, apples, and carrots, which he gave away to guests when they visited (see figure 9.1). America as the land of opportunity rang true for the peasant boy from Central Asia. Altay's motto was "If a man works hard, he achieves good fortune."

Figure 9.1: Azamat Altay with his former boss at Columbia University Robert Karlowich in Altay's backyard in New York City in the early 1970s. Source: Photo courtesy of Robert Karlowich.

But there was a price for that good fortune. His work at Columbia kept him up to date on happenings in Kyrgyzia, but it was also a constant reminder of his self-imposed exile and lack of contact with his family. Occasionally, he got reports from his home village. In the mid-1960s, he had met a Kyrgyz man visiting the United States on a four-month exchange program. Joldosh Jusaev was a collegial fellow without the suspicion Altay normally encountered among visiting Kyrgyz. Like Altay, Jusaev came from the Issyk Kul region, and upon his return he offered to deliver a message to Altay's father.

Here, Altay thought, was a chance to reconnect with his father. If Jusaev found his father, then maybe the Soviets would let his father visit him. It was a long shot, to be sure, with Altay a prominent name on the Soviet "blacklist" for Central Asia. Jusaev wrote back a short while later. He had traveled to Altay's home village on the southern shore of the lake in 1965 and located Altay's first cousin Bekboo, the son of his father's younger brother. After explaining to Bekboo that he had seen Altay in the United States and sharing a letter Altay had written, Jusaev was coldly rebuffed. "We don't have a relative named Kudaibergen. We don't know him," Bekboo said, refusing to let Jusaev enter his house.

A discouraged Jusaev set about finding someone in the village who could lead him to Altay's father. He was eventually told that Kojomberdi Teke uulu had died several years earlier. When Altay learned the news, he was crushed. He imagined his father dying a lonely man, troubled until his last days by the fate of his ostracized son. Stranded in the United States, there was no way Altay could fulfill his duties as a filial son and bury his father according to Islamic custom.

—⁓—

In his private grief, Altay recited prayers from the Koran and consoled himself in his living room. In the evenings after work, amidst book shelves lined with some of the five thousand books on Central Asian history, literature, and culture that he had amassed over the years, he would slide a record of Kyrgyz folk music out of its cover and place it on his phonograph. While the evening ebbed into nightfall outside his front door, Altay would let centuries-old melodies of Central Asia transport him back to the mountains and pastures of his youth.

And he read Aitmatov's books. They were all there on his bookshelves, from *Jamilya* to *The White Ship*. In an era before cable television, e-mail, and the Internet, Aitmatov's stories were Altay's lifeline to home. For a man whose own memories had been dimmed by the passage of time, Aitmatov's writing was like literary postcards. Hadn't Aitmatov chosen Lake Issyk Kul as the setting for *The White Ship*? The forests around the logging camp, the blue lake, the winding roads into the mountains— Altay knew the setting well. He still remembered Aitmatov's description of the lake in an earlier short story:

> Bluish-white waves, as if led by the hand, broke one after another onto the yellow shore.
> The sun dropped below the mountains, burnishing the lake's distant waters with a rose color.
> On the other side of the lake, the purplish ridges of snow-covered mountains appeared in the distance.[9]

And then there were Aitmatov's characters: independent-minded Jamilya upending norms by fleeing with the rootless Daniyar, and deserter Ismail, a betrayer in the eyes of the Soviet government, whom Aitmatov had dared to portray as a distraught man with feelings. Both stories spoke directly to Altay's personal experience of alienation. As he had been reminded countless times, he was a persona non grata in the Soviet Union, a man who couldn't even attend his own parent's funeral, just like Ismail. But here was Aitmatov making a heroine of a tradition breaker and humanizing a traitor.

At a time when other Kyrgyz were ostracizing Altay, Aitmatov's prose was a comfort. "Chingiz is an honest man," Altay would tell himself. "He's not afraid."[10]

Back in Frunze, Aitmatov kept watch as Beishenalieva's health declined in 1973, visiting every morning on his way to work. Watching illness debilitate his soul mate took a toll on the haggard Aitmatov, so much so that Beishenalieva wondered how he would manage without her. One day she spotted him from her hospital window, leaning against the front gate, his shoulders heaving and his hands covering his face. "How will he be without me?" she asked herself.[11]

Bübüsaira Beishenalieva died on May 10, 1973. Discarding etiquette, Aitmatov cried openly at her funeral at the State Opera House. "How would people know that in losing Bübüsaira, I almost lost myself," he would say later.[12] Party officials sitting nearby bemoaned his lack of composure and considered escorting him from the hall. "A married man, with a family," they whispered haughtily.

It was shameful sniping from party functionaries who wouldn't let up even in Aitmatov's moment of sadness.

—⁘—

In the face of official constraints, Chingiz Aitmatov continued to produce bold works. Not long after finishing *The White Ship*, he wrote his first play (see figure 9.2). A cooperative endeavor with Kazakh playwright

Figure 9.2: Chingiz Aitmatov at his writing desk in Frunze in 1972, about the time he was writing the play *Ascent of Mt. Fuji*. Source: Central State Archives of the Kyrgyz Republic.

Kaltai Mukhamedzhanov, *Ascent of Mt. Fuji* exposed how paranoia fostered by Stalin's leadership style had infected Soviet society down to the level of a group of four Kyrgyz men who meet for a picnic decades after World War II. The play's name came from a Japanese tradition according to which every Buddhist, at least one in his life, is supposed to climb Mt. Fuji to confess his sins.

The dramatic tension in the play is heightened by the presence of Aisha-apa, the men's childhood teacher, who asks about their forgotten comrade Tsabur. She is the men's collective conscience, the metaphorical holy mountain, and in her presence the men debate who caused Tsabur's downfall by informing Soviet military authorities about one of his pacifistic poems.

By giving the men high rankings in Soviet society—agronomist, professor, journalist, and teacher—Aitmatov underscored how societal standing was at odds with moral and ethical values, meaning that the higher up a person was on the Communist Party ladder, the more likely he would compromise himself. Careful listeners detected Aitmatov's exposure of the duplicitous nature of Soviet communism when he has a character say, "One has to first be honest with oneself before embarking upon universal schemes to save humanity." In other words, how could the morally bankrupt Soviet Union dare to spread its model through worldwide revolution?

Aitmatov may have understood Mt. Fuji as a sacred place, but Kyrgyz Communist Party head Usubaliev thought differently. He had been trying to derail Aitmatov for decades. Under his watch, the Kyrgyz Communist Party had not allowed a single one of Aitmatov's books to be published in the Kyrgyz language since 1964, the year after he won the Lenin Prize.

In July 1973, Usubaliev mounted another attack. In an address to Kyrgyz Party officials, he criticized writers and poets for abetting a dangerous drift in the republic toward anti-Russian and anti-Soviet attitudes. While he didn't name Aitmatov personally, Usubaliev targeted his rival in pointed comments about writers having "a mountain fetish" and glorifying the past. He denigrated them for portraying the mountains as if they were a narcotic, that "produces an active influence" on people."[13] The Communist Party chief then rolled out the staid ideological retort, calling on writers and poets to praise the Soviet Communist Party and the help of the Russian people for creating social progress in the Kyrgyz Soviet Socialist Republic.

With his myopic and inflexible approach to the world, Usubaliev rejected Aitmatov's literary lyricism—in this case, the use of soaring mountains as a metaphor to express man's striving to improve his spiritual well-being. Doctrinaire communists had no use for Mt. Fuji. The spirit for them was a materialistic currency to be channeled by ideology and shaped by groupthink.

In the face of such blockheadedness, Aitmatov persevered, driven by a desire to expose the betrayals of the past. Writing for him had always been personal. Like writing about a fatherless boy in *The White Ship* or indomitable women characters in *Face to Face* and *Mother's Field*. Propelled by unanswered questions about his father's death—and the unacknowledged guilt in Soviet society for the Great Purges—Aitmatov had penned the *Ascent of Mt. Fuji*.

For below the surface of the accomplished writer still lingered a traumatized, sensitive boy. "We are temporary creatures here on earth," he would tell a group of Western correspondents visiting Frunze in June 1974. "Helpless snowdrops grow in the mountains. People rip them up and take them to the city. The torn flowers remind me of ailing children with drooping heads. One might speak of genocide of flowers. It seems a trifle, but it can be serious. A human being grows from such trifles."[14]

Ascent of Mt. Fuji was a continuation of Aitmatov's mission to resurrect honesty, to erect "barricades in the defense of truth."[15] To let the play go forward, Aitmatov reportedly appealed to powerful Kazakh Party boss Dinmukhamed Kunaev to intervene with Soviet authorities, including possibly Soviet leader Leonid Brezhnev.[16]

—•—

Altay and Ginsburg's efforts to organize a visit to the United States for Aitmatov bore no fruit. Like all Soviet citizens, Aitmatov was a captive of the system, unable to travel overseas without government authorization. He himself pushed the issue by asking Ginsburg to arrange an invitation for him. But his signature on the public denunciation of Sakharov in 1973 was apparently a complicating issue. It seems his participation in the campaign was an obstacle on the American side. Altay writes in his memoirs that Ginsburg had refused to help Aitmatov on account of his support of the campaign against Sakharov. In any case, Aitmatov appears to have halted correspondence with Ginsburg out of fear that discussion of such a sensitive political topic might doom him to an even longer wait.

But with détente under way—and the skies above America and the Soviet Union filled with space activity connected to the approaching Apollo-Soyuz hookup in July—the stars started to align for Aitmatov to visit the United States. The occasion was the decision of Arena Stage, a cutting edge American theater company, to stage the *Ascent of Mt. Fuji*.

If any theater company in the United States was well positioned to take advantage of a warming in US-Soviet relations, it was Arena Stage. By the 1970s, Arena Stage had established itself as the premier theater company in Washington, DC. Delivering on average a show a month, it had become a darling of politically staid Washington. It was even touching the hearts of supposedly Cold War enemies, with the wife of the Soviet cultural attaché reportedly shedding tears after an Arena Stage production.[17]

That kind of reaction boded well for Arena's international work, the prospects for which were looking bright during the détente era. In 1973 Arena Stage was selected by the State Department for an innovative cultural exchange to present American plays in the Soviet Union.

Arena Stage's "comparative advantage" was its "Russia connection." Zelda Fichandler, who was running the theater company after two decades of directing plays, had been a Russian language and literature major at Cornell University. Director Alan Schneider was a native Russian speaker, having been born in Russia before immigrating with his family to the United States in the early 1920s. Under their direction, Chekov's plays were a mainstay on the theater's bill.

But the ties went deeper. Arena Stage preferred the Stanislavsky method, an approach to acting developed in Russia in the early twentieth century in which actors were expected to absorb themselves completely in the emotional lives of their characters. A warmhearted, deep-thinking woman, Fichandler liked to describe the Stanislavsky method as "know-ing the human heart in all its complexity."[18]

The Washington, DC, theater company prepared two staples from its repertoire for performances in the Soviet Union in October 1973: *Our Town*, Thornton Wilder's poignant play about life and death in a small town in New Hampshire; and *Inherit the Wind*, the controversial play about defending intellectual freedom in the 1920s in the American South. On September 29, sixty-eight members of the troupe—actors, di-rectors, makeup artists, lighting crew, and sound technicians—boarded a Trans World Airways plane at Dulles Airport. Below them, the plane's cargo section held crates with ten tons of scenery, costumes, and props, along with a live monkey jumping around in its cage. Yes, Arena Stage had to take its own monkey—as a stage prop for *Inherit the Wind*—after word came from the Russian tour organizer that Russian monkeys were "busy and booked up."[19]

Performances in Moscow and Leningrad were "smashes," with sell-outs all fourteen evenings. Reviewers raved about *Our Town*. "It touched some kind of common chord," wrote Vera Maretskaya in *Literaturnaya Gazeta*. "It told us in a simple but masterful way of our universal fate."[20] Off stage, Americans and Russian actors shared meals, stories and shots of vodka. The Americans returned home, with the parting words of Sovremennik's youthfully irrepressible director Oleg Tabakov still in their heads. "In Russia, artists cannot really do anything; only politicians can," Tabakov had said to the assembled collectives of Arena Stage and Sovremennik Theater. "But artists can point out what has to be done."[21]

—⁓—

Two years later, Zelda Fichandler was poring over a copy of *Ascent of Mt. Fuji*—shortening sentences, erasing needless repetition, and adding *le mot juste*—to ready the play for the American stage. Edits in red, green, and gray pencil climbed up and down the pages of the script. Fichandler registered her reactions to the play's narrative line and scribbled notes from her own life in the margins, about times when she had found herself as conflicted as Aitmatov's characters.

Cognizant of the travails happening in American politics, like the fallout from Watergate and the Church hearings about the CIA's covert activity in toppling foreign governments, Fichandler believed the play had universal appeal: "This play has much to say to us, here and now," marketing materials touted. "Here in the nation's capital, now in a time of tumultuous dilemmas of conscience."

Arena Stage seemed to be taking Oleg Tabakov's words to heart. Indeed, themes of betrayal, dishonesty and ethical cowardice had gripped Fichandler and Schneider when they had seen the Sovremennik Theater perform the *Ascent of Mt. Fuji* in Moscow in 1973 and had helped convince them to stage the play in Washington, DC.

But Fichandler believed Arena Stage could do a better job with set design. Rather than doing the play in a circle, like a psychoanalytic help group as Sovremennik Theater had done, Arena Stage would create a mountainous setting. On the fringes of the stage, accomplished set designer Ming Cho-Lee crafted a mountain, which surrounded a yurt. The mountain rose up gradually from center stage, with nooks and crannies for the characters to sit in as befitting a picnic in the countryside. Male characters wore an assortment of Central Asian hats, including a skullcap and the distinctive Kyrgyz conical kalpak.

In May 1975, Fichandler was heavy into rehearsal schedules, with performances slated to start in June. There were small details to attend to—like how to procure a copy in Kyrgyz of Tsabur's pacifist poem. Fichandler wanted to put the Kyrgyz version on the cover of the playbill, but they had only the Russian and English versions. Arena Stage's director of press and public relations Alton Miller fretted: Russian language translations were one thing, but where could he possibly find a person who knew Kyrgyz?

Using contacts, likely including Mirra Ginsburg, Miller found his man. After speaking with Azamat Altay in New York, he informed Fichandler that he had found someone at Columbia University, "a Kirghiz, one of the very few in this country."[22] Altay made quick work of the request, locating the latest issue of a literary journal in his library and then translating the poem into Kyrgyz. When Arena Stage offered him free tickets as compensation, Altay suggested that the theater, instead, invite Aitmatov to Washington to see the play.

Sensing an opportunity to stretch détente even further, Arena Stage persuaded the US State Department to invite Aitmatov as part of a US-Soviet cultural exchange. Aitmatov got a US visa, and the Soviet government apparently concurred with Aitmatov's travels during a period of warming relations.

Aitmatov penned a quick note to Ginsburg, saying he was set to arrive in Washington on June 24, 1975. Writing cryptically, he appeared to allude to obstacles that had delayed his trip, including possibly his signature on the Sakharov letter: "People situated in different parts of the world and in different political systems can't always understand the situation of the other, and the whole complex of daily circumstances which flow through the life of another individual." But discussion of the past receded. Aitmatov was on his way for his first visit to America. "For me this is a big event to cross oceans in an effort to get acquainted with American people," he wrote.[23]

Reviews in June 1975 praised Arena Stage's production of *Ascent of Mt. Fuji*. Fichandler's directing and Ming Cho Lee's dramatic mountainous stage succeeded in transporting American audiences to an exotic land. *Newsweek* cited "Fichandler's well-staged, well-acted production" as "a provoking cultural event."[24] The *Washington Post* lauded Fichandler for finding "the inner rhythm, the breathing within the play."[25]

Fichandler herself was surprised at the positive response. "I didn't think anyone would come," she recalled in an interview many years later. "In the first act nothing happens, just talking and slicing eggs, eating fruit. But the audience felt inside the private, moral, mysterious, spiritual experience. You can tell by the breathing. You can make an absence of noise. That was the sound of the audience."[26]

Aitmatov was in the audience for the July 4 performance. In his hand, he held the *Ascent of Mt. Fuji* playbill, with Altay's translation of Tsabur's ill-fated poem in Kyrgyz prominently featured on the front cover. Shortly thereafter, Arena Stage's production unfolded before him just the way he had imagined. An American troupe in the midst of the Cold War had read his mind.

At the end of the show, Aitmatov climbed up to the stage himself, following in the footsteps of the American actors. The crowd gave him a standing ovation. "Spasibo," he said in gratitude, clapping along with the crowd. Against the backdrop of Arena's creative stage, with the picnic area nestled into rolling hills rising from behind center stage, Aitmatov hugged each member of the cast.[27]

At a time when the US press was focused on Alexandr Solzhenitsyn's arrival in America earlier in the year after his expulsion from the Soviet Union, some American observers seemed to be catching onto Aitmatov's growing voice inside the Soviet Union. *Newsweek*'s review of the play had pointed to the influence the Kyrgyz writer wielded by staying inside the Soviet Union.[28]

Indeed, although dissident writers like Solzhenitsyn and Brodsky would always hold sway in America, there was a growing awareness that writers like Aitmatov merited attention. The *Washington Post*'s correspondent in Moscow, Peter Osnos, echoed the sentiment in several articles, including one entitled "The Writers Who Stay." He mentioned Aitmatov in the context of Soviet writers who battle censors "behind their desks and in their minds."[29]

On Thursday, July 17, as Soviet and American spaceships maneuvered a hundred miles above the earth for their historic linkup, Azamat Altay began his day by reading a review of the Bolshoi Opera's performance of *Boris Godunov* at the Metropolitan Opera House. The review was similar to the reviews of Bolshoi performances that had run in the *New York Times* the previous weeks. In fact, with the Bolshoi in residence for a month at the Met, the reviews had become repetitive—about the convincing cast, superb orchestra and commanding conducting.

But eagle-eyed Azamat picked up a wrinkle: the company's new Boris Godunov was "oriental in appearance" and came "from Kyrgyzia, a Soviet Central Asian republic near Tibet."[30] Always on the lookout for Kyrgyz, Altay tracked down his compatriot—bass singer Bolot Minzhilkiev—and drove to his hotel. From the concierge's desk, he dialed Minzhilkiev's room.

"I am a Kyrgyz who by the hands of fate has ended up in alien lands," Altay introduced himself. "I work at Columbia University and would like to meet you."

"I am also Kyrgyz, *agai*," the thirty-five-year-old opera singer responded with alacrity, addressing Altay with the respectful title for older men. "Give me five minutes."

Although the Bolshoi troupe had strict orders forbidding contact with American citizens, the free-spirited Minzhilkiev paid no mind to the KGB guards in the lobby and headed out the door with Altay. He ignored them not because he was a world-traveling opera singer, but because, for him, a Kyrgyz anywhere in the world was a blood relative.

A few weeks later in Washington, DC, Minzhilkiev would make a scene by threatening not to perform unless a Kyrgyz couple visiting from Germany were seated. When told there were no tickets left, the Kyrgyz soloist tore off his wig and stalked away from his makeup chair. "Find tickets for my relatives or I won't perform," he demanded. In a panic, with the performance about to start, the theater administration offered the only seats left—the presidential box. After singing an aria, Minzhilkiev would bow to the couple in the box and then to the audience. Believing they were in the presence of VIPs, the American audience would turn toward the box and cheer. Minzhilkiev had turned simple Kyrgyz into royalty.[31]

Over dinner at Altay's house, Minzhilkiev and Altay talked of their common roots in the Lake Issyk Kul region, the manaschi Sayakbai Karalaev, who had died in 1971, and, of course, *kymyz*, the fermented mare's milk they both loved. Minzhilkiev regaled Altay with the story about how the Bolshoi Opera, reacting to criticism in the New York papers of the two soloists they had brought over, had summoned him from Moscow at the last minute for the July 15 performance.

A few days after his meeting with Altay, a Russian KGB colonel warned Minzhilkiev about unsanctioned contact with foreigners.

"Bolot, if you see our enemies, don't approach them," the colonel said.

"If your Ivanov leaves, then Petrov stays," Minzhilkiev shot back. "But we Kyrgyz are a small people, and if we don't support one another, we will disappear from this earth."[32]

—⁓—

During dinner with Minzhilkiev, Altay got a call from Mirra Ginsburg. "Chingiz Törökulovich has been asking about you," she said. "Here's his number at the hotel."

Aitmatov's outreach to Altay can be traced back to the seeds Gins-burg and Altay had planted as well as to Altay's cooperation with Arena Stage on inviting Aitmatov. But Aitmatov's desire to meet Kyrgyzia's most reviled dissident also had roots in the Kyrgyz people's desire to stay connected, just like Minzhilkiev had explained to the KGB colonel. Blood, indeed, ran thicker than devotion to the Party. In fact, Aitmatov had likely first heard of Altay decades earlier from his mentor Auezov, that consummate friend of the Kyrgyz people and champion of Central Asian culture and history, after Auezov's meeting with Altay in 1959 in New York.

Now, sixteen years later, Azamat Altay had a chance to meet another Central Asian legend. After a quick conversation on the phone with Ait-matov, Altay snatched up his Aitmatov books and loaded them in the car. For Altay, the books had been like fellow travelers with him on his personal odyssey, and they deserved to meet their maker. He, Saniye and Minzhilkiev raced to the hotel.

Any concerns about inconveniencing the great Aitmatov disinte-grated as the two men embraced in the hotel lobby. The group then strode past KGB guards on the way to Aitmatov's room, where his adult son Sanjar was waiting. There, while Saniye, Minzhilkiev, and Sanjar car-ried on a conversation in Russian, Altay and Aitmatov, two men divided by the Cold War but linked by a desire to keep Kyrgyz culture alive, talked animatedly in their native Kyrgyz.

The scene was an uncanny, terrestrial version of the dramatic events that had happened earlier in the day. At noon New York time, Apollo had achieved a firm linkup with Soyuz over the Atlantic Ocean, 620 miles west of Portugal. In a culmination of three years of joint work by the Cold War rivals, Soviet cosmonaut Aleksei Leonov welcomed American astronaut Tom Stafford through the hatches with a hardy handshake. President Ford and General Secretary Brezhnev sent congratulatory messages to the crews.

Aitmatov had watched the actual hookup live on TV earlier in the day with American writer Kurt Vonnegut. The meeting was one of Aitmatov's official duties as a representative of the Soviet Union. The two writers discussed the last link up between the countries at the Elbe River in Germany when American and Soviet soldiers met after the surrender of Nazi Germany. A captured American soldier at the time, Vonnegut related how he himself had been freed by Soviet soldiers from a prison camp.

With the debut of his play and the space hookup happening before his eyes, Aitmatov had spoken that day of the need for the two countries to step down from a "boxer's stance" and take heart from the day's events. The space hookup was a time of mutual achievement that gave rise to hopes that cooperation could spread to other fields. "What's happening in space," he said, "elevates us all in our own eyes and shows what we are capable of."[33]

In Aitmatov's hotel room that evening, a celebratory atmosphere prevailed, but of a far different nature. The impromptu gathering of Kyrgyz in New York, though unpublicized, had as much significance for the Kyrgyz people as did the Apollo-Soyuz handshake, maybe more. It represented a coming together of the disparate parts of the Kyrgyz elite: two leading cultural lights of Soviet Kyrgyzia in the same room with the founding voice of the Kyrgyz Service of America's Radio Liberty—a Kyrgyz Hall of Fame, if you will.

What unified them was blood, and the simple joy of connection that stood as an affirmation that the Kyrgyz people were living, existing, and staying together, even across ideological divides that seemed insurmountable to so many—the day's events notwithstanding. The Kyrgyz Ivanov had met the Kyrgyz Petrov: Altay on the outside openly hostile to communism; Aitmatov on the inside, a careful operator whose voice for change was starting to resonate like the deep bass voice of their countryman Minzhilkiev across the room.

Before leaving in the wee hours of the morning, Aitmatov signed a copy of *Farewell, Gulsary* for Altay. The words were simple and short— "To Kudaibergen, my fellow countryman, in memory of our meeting"— but they meant the world to the disconnected Altay. In return, Altay invited Aitmatov to visit his home in Queens to see his book collection. So, the Kyrgyz party continued two days later at Altay's house. But there was a disquieting note: Aitmatov's son Sanjar, who had been part of the first gathering, stayed behind in the hotel—"as a hostage" according to Altay's niece Gulnara Turganbaeva.[34] Evidently, the KGB wanted some leverage over the freely moving Aitmatov.

Figure 9.3: Chingiz Aitmatov and Azamat Altay at Altay's house in Queens, New York, on July 19, 1975, during Aitmatov's first visit to the United States. Source: Photo courtesy of Gulnara Turganbaeva.

On the way home after picking up Aitmatov at his hotel, Altay navigated his car through a torrential downpour that had flooded streets. Taking a detour, they made it to Altay's house in Queens. Once inside the house, there were guests from the Tatar community in New York, "endless" discussions, food, and singing. The gathering went on until three in the morning, and pictures of the evening show a relaxed Aitmatov reclining on a sofa with Altay and a Tatar guest (see figure 9.3). Altay would write a few weeks later to a friend, "I felt that evening as if I were the happiest man."[35]

Not long after the New York rendezvous, a human saga played out in Kyrgyzia. In the fall of 1975, Tenirberdi Alapaev knew he had to act fast if he was going to die in peace. He dispatched his niece Kasida to contact the Aitmatov family. When Kasida found out Chingiz Aitmatov was traveling, her uncle asked her to find Chingiz's sister Roza. After forty years, Alapaev, the man who had shared a cell with Törökul Aitmatov in the 1930s, was ready to unburden himself.

"I have an uncle, the brother of my father," Kasida told Roza when they met in Talas at a funeral. "In 1938 my uncle sat in the same cell as your father, Törökul Aitmatov."

Roza Aitmatova was taken aback. She had expected another hanger-on asking her to intercede with her brother for help with housing or the purchase of imported medicine. But the mention of her father's name changed everything.

"Where is your uncle?" Roza asked anxiously. "Is he alive?"

Kasida said Alapaev was weakening by the day, his lungs wracked by tuberculosis. The two women hurried to Talas Hospital. Barely able to stand up, Alapaev was coaxed into conversation by Kasida.

"You have your father's eyes," he told Roza.

Then raising his eyes to the ceiling, the slight man with deep creases in his face said: "I thank God that this meeting has come to be. Now I can die quietly. If I meet with Törökul up there in heaven, I won't be ashamed to look him in the eyes."

A gentle man, Alapaev started his story. In 1938, he had shared a jail cell with Törökul Aitmatov and six other men in the Frunze Prison. Alapaev related how, after being beaten by prison guards, he had been left on the cell floor. Törökul had cleaned his wounds and let the battered Alapaev take his turn on the lone metal cot in the center of the room, the prisoners' only relief from the cell's cold cement floor.

Alapaev told Roza he had been struck by Törökul's dignity and how the high-ranking communist official had borne his hardship with equanimity. Rail-thin from prison gruel, Törökul had confided in Alapaev on that first day of their acquaintance. "The time will come when people will figure out what's going on, and you will go free," he told Alapaev. Then referring to the NKVD, he added, "They will eliminate [the rest of] us, however, and they will likely do it very soon. They don't want to leave any traces of their crimes."[36]

Roza listened transfixed as Alapaev recounted Törökul's last days—Törökul's insistence that he was innocent, his message to Chingiz to oppose injustice, and the system of signals he would use to convey the outcome of his trial so that Alapaev could inform the family what had happened to their father.

Alapaev didn't get any signals and never saw Törökul again.

———

Though just sixty-three years old, Alapaev's wasting body made him look much older to Roza Aitmatova. He had survived twenty years of exile in Siberia. During one of those years, on an emotional night when he was drunk and despairing of ever returning to Kyrgyzia, he threw his coat into a river. Tucked in an inside pocket was the toiletry bag Törökul had entrusted to him.

During Khrushchev's rule, Alapaev ended up returning to Kyrgyzia, but he was a broken man physically and had to undergo periodic treatment for his damaged lungs. One time his roommate in the recuperation clinic was a young man who read books day and night. Curious, Alapaev asked for a book. When he flipped the pages to one of the stories, he read the epigram: "Father, I don't know where you are buried. I dedicate this book to you, Törökul Aitmatov. Mother, you raised us four. I dedicate this book also to you. Nagima Aitmatova."

When Alapaev saw the author's photo in the book, he saw Törökul's expression and thoughtful gaze. It clicked. The author was Törökul's eldest son, whose name had been sewn on the toiletry bag. The story was "Mother's Field." Here was a chance for Alapaev to make good on his promise to Törökul, but he prevaricated. Instead of acting on his promise to be a living link to the Aitmatov family, he had again been overcome with shame for having thrown away the bag. Whenever he sat down to write a letter to Chingiz to explain himself, he ended up never finishing, he told Roza.

"Forgive me," a sobbing Tenirberdi asked Roza that summer day in the hospital. "Forgive me."[37]

Alapaev died two weeks later.

10

Standing Up to Injustice

Out for an evening stroll in Munich in February 1981, Azamat Altay had time to reflect on the turn of fate that had brought him back to Radio Liberty in 1979. After a long career working in libraries, he had been looking forward to spending his retirement in Queens on the porch of his house and tending his vegetable garden. But in 1978 Radio Liberty officials made an appeal. The Kyrgyz Service was in dire straits, they said: the director of the Turkestan Department had died suddenly two years earlier, and the longest-serving employee of the Kyrgyz Service had been diagnosed with heart disease.

"If you don't continue what you started, then the Kyrgyz Service may have to close," a Radio Liberty official told Altay in New York.

The pitch worked. Altay and Saniye uprooted themselves and returned to Europe far more comfortably than when he had left the continent two decades earlier. Indeed, when he was in the radio studio, dressed in a suit and wearing glasses with his silvery gray hair combed back over his head, Altay looked like a Westernized *aksakal*.

A loud boom jolted Altay out of reminiscing. It was nearly 10 p.m., and, ready for bed, Altay paid little mind to the sound coming from the direction of the English Garden, the public park where the Radio Free Europe/Radio Liberty (RFE/RL) office was located. The next morning, however, brought grim news.

An explosion had destroyed a wing of the building, wounding four employees from the Czechoslovak Service. Altay breathed a sigh of relief when he learned no one from the Kyrgyz Service had been hurt. The only damage to the Kyrgyz Service, which was located next to the

Czechoslovak Service, was broken windows and damaged typewriters. All told, the multiwinged Radio Liberty building suffered $2 million in damages.

—⁓—

Radio Liberty was apparently doing its job too well. Documents from security files made available after the collapse of communist regimes reveal that Romania, concerned over the impact of RFE's broadcasts on its population, instigated the attack, with support from other communist countries.

The mastermind behind the bombing was Carlos the Jackal, a Venezuelan-born radical Marxist. Born Ilich Ramirez Sanchez, Carlos had made a name for himself in the 1970s and 1980s for his violent work on behalf of Arab nationalist causes. But with close links to intelligence services of the Soviet bloc, he also did the dirty work of communist regimes. Romanian Security Services reportedly paid Carlos a million dollars to carry out the operation and supplied bomb-making equipment, walkie-talkies, pistols, and hand grenades.

On the evening of February 21, a Swiss member of Carlos's group attached forty-four pounds of plastic explosives to a wall at ground level just outside the offices of the Czechoslovak Service. After the detonation, the culprits escaped in getaway cars. Carlos, who directed the strike from a safe house in Budapest, remained at large for another decade, organizing bombings on French trains and against French interests overseas, which earned him the reputation of being "one of the world's most brutal terrorists."[1]

Carried out at a low point of the Cold War—just after the Soviet invasion of Afghanistan in 1979 and the U.S. boycott of the 1980 Olympics—the attack exposed the risks inherent in Radio Free Europe/Radio Liberty's work during the Cold War.

—⁓—

In December 1979, Soviet tanks and troops invaded Afghanistan in a bid to prop up Afghanistan's communist leadership against Islamist insurgents, or mujahideen, as they were known in the West. It was a watershed event, marking the first time Soviet troops had intervened in a country outside Europe. The invasion affected Soviet Central Asia in particular because, contrary to previous military strategy, Muslim soldiers from the Central Asian republics participated in the invasion.

Historically, including during World War II, the Soviet Union had preferred to use Slavic soldiers instead of non-Russian soldiers from the Caucasus and Central Asia whose loyalty was in question. But in Afghanistan, partly because of the belief that soldiers who shared a religion (Islam) and languages (Uzbek and Tajik) with parts of the Afghan population would be more effective, soldiers from Central Asia were at the vanguard of the Red Army's invading forces.[2]

Worldwide condemnation, particularly from the United States and Europe, rained down on the Soviet Union for its invasion. At Radio Liberty, the Kyrgyz Service, capitalizing on heightened interest since Kyrgyz soldiers were among the Soviet invasion forces, translated and broadcast reports on the invasion filed by the station's correspondents, thus providing an alternative to Soviet state-run media.

As news of the Soviets getting bogged down in Afghanistan filtered into Kyrgyzia, the republic's communist leadership became incensed. The familiar voice of anticommunist Altay, on the air after a nearly twenty-five-year hiatus, must have vexed them even further. The last thing the communists in Kyrgyzia wanted was for Altay's name recognition in his homeland to rise. So, they set out to derail him.

Over the decades, "renegade" Altay had fended off KGB attempts to lure him home—like the preacher's letters praising him and the kolkhoz chairman's plea to return to the Soviet Union. He had proved too hardened for such indirect approaches. So, the Kyrgyz KGB designed a more personalized approach. They recruited a Kyrgyz scientist who had received an invitation to travel to the United States in the late 1970s and hatched a plan "to wake up Altay's love for his homeland" and convince him to return home.

The KGB knew that Altay was prone to melancholy. So, in addition to standard gifts like a souvenir whip and kalpak, the Kyrgyz KGB gave geologist Bektash Iliyasov a cassette tape with Kyrgyz melodies played on the three-stringed *komuz*. During a two-month training camp in

Frunze before Iliyasov's departure, KGB officials rehearsed Altay's "entrapment." Iliyasov would invite Altay to a dinner with other members of the Soviet scientific delegation. "To get him nostalgic, turn on the music when you are setting the table," the KGB operatives counseled. "Then address him as 'brother.'"

Upon arrival in New York, Iliyasov contacted his KGB handler who arranged for food to be flown up on an Aeroflot plane from Washington, DC, and provided money to pay for expenses related to the operation. The trap was set. But once Altay arrived at the dinner, he was not fooled. He immediately sensed that Iliyasov was part of a KGB trap. "Don't trouble yourself," Altay chided Iliyasov.

Altay then turned the tables on the scientist. He complimented the geologist on getting invited to the United States and conversed with him about Kyrgyzia under communism. Over the next three months, Altay showed Iliyasov life in America, inviting him to his house and for a picnic in the woods outside New York and impressing upon the KGB agent how he had continued to be a patriot of Kyrgyzia despite living in the United States. He even gave Iliyasov a tour of his personal library and recounted to him the founding of Radio Liberty. "This man was simple, smart and articulate," Iliyasov recalled years later.[3]

Iliyasov reported his failure to his KGB handlers. He didn't, however, tell them that upon his return to Kyrgyzia, he became a regular listener of Radio Liberty broadcasts, taking a Latvian-made portable radio to the mountains to catch the shortwave signal.

———

With Altay parrying soft approaches, the KGB launched a mean-spirited propaganda campaign. If they couldn't stop "supply" from abroad, then they would try to blunt "demand" at home. In 1982, communist authorities broadcast a documentary film castigating Altay called *The Waves Die on the Shore*. Articles appeared in the state-controlled Kyrgyz press detailing Altay's "traitorous" life and his "CIA-funded" work at Radio Liberty.

A one-two combination appeared in *Sovetskaya Kyrgyzia*, the newspaper of the Communist Party of Kyrgyzia, in early 1982. A letter signed by five elders from Altay's home village accused Altay of being a triple agent for the United States, West Germany, and Turkey—a versatile man, indeed. The elders pounced on his name change: "How many years has it been since you forgot your name?"

Then the authors attacked Altay for not being sufficiently religious, criticizing him for not washing his hands before he prayed. It was time, the village elders counseled in their denouement, for Altay to make amends for bad decisions because, at age sixty-two, he was the same age as the Prophet Muhammad when he died.[4]

It was a curious tack by the KGB—using citizens from an avowedly secular state to make a religious attack—and smelled as if the Kyrgyz KGB, having failed in other attempts, was running out of "ammunition" for its attacks against Altay.

The elders' letter set the stage for the reappearance of preacher Jeyenbekov. In his published letter, Jeyenbekov no longer referred to himself as Altay's "friend from the Haj," but he castigated Altay for being a sentimental crybaby who had tried to sow divisions in the Kyrgyz delegation in Mecca some twenty-five years earlier. Taken with the elders' letter a month before, it was obvious that Jeyenbekov was the KGB informant who had supplied the information about Altay's supposedly wayward religious practices at the hajj.[5] Jeyenbekov's weak cover was completely blown.

In the fall of 1982, the KGB took the campaign against Altay to the airwaves, with Kyrgyz State TV broadcasting a film about him called *Disdain*. The documentary film referred to Altay as a coward and charged that Radio Liberty was using CIA funding to pour "tubs of dirt" on the Soviet Union.

The campaign gained momentum, evidently to combat Kyrgyz Service reports about declining living standards in Soviet Kyrgyzia. A letter from a resident of Altay's home village trumpeted the arrival of a new furniture store in the village. A Communist Party official from Frunze piped in: "The vile bark of the servants of imperialism cannot stop the victory march of Soviet society."[6]

—⁓—

In 1983, Altay started noticing suspicious men trailing him in Munich. When he departed from work in the evenings, he would spot two men standing on the street corner. As he crossed a bridge in the neighborhood, they would edge closer, and in the late evenings they would spy on his apartment from across the street. There were also disturbing calls at night: when Altay picked up, the other side would abruptly hang up.

The KGB had made clear its displeasure with Altay's work. Unable to dissuade him using agents and propaganda campaigns, would they now try to kidnap him? Or maybe even eliminate him? They had done so with the Bulgarian dissident writer Georgi Markov. In 1978 the Bulgarian Intelligence Service, with help from KGB poison specialists, had engineered a pass-by assassination while Markov was waiting for a bus in London. The assassin stabbed him in the leg with an umbrella—purchased by the KGB's main residency in Washington, DC, incidentally—that released a pinhead-sized ricin pellet. Markov, a reporter in the Bulgarian Service of the BBC at the time, died four days later when the poison spread throughout his body.[7]

The surveillance in Munich lasted for about a year before Altay, aware that Markov had worked for Radio Free Europe before joining BBC, brought the matter to the attention of Radio Liberty's Security Department. Only when Radio Liberty security personnel started following the two men did they disappear, as covertly as they had sprung up.

The propaganda pieces and KGB's failed campaigns against Altay were the best confirmation that he had developed name recognition among those Kyrgyz—including at least one KGB informer—brave enough to listen to Kyrgyz-language broadcasts. There was even tacit recognition among the propaganda that Altay was effective: "He sows the seeds of doubt in the souls of listeners and gradually nurtures it."[8]

———

Chingiz Aitmatov's *The Day Lasts Longer Than a Century* was published in the dark years of Brezhnev's gerontocracy. Détente had crumbled, living standards were stagnant, and human rights heavily suppressed, with the internal exile of dissident Andrei Sakharov in 1980 a bellwether.

Soviet citizens, particularly youth, were in quiet rebellion against their drab society, craving Western clothes and rock-and-roll music. Around hotels where tourists were segregated, black market traders started to

appear. Usually young men with broken English, they were the risk tak-
ers of Soviet society, speculators hoping to catch a foreigner's eye to trade
Soviet kitsch for jeans or cosmetics or to exchange dollars for rubles at
two to the three times the official rate.

The aging Brezhnev himself became the butt of jokes, told sotto voce
among friends. One popular joke described a Brezhnev aide informing the Soviet leader that the Americans had sent a man to the moon.
Brezhnev replies that the Soviet Union will rocket a man to the sun.
When his aide politely remarks that the rocket will burn up, Brezhnev
answers, "Okay, we'll launch at night."

In the midst of the gloom, Aitmatov had holed himself away in an elite
government compound on the shores of Lake Issyk Kul. It was his favorite place to write, and he retreated there whenever he could. Sequestered
in a dacha in the birch forest and surrounded by piles of books, he wrote
nonstop during the winter of 1980, taking breaks only to eat and sleep.
It was as if a literary fury were percolating up to the surface, the words
pouring onto the paper in his flowing longhand over the course of four
months. Years later, a Kyrgyz journalist would say the book was written
by God through Aitmatov's hands.[9]

The Day Lasts Longer Than a Century became the most popular book
in the Soviet Union almost overnight when it was published in the November 1980 issue of Novy Mir. University students in Moscow guarded
scarce copies of the novel as if they were tamizdat, lending them to eager
readers for just twenty-four hours. American correspondents in Moscow
reportedly had copies of the Novy Mir issue made in the United States
and sent back to the Soviet Union to distribute to their Soviet friends.

The story features a Kazakh man named Edigei who, after a day's
effort, fails to bury his longtime friend in the cemetery of their remote
village. Aitmatov fills in Edigei's daylong journey with flashbacks about
his life as a soldier in World War II and as a railroad worker in the Kazakh
steppe. Edigei is an exceedingly likable protagonist—fallible, hardworking, and human to the core.

The Day is a multilayered tour de force whose exotic setting—a
remote railroad depot in the Kazakh steppe with camels and dust

storms—masks profound truths about the dehumanizing Soviet system. The craftsman Aitmatov conveys the novel's deeper meaning through levels of subplots. The first level describes Edigei's journey to bury his friend Kazangap and the obstacles he faces along the way, including a lack of reverence in Sovietized Kazakh society for burial rituals and cemeteries.

The second level introduces the legend of the *mankurt*, for which the novel became famous. Aitmatov uses the ancient legend, which has roots in the *Manas* epic, to warn readers about the danger of forgetting their heritage.[10] In the novel a young warrior is captured by Kalmyk invaders during times of turmoil hundreds of years earlier. To make sure the enemy soldier never fights again, the Kalmyks torture him by placing a dried camel-skin cap over his head. As the leather contraption shrinks in the midday heat, it either kills the warrior or renders him senseless, fit only to be a slave. In Aitmatov's version, the *mankurt* is so deprived of human emotion that he fails to recognize his own mother, who has come looking for him, and shoots her dead with an arrow.

The third level takes readers into outer space where a joint Soviet-US space mission has made contact with living beings on another planet. The joint Soviet-US crew radios back to earth that they have discovered extraterrestrials who have something to teach earthlings in the way they govern peacefully and plan for the future. The superpowers convene and, on the basis of narrow interests to preserve their supremacy on earth, decide to erase all memory of the discovery of a better way of life. They cut the pioneering astronauts off from earth by deploying a ring of space-based rockets.

While a bit fantastic, the galactic story ties into the novel's climax when rockets are fired from a Soviet military base that is encroaching upon the village cemetery. The launch of the rockets sends Edigei fleeing into the steppe with his camel and dog. But the launch accentuates the distance between Edigei and two Soviet-made *mankurts*: a Kazakh guard at the military base who insists on speaking Russian and Kazangap's cravenly opportunistic son, an official in the local Communist Party, who ridicules traditions from the past.

—⁂—

Aitmatov's mastery as a writer is evident in the way he connects the metaphor of the mankurt to US-Soviet relations and to Edigei's struggles. By forming an impenetrable ring around earth that effectively shuts out new knowledge, the rockets are akin to a *mankurt*'s cap. In the same way the missile ring shuts off learning, the soldier and Kazangap's son, by refusing to honor traditions—the son even suggests burying his father near the railroad tracks—are willfully ignoring the accumulated knowledge from the past and, thus, embody *mankurts* come to life.

The skillful Aitmatov wrote the book on several literary planes, thus making it harder for censors to distinguish a distinct anti-Soviet line. Indeed, he earned praise from some Soviet critics for focusing the book on a simple workingman who benefits from technological progress, be it a tractor or railroads.

But what Aitmatov gave with one hand, he deftly manipulated with the other. Edigei's raison d'être may be building communism to orthodox critics, but to those privy to Aitmatov's inner world Edigei's essential human worth derives from his drive to preserve the history and culture of Central Asia and, equally important, maintain self-dignity. Edigei's character in the book proved that, while taboos on the expression of religious faith and nationalist feelings were demoralizing, people could still live inner lives of the spirit. Such people existed as strong, self-reliant, and uncompromising figures.

As he had done with *The White Ship*, Aitmatov drew on personal tragedy to build a searing narrative that condemns the totalitarian system. Returning to the theme of a family deprived of its father in *The White Ship*, Aitmatov describes village resident Abutalip on a train taking him to the labor camps. As the train passes through the village, he spots his house and sees his wife and children through the window. The scene is reminiscent of what Aitmatov's own father may well have experienced in January 1938 on the train transporting him from Moscow to Frunze, when he passed near Sheker.

For Aitmatov, the crux of *The Day* was the struggle to be free—a journey the free-spirited Kyrgyz people had been on at least since the chronicle of Manas was started in AD 800. But in the twentieth century, their weapons were not spears and bows but their own mental fortitude. To give themselves the best chance to be free—in their minds if not in the sovereignty of their countries—Central Asians had to halt cultural dissolution and refuse to become willingly made *mankurts*. By remembering history and respecting traditions, people could reclaim a sense of community, shared heritage, and dignity. That was Aitmatov's message.[11]

When read as three stories linked together, *The Day* was a condemnation of the Soviet system—the whole system, not just its Stalinist perversion. The experiment to build a Soviet man, Aitmatov concluded in *The Day*, had produced morally degraded and spiritually vacuous citizens who refused to question the state's ideology. The word *mankurt*, in fact, would reappear several years later across the Soviet Union during demonstrations for independence. Peaceful demonstrators in the Baltic republics carried posters saying "We are not *mankurts*."[12]

Chingiz Aitmatov had a successful record of publishing books with controversial themes, but *The Day* pushed the limits of what was acceptable in Soviet society. The story of its publication is a testament to the efforts of two men, Aitmatov and *Novy Mir* editor Sergei Narovchatov, striking a blow for freedom using their wits and bravery.

Were it not for the courageous efforts of Narovchatov, *The Day* might never have seen the light of day. Aitmatov and Narovchatov, who became *Novy Mir*'s chief editor in 1974, battled Soviet authorities for months leading up to the printing date. Censors asked that the title be changed, that the negative characterization about a KGB official be softened, and that the tragic ending—in which the unfairly maligned Abutalip is tortured and commits suicide—be replaced. Aitmatov bristled but ultimately had to relent. It was a tormenting process as he saw his book get whittled down. But the core of the book remained intact, and it got approval to be published.

Then Aitmatov got a call in the summer of 1980 while he was in Moscow with his soon-to-be second wife, Maria, whom he had met in Frunze in the mid-1970s. He learned that, even though his novel had received the green light, Communist Party officials had put a halt to the book's printing. It was the same kind of last-minute panic that had shelved *Novy Mir*'s publication of Solzhenitsyn's *Cancer Ward* in the late 1960s.

In despair, Aitmatov called Narovchatov, and the two men strategized for an hour while Maria waited in the car. Disregarding protocol, which would have had him bow to the party's concerns about controversial themes, Narovchatov, whose own father had been exiled to Siberia in the 1930s, ordered the print run to proceed, taking responsibility himself for any negative consequences. His bold decision paid off; issues of the November issue of *Novy Mir* were bought up quickly from news kiosks.

—*~~~*—

Radio Liberty estimates that by the early 1980s as many as one in four Soviet adults was listening to programs emanating from the West, with Radio Liberty listeners accounting for up to 40 percent of those listeners.[13] Solzhenitsyn himself gave Radio Liberty perhaps its biggest advertising coup in the 1970s when he said, "If we ever hear anything about events in our country," it's through Radio Liberty.[14]

The US-funded radio station had established a reputation for hard-edged programming that was giving listeners across the Soviet Union insight into repression in the Soviet system. Broadcasts had relayed back into the Soviet Union the transcripts of the Sinyavsky and Daniels trial and taboo writings of Sakharov and Solzhenitsyn. When Stalin's daughter, Svetlana Alliluyeva, defected to the United States in the late 1960s, Radio Liberty made sure to broadcast her memoirs. In fact, in those days the radio station received so many documents smuggled out of the Soviet Union that it established an archive to vet and store them.[15]

Contrary to Soviet propaganda about Radio Liberty using CIA funding, the radio venture had ceased to be funded by the CIA in 1971, instead receiving a direct financial injection from the US Congress. There was robust bipartisan support for the radio station on Capitol Hill. Republicans liked its anticommunist slant, while Democrats supported its pro–human rights and pro-democracy angles. In fact, a virtuous circle ensued when interviews of Soviet travelers to the West revealed deep interest in the programming of Radio Liberty's language services. That, in turn, led to more funding.

The arrival of Zbigniew Brzezinski as President Jimmy Carter's national security adviser in 1976 boosted the station's position even more. A Pole by birth, Brzezinski had a visceral understanding of what it meant to be a captive nation and appreciated the power of nationalism to thwart Soviet assimilation policies. A first indication of a growing role for radio was when Brzezinski tapped RFE/RL veteran Paul Henze to build a Soviet nationalities program as part of the National Security Council (NSC) apparatus.

In his approach to dealing with the Soviet Central Asia, Henze was influenced by Altay's old friend Alexandre Bennigsen. As a professor of Turkic studies at the University of Chicago, the urbane Bennigsen was bucking the consensus that the Soviet totalitarian system had squashed traditional values and religious inclinations in Central Asia. Instead, Bennigsen believed that the Central Asian republics, despite the overt Sovietization of life, were still steeped in religious customs and the Turkic and Persian traditions which had defined living for centuries.

For years on trips to the US Bennigsen had been dismissed by Soviet scholars for his pie-in-the-sky views. But in the 1980s Bennigsen's nuanced view that Central Asians were "practicing" Islam in an informal way was gaining traction. Practices handed down through generations like the conduct of funeral rites and holiday celebrations were serving as a bulwark against assimilation into Russian culture. Bennigsen's belief that elites in Soviet Central Asia were resisting Soviet social engineering started to enjoy popularity among US government officials. Here the connection is clear between what Bennigsen—and Altay believed—and what Aitmatov, with a character like Edigei setting out to bury his friend according to Islamic rites, was writing.

Thanks in part to Henze, funding for Radio Free Europe/Radio Liberty increased in the Carter administration. It continued to climb with the arrival of President Ronald Reagan in office in 1981 in line with his administration's policy to communicate the superiority of the American system over communism.

Reagan's strategy to oppose the Soviet Union pivoted on the belief that the Soviet Central Asian republics were the vulnerable underbelly of the Soviet empire. Moscow's troublesome war in Afghanistan and evidence of a nationalist spirit in Central Asia fed the desire of policy makers in the Reagan administration to exploit weaknesses in their superpower rival. In concert with an arms buildup by the United States, Bennigsen's views provided support for a policy of chipping away at the Soviet monolith from the border regions. In 1985, President Reagan

himself voiced his determination to show "the captive nations that resisting totalitarianism is possible."[16]

Sensing more operating room, RFE/RL's language services edged
forward since the Soviet republics were, in the opinions of Radio Liberty staffers like Altay, "captive nations," just like the Eastern European
satellite states. With support at the highest levels of the US government,
Radio Liberty was about to enter its "golden period."

In July 1981, while *The Day* was still enjoying popularity across the
Soviet Union, even the staid Soviet Writers' Union had to praise Aitmatov. First Secretary of the Soviet Writers' Union Georgi Markov held
up Edigei as an exemplary worker and lauded Aitmatov's multileveled
stories and use of folktales.[17] It was a remarkable speech for the conservative Markov. The approving tone showed that, while Aitmatov's novel
may have touched sensitive subjects, it still fell within the realm of accepted prose. Or maybe Aitmatov was helping to widen the realm of the
permissible. That's what it seemed like given a kinder, gentler message
emanating from the Soviet Communist Party.

Chastened after the disintegration of the Polish Communist Party in
the face of pressure from the Solidarity Trade Union in 1980, the Soviet
government started to moderate hard-line policies, including its han-
dling of its own national minorities. Soviet leader Brezhnev led the way,
acknowledging that the nature of problems in a multinational state demanded that the party "pay close attention to the voice of the masses."[18]

Nevertheless, the cautious Aitmatov, mindful of the fate of his father,
built layers of postpublication protection around his stealthily crafted
novel. During this period of Soviet vulnerability, he chose his words
carefully, noting Edigei's Soviet persona—his ennobling war experience
and his simple roots. Here the master craftsman took advantage of the
"flexible" hero he had cultivated, emphasizing the sides of Edigei that
could answer to Soviet literary protocols.

Should someone suspect from reading *The Day* that Aitmatov was
intimating that Russia's dominant culture was squeezing out native traditions in Central Asia, in public Aitmatov came across like a Russian
patriot and convinced communist: "Love for the Russian language,"

he said in 1982, "is an expression of love toward the language of the revolution."[19]

When discussing the Soviet man, Aitmatov was as cunning—or complicated—as he had ever been. In 1982, he declared that the Soviet Union had "proved the advantages of the new social order," adding that the country's main accomplishment had been "the birth of a new man."[20]

How could it be that this Soviet man whom Aitmatov praised as the crowning achievement of communism was the same man Aitmatov himself had skewered as a *mankurt* in *The Day*?

Aitmatov's public statements were his reckoning with the complicated Soviet reality in which he existed. It was a reality in which the tragic fate of his father was predominant: Törökul Aitmatov had been cut down at the pinnacle of his career—an ever-present reminder of the system's sudden, brutal power. Naturally, Aitmatov looked to protect himself from a similar fate. But things were not so black-and-white all the time. Aitmatov himself had much for which to be grateful: he had benefited from the Soviet system in terms of education, vocation, promotion, and access to the outside world. And he was indebted to things Russian—language, literature, and acquaintances—for playing an instrumental role in all his advances.

At the same time, like other Soviet citizens, Aitmatov had learned to "game" the system by using leverage—in this case, his adherence to literary protocol—to procure benefits. Public statements showing him as a supportive communist were partly sincere and partly a way to ensure that he maintained the personal lifestyle and preserved the creative space to work as a writer in the Soviet Union. They were his price for freedom.

Aitmatov was walking a tightrope, proceeding cautiously but doing sleights of hand and foot, which while daring to a knowing audience, never led him to fall. A close colleague would say many years later about the conundrum inside Aitmatov: "He could not lie when he sat behind a desk."[21]

—⁓—

Aitmatov's thinking on the danger of nuclear war illustrated his double life. In public, he followed the party line, railing against US imperialism for policies that were driving the world to the edge of a nuclear apocalypse. In the 1982 interview in which he extolled the Soviet man, he accused the West of convincing its citizens that it could win a nuclear war against the Soviet Union.[22]

But in his writing Aitmatov was sending a warning about the potential for a nuclear holocaust and assigning equal blame to the Soviet Union and United States, who together controlled the vast majority of nuclear weapons. That joint culpability was evident in *The Day*. Contrary to Soviet propaganda, which would have placed blame solely on the United States for setting up the missile ring around the earth, Aitmatov made the decision a joint one taken by both superpowers.[23]

It was all part of the riddle of Aitmatov. In public life, he blended in as if not to bring attention to the expansive gift that he harbored inside. Communism intruded on a citizen's daily life, as Aitmatov well knew from the scolding he took about his affair with Beishenalieva. But it couldn't suppress his rich interior life, the place he could retreat to and find solace. And that inner life afforded Aitmatov a unique vantage point. A friend would say years later of Aitmatov's particular perch: because he was from a small place, he could look at history from above, like a bird. Aitmatov saw beneath dissembling and prevarication and picked up on trends and human currents. And as he aged, his concerns would transcend the Soviet Union to take up the world—the arms race, environmental degradation, terrorism and religious extremism. "We must not think anymore within the context of our country," he would say. "For global crises, we need global solutions."[24]

Even in family life, Aitmatov didn't give many hints of what was percolating inside. He might spin an entertaining bedtime story for Eldar and Shirin, his children by his second wife Maria, but then would retreat to the privacy of his writing, where it seemed another consciousness would take over, this one propelled by brutal honesty (see figure 10.1). Like Sheker, his writing was a refuge from an unpredictable and fickle outside world, a place where he could try to resolve the angst—personal and existential—besetting him.

His creative talents spawned books that were entire metaphors. A few years before *The Day* he had telegraphed his contrarian stance about nuclear weapons in a short story that explores the responses of man when

Figure 10.1: Chingiz Aitmatov with his son Eldar and daughter Shirin in the early 1980s outside Frunze. Source: Central State Archives of the Kyrgyz Republic.

he is put in an extreme situation. In his first piece of writing set outside Central Asia, titled *The Piebald Dog Running along the Seashore*, Aitmatov portrays a Nivkh family—distant relations of Alaskan Eskimos—caught in a deep fog while on a seal-hunting expedition off the coast of northeastern Siberia.

Running out of water after several days on the ocean, the grandfather voluntarily slips into the water to his death, leaving an uncle, father, and teenage boy in the fogged-in kayak. Crazed from a lack of water, the uncle gulps seawater and jumps overboard. Finally, with water supplies dwindling, the father sacrifices himself in hopes his son can make it home. The son ultimately makes it back to shore when the fog clears.

While there are tragic losses, Aitmatov's teaching moment comes in the conduct of the older generations—the grandfather and father—who give up their lives for the young boy. As the oldest, the grandfather takes on the responsibility of doling out the water reserves, leaving himself as the last recipient and giving himself the smallest dose. The men sacrifice themselves by age in a solemn order decreed by nature. A reverence for life is conveyed through death. Aitmatov's story about the Nivkhs is a parable about humanity's plight at the end of the twentieth century: nations would have to row together to escape the "nuclear fog," and the "elder" nations would have to lead by example.

—⁓—

The downturn in US-USSR relations at the start of the 1980s prevented follow-up meetings between Aitmatov and Altay. Plus, Altay's affiliation with Radio Liberty made him "toxic." But Aitmatov continued to "speak" to Altay through his writing, like a natural counterweight to the propaganda attacks. In *The Day*, Aitmatov sympathetically portrayed former POW Abutalip who, like Altay, is captured by the Germans, escapes, and joins partisans to fight against the Nazis. Except Aitmatov has Abutalip return to the Soviet Union where he is hounded and meets an untimely death, just the sort of grim fate Altay had avoided by jumping lines.[25]

Whether or not Aitmatov had Altay in mind when he wrote *The Day* is hard to determine. But several years later, when Altay and Aitmatov would meet in 1988, Aitmatov would inscribe a copy of *The Day* with words that make clear a link in the writer's mind between Altay and Abutalip. "I dedicate this to Abutalip, who is alive," Aitmatov wrote on the front page, "and he is Azamat Altay."

But it was the *mankurt* theme that likely resonated most deeply with Altay. Through his work at the Turkic collections at New York Public Library and Columbia University, Altay had cataloged versions of *Manas* and the banned works of writers such as Kasym Tynystanov. And Aitmatov knew himself from a tour of Altay's home library in 1975 that the "American Kyrgyz" was keeping Kyrgyz heritage alive in his personal collection.

It's highly unlikely that Aitmatov was doing this intentionally for Altay. Rather, Altay's plight was so common—more than five million

Soviet soldiers were captured by the Germans during the war—and his response to the trampling of his culture so logical that Aitmatov's narrative swept up Altay's personal story in the telling.

In the absence of personal contact, Altay closely followed Aitmatov's public statements from Munich, where in 1983 Altay had been promoted to chief editor of the Kyrgyz Service. He understood the complicated calculus of being a popular writer in the Soviet Union—the pressures the communist regime exerted and the contortions writers had to perform in response. Altay instructed his staff, some of whom had never lived in Soviet Kyrgyzia, that Aitmatov's pronouncements in favor of Soviet policy— against the West or supporting the Bolshevik Revolution—should be viewed as payment to keep his literary oxygen flowing. They were compromises Aitmatov had to make. "Take a 'soft' approach towards Chingiz Törökulovich," he would advise them.[26] He counseled his staff to limit mention of Aitmatov in broadcasts so as to avoid making him look like a "darling of the West" and becoming the subject of criticism. This was particularly important during the sharp downturn in relations in the 1980s.[27]

Paradoxically, this put newspaper and radios outside the Soviet Union in charge of Aitmatov's fate: by regurgitating back to Soviet listeners a neutral profile of Aitmatov, editors like Altay could help preserve his space to write. As the saying goes in Russian, "The quieter you travel, the farther you will go." It was a delicate balance that Altay handled superbly.

As well as being advocates of individual liberty and "survivors" of totalitarianism, Chingiz Aitmatov and Azamat Altay connected on other levels. Raised in the godless Soviet Union, Aitmatov described himself as an atheist, but the more he wrote, the more he became interested in issues of religion and faith.[28] He had pushed limits of Soviet belles lettres in *The Day* by portraying his socialist hero Edigei as a spiritual, if not religious, man.

In the book's final chapter, Aitmatov describes Edigei appealing to God after saying prayers over the shrouded corpse of his friend Kazangap: "I want to believe that You exist and You are in my thoughts when I come to You with my prayers. In fact, I speak through You to myself, and at such times I am given the gift of thinking."[29]

For all its powerful political implications—against dictatorial repression and in support of national identity—*The Day* was an uplifting work of the spirit, particularly for a small national minority like the Kyrgyz. A Kyrgyz intellectual, who was studying in high school when Aitmatov's novel came out, called *The Day* a "spiritual inoculation."[30] For some, that meant a book that gave them clues on how to conduct their lives with dignity and compassion; for others it spurred them to believe in something greater than themselves. And still for others, it was a warning not to become a *mankurt.*

Aitmatov had signaled the novel's spiritual thrust by taking his epigraph from the *Book of Lamentations*, written by the Armenian monk Grigor Narekatsi in the tenth century:

> This book I offer instead of my body
> And this word instead of my soul.

With the epigraph echoing Jesus's words to his disciples at the Last Supper, it was no surprise that Aitmatov himself spoke of writing the novel as being an "opening" of his soul.

Aitmatov had been consumed by Narekatsi's book since receiving it as a gift from the Armenian poet Levon Mkrtchian in the 1970s. The Armenian saint's utter humility in judgment before God—tirelessly recounting his own sins and weaknesses—had moved Aitmatov profoundly. Aitmatov understood that Narekatsi was doing a final accounting of himself, that in appealing to God he was confronting his own internal measure—his conscience. It was just the sort of moral exercise that was so lacking in a Soviet people robbed of religious devotion and alienated from spiritual pursuits.

Narekatsi's story connected to themes of moral accountability that Aitmatov had developed in *Ascent of Mt. Fuji.* Indeed, here was an example of the rich patchwork of the Soviet Union—Armenians facing Europe and the Kyrgyz on the border with China, communicating with each other in Russian—fostering a moral discourse.

—~~—

At the same time Aitmatov was crafting Edigei's character, Azamat Altay was working on a side project to translate the Bible into Kyrgyz.

Altay's work translating the Bible was not because of a conversion to Christianity. He remained Muslim his whole life, insisting on marrying a Muslim woman, and, while not a regular at religious services, adhering to Muslim customs, such as reciting prayers and celebrating holidays. In 1970, he had joined other Radio Liberty employees in signing a petition for a prayer room for Muslim staff members.

Rather, when he was approached in 1973 to produce the first Kyrgyz translation of the Bible, Altay likely accepted because he understood the place of the holy book in Western culture and appreciated its wisdom and life lessons.[31]

In fact, in their tolerant approach to religions, both Aitmatov and Altay were drawing on a Central Asian tradition of tolerance. Though Muslim or followers of their own native religion Tengriism, the Kyrgyz over the centuries have welcomed other religions, particularly Christians, and today live side by side with hundreds of thousands of Russian Orthodox Christians in independent Kyrgyzstan. That tolerant approach stretched back to the period after Jesus' death when the first Christians led by the wandering apostle Thomas trickled into the area known as Kyrgyzstan today. In part because they adapted to the local conditions by holding services in yurts and provided medical care, Christian missionaries were generally welcomed in Central Asia. Nomads felt a connection with the figure of Jesus; in him they saw a powerful shaman who had healed the sick and triumphed over death.[32]

The next Christians came in haste, fleeing Roman persecution in the second and third centuries. They arrived as outcasts from the Byzantine Empire. Then, expelled in the fifth century AD over a dispute with the Byzantine Orthodox Church, the Nestorians made their way east along the Silk Road, eventually finding refuge among Zoroastrians and Buddhists in Central Asia.[33] From their perch in Central Asia, the Nestorians took the Gospel into China, Mongolia, and Tibet. Gregorians followed the Nestorians, arriving in the early sixth century from Armenia.

Christians continued to exist in distant outposts after conquering Arabs introduced Islam in the eighth century. According to the Catalan Atlas, made in 1375 on Majorca, there was an Armenian monastery on the shore of Lake Issyk Kul, complete with a double-towered cathedral with a terra-cotta roof. Notes accompanying the map indicate the existence of relics of St. Matthew at the church.

How St. Matthew's remains ended up at the eastern edge of the lake remains a mystery, but Russian Orthodox historians contend they were brought for safekeeping by some of those Christians fleeing Roman persecution in the second and third centuries.[34]

—–••••–—

In his biblical translation work, Altay worked closely with Boris Arapovic, a Swedish citizen of Croatian descent who founded the Institute for Bible Translation (IBT) in Stockholm in 1973. Arapovic's project to introduce the Bible to the non-Slavic peoples of the Soviet Union in their native language was one of many Western initiatives intended to expose the closed-off Soviet Union to outside influences, be they anti-Soviet journals, Western books, or the Gospels.

In fact, realizing that there was a kinship between moving the Holy Word across closed borders and broadcasting forbidden news across the airwaves, Arapovic moved to Munich in March 1973 to recruit translators from among Radio Liberty employees. Staff from virtually all the non-Russian language services—Avar, Karachy-Balkar, Karakalpak, Kazakh, Tajik, Turkmen, Uighur, and Uzbek among them—signed contracts with IBT. To make the translators' work easier, Arapovic provided them with Cyrillic-keyed typewriters supplemented with letters unique to their languages.

For the Kyrgyz language, though, Arapovic ranged farther, contacting Altay in New York because he was one of the few Kyrgyz with the linguistic ability to handle the task. Relying on copies of the New Testament in Russian, German, and Turkish, Altay set about translating the Gospels and typing his work using a custom-designed Kyrgyz-language typewriter provided by IBT. He finished translating the Gospel of Matthew in 1982, closing a circle of sorts with his own Lake Issyk Kul, the final resting place for some of the apostle's bones, according to legend.

The Bible translation work took Altay fifteen years, during which time he traveled to Paris and London for cram sessions with editors from IBT. The sessions were long and often complicated, with Altay orally retranslating his Kyrgyz version into Russian or German—depending on the language preference of the editor—and the editor then comparing the verbally conveyed text with a New Testament text in Russian or German. In this way, IBT succeeded in distributing to various parts of the Soviet Union the first Bibles many Soviet citizens had ever seen. Altay's translation became the basis for subsequent translations of the Bible that are in circulation in Kyrgyzstan today.

—⁓—

In July 1980, Altay traveled to Zurich with a Kyrgyz colleague from Radio Liberty to attend a Soviet cultural festival featuring Kyrgyzia. They met up with a Kyrgyz musical troupe. Among the artists was opera singer Minzhilkiev, the man who had greeted Altay so warmly in New York in 1975. The two men embraced and reminisced about Altay lending Minzhilkiev $200 to replace the portable stereo that had been stolen from him in New York. Minzhilkiev had not forgotten Altay's generosity and wanted to repay him.

"Agai," Minzhilkiev said, addressing Altay respectfully as he handed him a present, "I shot an animal and had this hat made from the fur."

As Minzhilkiev extended the gift, Altay noticed that KGB agents were watching the group's every move. Even when they jumped in a taxi and went to bar, a KGB agent followed, taking a seat in the corner (see figure 10.2). Finally, to elude the KGB agents, they went to Altay's hotel room in Zurich. Raising their glasses, they wished each other health. Then one of the Kyrgyz artists addressed Altay: "Azamat Agai, I think we will meet again. We are going to have a happy life."

Altay joined in, proposing a toast to a brighter future: "Here's to the Kyrgyz people achieving their freedom and to Kyrgyzia becoming independent!"[35]

—⁓—

Altay's toast was wishful thinking, but in the Soviet Union, change was afoot. The decrepit health of Soviet leaders signaled the start. After the death of Brezhnev in office in November 1982, two successive general secretaries, Yuri Andropov and Konstantin Chernenko, followed suit. Andropov succumbed to kidney disease in February 1984, and Chernenko passed away about a year later in March 1985. Three leaders in a little

Figure 10.2: Altay (*far right*) with Bolot Minzhilkiev (*second from right*) and other Kyrgyz at a bar in Zurich, Switzerland, during Minzhilkiev's visit with a Soviet Kyrgyz artistic troupe in 1980. Source: Photo courtesy of Gulnara Turganbaeva.

more than three years. Even the secretive Soviets couldn't hide this. It looked like the mighty Soviet Union didn't have any young leaders to call on.

Then came the announcement that Mikhail Gorbachev would be the next general secretary of the Communist Party. At fifty-four, Gorbachev became the youngest man since Stalin to rule the Communist Party. He projected a vitality highly unusual for Soviet leaders, wading into crowds of Soviet citizens to exchange banter and appearing at parades with his wife, Raisa, and their children.

On the policy front, Gorbachev consolidated control over the Communist Party. He named younger colleagues to top positions in the Politburo while at the same time frankly acknowledging problems, like economic stagnation and restive national minorities. But proceeding cautiously, Gorbachev proposed only to tinker with the centrally planned economic system. His lone concession was that factories needed to produce more consumer goods and fewer industrial products.

In foreign policy, however, Gorbachev made an immediate mark. Unlike his stodgy predecessors, he was open-minded and eager to listen to experts. He sought to defuse the dangerous superpower standoff by agreeing to meet President Reagan at a summit meeting in the United States in 1985. His point man on foreign relations, the newly appointed foreign minister Eduard Shevardnadze, earned praise from American leaders for being a quick study with a creative mind.

But Gorbachev's immediate impact came in the realm of freedom of expression. In December 1985, Aleksandr Yakovlev, a Gorbachev appointee as the Communist Party's chief ideologist, announced at a gathering of some of the country's leading writers that there would be more openness or glasnost in Soviet letters. Both Yakovlev and his boss knew the change would open the Soviet leader up to critical comments, but they were ready. "Criticism is a bitter medicine," Gorbachev himself would write in 1987. "But sickness makes it necessary. You may wrinkle your face but you take the medicine."[36]

––––⁓⁓⁓––––

At a time in the 1980s when the world faced the risk of man-made nuclear apocalypse, Chingiz Aitmatov's novel *The Day* had summoned man to heed his internal compass. Through a carefully chosen epilogue and by extension through the life of his hero Edigei, Aitmatov hoped to galvanize readers to accept direct responsibility for their actions and for the world as a whole. Only then could solutions be found to earthly problems like the nuclear standoff and environmental degradation.

For Aitmatov, the sanctity and autonomy of the individual was a sine qua non for human progress. In this sense, the Soviet Union was a backward invention, whose conception of a man as an instrument of manipulation was entirely antithetical to growth, maturity, and, most important, the development of a humane conscience. In *The Day* Aitmatov had diagnosed the Soviet Union as sick. With his clever prose, masked in folk tales and cosmic discoveries, he had administered substantial doses of the "bitter medicine" Gorbachev himself would prescribe in 1987. But Aitmatov's message was broader—to mankind as a whole. Address yourself through God. Develop a conscience. Lead a clean spiritual life. Learn to live together.

In this sense the writer from Kyrgyzia had burst the seams of his small republic and become universal. And for this reason he was a kindred spirit of Gorbachev, who was embarking on one of the most challenging governing tasks of the twentieth century—to remake the world's largest country. The two men were linked by their desire for reform, with Aitmatov bringing the spiritual message to rehumanize communism and Gorbachev taking on the challenge of restructuring the behemoth planned economy.

11

Waves of Change

Because of strict control over the movement of people and the media, the Soviet Union's embarrassments—and shameful behavior—had mostly been shuttered from the world and hidden from its own citizens. Not so with the teenage pilot from West Germany who landed his plane on Red Square on the evening of May 27, 1987. A video captured by a British tourist in Moscow laid bare the facts.

A single-engine propeller plane buzzes above the Kremlin walls, then circles back over St. Basil's Cathedral before landing on a four-lane bridge. A crowd of curious Muscovites and tourists gathers as the white Cessna taxies to a spot near Red Square. Out climbs a young man sporting tinted glasses and a red aviator's jacket. "I am here on a peace mission from Germany," the pilot told the gathering crowd. Identifying himself as Matthias Rust from Hamburg, West Germany, the nineteen-year old amateur pilot announced that he had flown across western Russia to present his plan for a nuclear-free world to Soviet leader Mikhail Gorbachev.

In a colossal failure of Soviet air defenses, Rust had flown unobstructed across four hundred miles of Soviet airspace. It was a brash stunt that could have gotten him killed—just by a Soviet jet directing its exhaust at the Cessna. But instead Rust became known as the precocious teenager who shamed the Soviet Union. That Rust broke through Soviet air defenses on the national holiday honoring border guards added insult to injury.

In reaction to Rust's bizarre stunt, Soviet Premier Gorbachev convened an emergency meeting of the Soviet Politburo and then fired his defense minister and commander of air defenses. Hundreds of others lower down in the military hierarchy lost their jobs as well. Some say it was the biggest overhaul of the Soviet military since Stalin's purges fifty years earlier. For Gorbachev, who was rolling out his plan to reform the Soviet Union, the Rust debacle was a continuation of bad news. It followed the Chernobyl nuclear accident in April 1986, which spread radiation as far as Scandinavia. And it came amid the Soviet Union's faltering military invasion of Afghanistan.

Rust, who drifted into obscurity after serving fourteen months in Soviet jail, is remembered today as the young man who made history with an incredible flight that perhaps did more to defang the Soviet Union in the eyes of the world than any number of nuclear arms agreements with the United States.[1]

When asked several weeks later about the incident, Chingiz Aitmatov didn't mince words, posing the question Soviet citizens had been asking themselves since the improbable landing: how could an unskilled pilot evade supposedly sophisticated air defense systems and land "as if on an uninhabited island in the most holy places of our country, Red Square?"[2] Answers were few, but one thing was clear: the mighty Soviet emperor was wearing fewer clothes.

—◦—

About eight months earlier, Aitmatov himself had pulled a pioneering stunt of a different order. In line with Gorbachev's policy to open up to the world, Aitmatov had brought a group of foreigners to Lake Issyk Kul for one of the first—if not the first—citizen-initiated events to be held in the Soviet Union. Having in mind the lake's history as a crossroads of civilizations, Aitmatov chose Lake Issyk Kul as the venue for the unprecedented gathering. But the KGB objected, insisting that the lake remain off-limits because it harbored a secret torpedo testing facility and lay just on the other side of the mountains from communist rival China. Aitmatov ultimately prevailed using high-level connections, including the support of Gorbachev, thus opening the way for the international delegation to visit Kyrgyzia.

At the time of the forum, Aitmatov's voice on the Soviet political scene was amplified by the success of *Plakha* or *Executioner's Block*, his most recent novel. Serialized in *Novy Mir* starting in June 1986, the book was a best seller by Soviet measures of the day—long lines at book stores and worn edges of the journal shared among friends. Aitmatov's novel functioned as a test case for glasnost by discussing taboo subjects like narcotics trafficking and proselytizing in the Soviet Union, topics the government-controlled media was forbidden to address. Through the travails of protagonist Avdi, a lapsed seminarian, Aitmatov portrayed the Soviet Union as a soulless society gripped by substance abuse, corruption and the destruction of nature.

Aitmatov showed in *Executioner's Block* how Marxist doctrine had enslaved Soviet man, causing him to perceive enemies all around and cutting him off from evolving into a more empathetic and caring person. "We have to leave behind this narrow understanding of politicization which has begun to limit us," Aitmatov said in a 1986 interview. "We have to search for the threads that tie people together."[3] In the three stories that make up *Executioner's Block*, Aitmatov trumpeted a person's choice to make decisions freely. He highlighted how Avdi's freedom to grow is dependent on his individual choices, not institutional dictates. When Avdi's unorthodox views on religion cause him to be excommunicated, he declares in an echo of Edigei from *The Day*: "My church will always be within me."[4]

The goal of life, Aitmatov was saying, is self-development, and he held forth Jesus as the finest example of a human developing into a higher order of being. Steeped in a deep reading of the foundational texts of Western literature, including the Bible, Aitmatov established himself as a secular spiritualist or, as was popular to say in the West, a humanist. Like other humanist writers, his heroes sought practical moral wisdom that would provide them integrity and purpose. Aitmatov's deeply spiritual approach to life became a living, breathing philosophy of the need for man to develop morality and self-awareness.

Soviet dogma and class struggle were nowhere to be found.

—∿∿—

With the route to Kyrgyzia opened, intellectuals from around the world, including from "enemy countries" such as England, France, and the United States, arrived in Frunze in October 1986 as Aitmatov's personal guests. Playwright Arthur Miller, novelist James Baldwin, and futurist thinker Alvin Toffler and his wife, Heidi, represented the United States. The lake's natural beauty bowled them over. "Full of fish, surrounded by snow-capped peaks like Switzerland," said Miller. "Absolutely gorgeous."[5]

Lake Issyk Kul is, indeed, a sight to behold. Situated a mile above sea level, the 2,400-square-mile lake looks like an inland sea. The first Russian explorer to map the lake in 1856 called it a "blue emerald set in a frame of silver mountains."[6] Kirghiz say the lake breathes, and its water level rises and falls for reasons scientists can't fully explain. Underwater hot springs reportedly keep the lake warm enough to stay unfrozen in winter. More than a hundred rivers feed the lake, but, adding to its mystery, not one flows out.[7]

A route of the famed Silk Road—which over the course of fifteen centuries transported humans, goods, languages, and religions back and forth from China to Rome and spots beyond—traversed the south side of the lake. With its abundant supply of water, shade, and food, the lake was an ideal resting spot for weary travelers. Buddhist pilgrim Hsuan Tsang came through the area on his way to India about AD 620. After a rough mountain crossing, the monk wrote of arriving at the Great Qing Lake, as he called it, *qing* being the Chinese word for "blue" or "clear."

Hsuan Tsang's path crossed lakeside entrepôts active as far back as the fourth century BC. One legend relates that Alexander the Great on his way to conquer India around 325 BC left two Persian hostages on the south shore of the lake. The two young men, who had been kidnapped from prominent Persian families as a disincentive for their families to revolt, eventually despaired of returning home and settled on the southern shore. Other stories relate that Central Asian conqueror Tamerlane, who lived in the sixteenth century AD, had a summer palace on an island in the lake. And a grand story has it that the treasures of Genghis Khan are buried at the southern end of the lake. Attesting to the lake's presence in history, petroglyphs and ancient Tibetan inscriptions decorate stones on the lakeshore.

Whether or not the legends are true, local archaeologists say that at the bottom of the lake are at least five sunken cities, and exploration is in the initial stages. Artifacts wash up on the shore or are easily fetched by a diver with an aqualung. To date, thousand-year-old daggers, jewelry, sacrificial bowls, and sickles have been retrieved.

―――

Aitmatov and his team structured the gathering at Lake Issyk Kul around the nuclear standoff between the West and the Soviet Union. By collecting writers and artists from around the world, he hoped to generate worldwide support for Gorbachev's call for "new thinking" and an attendant de-escalation in tension. It was ambitious and perhaps naïve, but it was pure Aitmatov. Ever since Soviet space flights in the 1960s, the writer had been haunted by the words of a Soviet cosmonaut. Spying the distant earth through a window in his spaceship, the cosmonaut had recounted how the tiny earth resembled a baby that he could rock in the palm of his hand.

Meetings at Lake Issyk Kul were frank and refreshingly devoid of Soviet propaganda. As if to underscore that all participants were on equal footing, Aitmatov was the only Soviet citizen to take part in the discussions. Pictures from the historic event show participants posing and discussing issues in a relaxed manner against the backdrop of the lake's blue waters and snowcapped mountains. All fifteen participants signed the Issyk Kul Forum's final declaration, which included a clause inserted by the Toffler about the importance of open debate without fear of reprisal.

General Secretary Gorbachev got regular updates on the progress of the historic conference. He would later describe the forum's effect on rigid orthodox thinking "as if a bomb had gone off."[8] On their way back through Moscow, participants met with Gorbachev on October 16 in one of the Kremlin's elegant halls. The Soviet leader queried participants about their views of the groundbreaking conference. Then he took advantage of his international audience to declare that human values should have priority over class values. With Aitmatov at his side, like a midwife to free expression in the Soviet Union, Gorbachev consigned class struggle to the dustbin of history.

―――

In his first year in power, Mikhail Gorbachev proposed using traditional methods to reinvigorate the Soviet Union's stagnant economy. He called for strict labor discipline and firm action against corruption. But the international embarrassment caused by the Soviet Union's initial concealment of the Chernobyl catastrophe pushed Gorbachev's government to be more open with information. He officially proclaimed the policy of glasnost or openness in public life in early 1987.

As if triggered by Chernobyl, the intelligentsia from different Soviet republics started to speak out more stridently. Major themes at the Eighth Soviet Writers' Congress in June 1986 were the displacement of national languages by the Russian language and Moscow's control over the cultural life of individual republics.

Aitmatov himself weighed in shortly after the conference as the most prominent voice from Soviet Central Asia. In a long interview in *Literaturnaya Gazeta*, he specifically mentioned the words "perestroika" and "glasnost," citing the need for "big efforts" to change the patterns of thinking of Soviet people. He then turned to the Soviet Union's "nationality problems" and the need to respect the languages, literatures, and culture of the Soviet republics. Dismissing Soviet theory that all languages would eventually merge into one or two primary languages, Aitmatov pointed out the need to boost the titular languages that had suffered for decades at the hands of the Russian language. He noted that, though the Kyrgyz language had at least ten synonyms for the word "truth," local Kyrgyz-language newspapers with names like *Issyk Kul Truth* still used the Russian word for "truth," *pravda,* in their names.[9]

By 1987, Gorbachev's second full year in power, Aitmatov's criticisms had become more trenchant. His frank remarks would be packaged as piquant sound bites today. Of smelly and dank dwellings Soviet citizens called home, Aitmatov mused: "What have we made of our houses? High rise barracks?" he said. "It's as if we live to take revenge on ourselves." He compared a Moscow airport to "an unorganized evacuation of refugees during a natural calamity."[10]

"Until now so much was couched in hackneyed, sickeningly abused interjections about the most advanced society in the world," he said in July 1987. "This sugary self-bewitchment dimmed our vision of real and concrete things; we sought to ignore the fact that the world around us had outrun us in many races."[11]

It was Aitmatov, unhinged from Soviet control, open and raw.

On the subject of slavish obedience to dictators, he liked to tell a story he had heard decades earlier in his home village of Sheker. It was after Stalin's death. A village elder, perhaps stroking his beard, related a chilling apocryphal tale:

> Stalin was sitting with his closest aides. I'll show you how to control people so that they are completely subjugated, the Soviet leader said. Then he asked for a chicken to be brought in. Stalin started to pluck the chicken's feathers, one by one. Soon, the chicken was plucked naked, its reddish skin exposed.
>
> "Now, watch where the chicken goes," Stalin told his aides.
>
> The chicken wanted to flee its torturer, but outside it could be burned by the sun, and inside it was too cold. In the end, it hid under Stalin's legs. Stalin took out some grain from his pocket and fed the pitiful chicken. Then he started to walk around the room. The chicken followed, close at his heel.
>
> "So, you see," Stalin said, "people are like chickens. You pluck them, and then let them go. Then you can control them."[12]

The son of a purged party official had a prescription for curing his tormented society: glasnost had to be spread to the cult of Stalin. Here Aitmatov differed with Gorbachev, a man who had spent his life inside the communist system. Brushing aside a question about the damaging effects of Stalinism on Soviet society, Gorbachev had said in 1986: "Stalinism is a concept thought up by the enemies of communism and widely used to discredit the Soviet Union and socialism as a whole."[13] Aitmatov thought differently: "Only now," he said in 1987, "have we begun to free ourselves from being slaves of the personality cult."[14]

The differences of opinion likely reflected the men's positions: Gorbachev as a political figure constrained by political realities and Aitmatov as a cultural figure on the forefront of the forces unleashed by Gorbachev. But overall the two men were of one mind about the need for reform. That was reflected in Aitmatov's promotion to the highest levels of Soviet cultural life. In the spring of 1986 he was appointed to the leadership body of the Soviet Writers Union, making him one of the most influential people in Soviet letters.

Aitmatov saw clearly that the Soviet Union had a chance to change, and from his new perch he was not going to let the opportunity pass. To build the Soviet Union anew, citizens would have to face up to the inhumanity pervasive in society that was a direct result of the Stalinist legacy of repression and murder. State-directed development had failed miserably in cultivating morals and a conscience. Aitmatov was convinced that the path forward had to be grounded in individual freedom, with archetypes like Avdi leading the way.

—·ιιι·—

Aitmatov took up the task immediately in Kyrgyzia, where he was aided by a wave of personnel changes. In 1985 long-standing first secretary of the Communist Party Turdakun Usubaliev, who had ruled Kyrgyzia for almost twenty-five years—and who had sidelined Aitmatov by banning publication of his books in Kyrgyz—was replaced in a purging of the old guard. The dominoes continued to fall, with the party's ideology secretary and the heads of Kyrgyz State TV and Radio and the State Publishing Company all losing their jobs.

Also gone was Tengdik Askarov, replaced by Aitmatov himself as head of the Kyrgyz Writers' Union in 1986. There was an element of sweet revenge for Aitmatov in Askarov's departure. In 1984, Askarov had not mentioned Aitmatov in a major article discussing contemporary Kyrgyz writers. It was an intentional slight, meant to "punish" Aitmatov for his disclosures of corruption and amorality in Soviet Kyrgyzia in works such as *The White Ship* and *Ascent of Mt. Fuji*. During Askarov's tenure a play based on Aitmatov's *The Day Lasts More Than a Hundred Years* had been banned from the theaters of the Kyrgyz capital.[15]

So, after years of being ostracized from literary affairs in his home republic, Aitmatov had the political influence to make change. With glasnost gaining momentum, he climbed out of his literary fortress and took on the forces of repression that had saddled Kyrgyzia's development. He spoke openly about previously taboo topics, such as the importance of promoting the Kyrgyz language, and he personally led a campaign to rehabilitate purged writer Kasym Tynystanov. It was time to right historical wrongs.

If any figure deserved rehabilitation, it was Tynystanov, a self-educated man who became one of the republic's first writers, the first minister of education and the author of numerous textbooks on Kyrgyz grammar. But after purging him, the Soviet system had corralled memory of Tynystanov under its dark shadow. By the 1980s, the erudite poet and minister was a forgotten person, his publications on the Kyrgyz alphabet out of circulation and his name erased from history books. Even Khrushchev's thaw, which saw the rehabilitation of other Kyrgyz intellectuals, had bypassed Tynystanov.

There was no clearer example of Soviet *mankurtism* at work.

In November 1986, just a month after the Issyk Kul Forum, Aitmatov led a commission of the republic's leading writers that recommended that Tynystanov be included in a publication on the history of Soviet Kyrgyz literature and that his previously banned works be published. Stuck in old ways of thinking and paranoid about losing control, the Kyrgyz KGB resisted. The KGB's opposition reflected a retrenchment across communist institutions in the republic that had only deepened with news of protests in Kazakhstan in December 1986. Those protests and their subsequent violent suppression had put security structures in nearby Kyrgyzia on alert.

The ethnic nature of the protestors' demands in Kazakhstan were particularly disturbing. Troops dispatched to quell the demonstrators protesting the replacement of long-standing Kazakh party chief by an ethnic Russian had ended up clashing with the protestors, with several people killed and two hundred injured. The clashes rattled Kazakhstan, which had long been hailed as a "laboratory of the friendship of peoples."[16]

The Kyrgyz KGB feared that Tynystanov's rehabilitation could spark similar events in Kyrgyzia. A secret memo in February 1987 cited the potential for "politically harmful nationalism" on the part of "immature" Kyrgyz youth to spin out of control.[17] "Nationalism" was KGB code for hostility against people of Slavic descent. With 20 percent of Kyrgyzia's population comprising Slavs, the Kyrgyz KGB wanted to squash anything that it perceived might stoke conflict between majority ethnic Kyrgyz and minority Slavs.

━━━

Communist Party General Secretary Absamat Masaliev, who had replaced Usubaliev in 1985, picked up the thread of dangerous nationalism spun by the KGB. Masaliev, to be sure, was no reformer. A cautious communist from the south of the republic, he had been bolstered by advisers sent in from Moscow with a mandate to keep control of the situation.[18] So while glasnost was moving forward in the cultural sphere, security and intelligence remained under the tight control of the unreformed Soviet KGB.

Masaliev lashed out at threats to the domination of the Communist Party, like the expansion of glasnost in Kyrgyzia and the riots in Kazakhstan. Adhering to the adage that when problems at home threaten societal unity, look for a culprit outside, Masaliev attacked Radio Liberty, which had extensively covered Aitmatov's Issyk Kul Forum and more recently the suppression of the Kazakh protests. "The most active propagandist of nationalist ideas in our republic is the Kyrgyz service of Radio Liberty," he told a gathering of party members on February 21, 1987. "Traitors to our homeland work there," he continued, naming Altay and fellow Kyrgyz broadcaster Tölömüsh Jakypov.[19]

So, after a relatively quiet period following the 1982 nationwide campaign against him, Altay was again in the sight of the Soviet propaganda machine. In attacks against Altay, the KGB made sure to use his birth name as well, Kudaibergen Kojomberdiev, to discredit him in front of as large an audience as possible.

———

At the time of Masaliev's outburst, Radio Liberty was gaining listenership as it was exposing the weaknesses of the Soviet system. The station's coverage of the Chernobyl nuclear disaster in April and May 1986 had been a high point. Broadcasts had kept Soviet listeners informed about the spread of radiation and instructed them on decontamination techniques and protection of children at a time when the Soviet government was hiding the severity of the situation.

With the arrival of Enders Wimbush in 1987 as director of the non-Russian radio services at Radio Liberty, the Central Asian language services, which had long played second fiddle to the Russian Service, began to enjoy more prominence. Wimbush had an abiding interest in Soviet Central Asia: he had studied under Alexandre Bennigsen in the 1970s at the University of Chicago and specialized on Central Asian issues at the Rand Corporation. Like his mentor Bennigsen, Wimbush believed that distinct national identities had emerged in Soviet Central Asia in spite of the Soviet Union's efforts to craft a Soviet man.

Wimbush also knew Altay well, having worked with him to support Bennigsen's scholarship on Central Asia. Bennigsen had designed the research, Wimbush had done a good part of the writing, and Altay had culled newspapers and journals from Central Asia for primary material. The threesome had continued to meet in the 1980s, gathering in the summer at Bennigsen's vacation home in southern France to complete writing projects and brainstorm about the Central Asia republics charting a more independent path from Moscow.

With Bennigsen's ideas enjoying currency in Washington, DC, Wimbush implemented the group's common belief that the nationality problem—specifically, the desire of the Soviet constituent republics for more freedom from Moscow—was the Soviet Union's Achilles heel. He paid special attention to the five Central Asian services. Aware that the non-Russian services had been considered "stepchildren" in relation to the Russian Service, which employed ninety people and enjoyed high listener ratings, he bolstered the quality of the non-Russian language services by hiring new chief editors, obtaining better short-wave frequencies and increasing broadcast hours.

But he left the Kyrgyz Service largely alone. Under Altay's leadership the Kyrgyz Service was vexing Communist Party leadership in Frunze. It was said among the Kyrgyz that the most devout listeners tuned into Radio Liberty broadcasts like pious Muslims going to pray five times a day. In general, despite spending nearly a billion dollars to jam US-funded radio broadcasts—more than twice what the United States was spending on VOA, RFE and RL—the Soviet Union was losing the Cold War of the airwaves.[20] In an ironic twist, the mountains that helped isolate Kyrgyzia from the outside world provided good conditions for the reception of shortwave signals beamed from Munich. The word among listeners was: "The truth that nobody can tell at home you can hear on Radio Liberty."

For the Kyrgyz Service, that "truth" consisted of quality reporting in line with Radio Liberty's policy of supporting the national identity of the Central Asian peoples. Programs connected Soviet Kyrgyz to their brethren outside the Soviet Union, like a story about the harsh living conditions of Afghan Kyrgyz, who continued to suffer during the Afghan

War after fleeing Soviet power during the turbulent 1920s. Other broadcasts emphasized Kyrgyzia's pre-Soviet heritage and historic struggle against foreign aggressors, the subtle message being that "while the Soviets are trying to desecrate you, Radio Liberty will guard your national values."[21] It wasn't unusual for broadcasts to end with a reading from the Koran and its translation into Kyrgyz—recognition of the important role religious customs still played in Kyrgyzia.

In line with changing times, Kyrgyz Service broadcasters discarded the caution they had used in covering Aitmatov in the early 1980s. No longer concerned about generating a backlash against Aitmatov, Altay and his staff broadcast Aitmatov's subversive messaging back to Soviet Kyrgyzia (see figure 11.1). A long piece aired on November 3, 1986 about Aitmatov and the Issyk Kul Forum made no bones about associating the term *mankurt* with a member of "a captive nation." The implication of the

Figure 11.1: Azamat Altay in the broadcast studio at Radio Liberty's headquarters in Munich, Germany, in 1985. Source: Photo courtesy of Gulnara Turganbaeva.

broadcast was clear: just as the *mankurt* only recognized his subjugator, Soviet Kyrgyzia under communism answered solely to Moscow.

As astute observers of developments in their native land, Altay and his broadcast team were picking up Aitmatov's signals or, rather, reading his code—like how in *Executioner's Block* Aitmatov had conveyed a powerful message about Kyrgyz national identity by naming the novel's Kyrgyz protagonist Ürkünchiev. Kyrgyz speakers in Kyrgyzia and Munich immediately recognized the root *Ürkün*, the Kyrgyz word describing the flight to China in the wake of the 1916 uprising. Aitmatov was cleverly resurrecting a loaded topic that had been largely omitted from Soviet-era history books and general societal discourse. For those able to "read the tea leaves," he was making a political statement that Central Asia was being repressed under communism just as it had been under the tsar. If Aitmatov's initial writings had shown "veiled criticism" of the Soviet Union, the November 3 report said, then *Executioner's Block* pulled no punches: Aitmatov's newest novel demonstrated the Soviet people's "gradual moral degradation."[22]

⸻

During the *Perestroika* years, two filmmakers completed a documentary film based on the life of Chingiz Aitmatov. It was an audacious project that they had conceived as tribute to Aitmatov's prophetic voice. While Aitmatov had been struggling to get his work published in Kyrgyzia, the filmmakers—Konstantin Orozaliev and Valeri Vilenski—had been reading between the lines, deciphering his code and unraveling his folk tales. Quiet iconoclasts inside the State Film Company of Kyrgyzia, they had started work on the film in the early 1970s, and over the course of seventeen years it became a labor of love done on the side as they completed officially approved film projects. Orozaliev himself reportedly spent months in film archives across the Soviet Union working under the radar to collect documentary footage that matched periods of Aitmatov's life.

Once the film was ready in 1988, the Soviet Union was changing at a dramatic clip. The filmmakers arranged a private screening for Aitmatov. Arriving fatigued from a day's work, Aitmatov warned them he may nod off. But once the film started, Aitmatov watched, his head inclined to one side. From time to time, he sighed deeply as images of his family and of the grand, often tragic events of the twentieth century crossed the screen.

The film's footage was somber in tone, even mournful, to mark the unfulfilled promises of the Bolshevik Revolution. There was the desiccated Aral Sea, grainy images of nomads disassembling their yurts and a Christian church being destroyed during the 1930s. And there were pictures of the lost generation of Soviet Kyrgyzia's first leaders, including Törökul Aitmatov. The film had aged well with the passage of years, and it captivated Aitmatov as a visual corollary to his prose. "In such a foreshortening view, we see the mistakes we all made," Aitmatov said at the end of the screening.[23] Over the next three months, Aitmatov wrote a script for the film. It became his confession for the failed experiment of communism.

In the climax of his script, Aitmatov returned to the psychological theme that the Sheker *aksakal* had articulated decades earlier in the anecdote about Stalin plucking the chicken: "Spiritual slavery can be voluntary and desired. When people for many years are humiliated and not in a condition to oppose cruelty, they are prepared to deify this evil," he wrote. "Now we understand, all this was evidence of the spiritual sickness of our society, but we didn't know then." And then gaining philosophical altitude, as if in a spaceship hovering above the earth, Aitmatov spoke to men and women everywhere, whether they were trying to throw off the yoke of authoritarianism or living in a democracy. Fearful of mankind's arrogance, especially in an age of technological advances, he warned of environmental catastrophes on the horizon that might even engulf Lake Issyk Kul.

He so wished that the prideful hunter in *Farewell, Gulsary* who had met his doom on the mountaintop after eradicating a family of mountain goats could serve as an example of the need to live in harmony with nature. "Our descendants will judge us not by our good impulses and assurances but by the soil that we leave them," he said.[24]

Taking advantage of Gorbachev's more open policies, when time permitted, Aitmatov took breaks from his myriad duties inside the Soviet

Union. Mostly he traveled to Europe to talk about his books. During one of those trips in 1986 he met Lucien Leitess, the founder of a Swiss publishing company specializing in international authors. Leitess became for Aitmatov the Swiss version of Mirra Ginsburg, an intermediary who could introduce the writing of the Kyrgyz author into new markets.

Leitess had long had a hunch that Aitmatov would sell to a German-speaking audience. Reading Aitmatov's first short stories in German translation, he had been struck by the writer's connection to the animal world, the natural beauty of Kyrgyzia and his spirited characters, all themes Leitess believed would appeal to German readers. At Aitmatov's suggestion, Leitess's publishing company Unionsverlag published *Executioner's Block* in German. Thus began a series of trips to Europe to promote the book.[25]

At book readings for *Executioner's Block*, Aitmatov often found himself in church halls or old monasteries facing up to a thousand readers he couldn't communicate with directly. But Leitess's literary sense, just like Ginsburg's intuition about Aitmatov in America, proved right. German audiences were enthralled with Aitmatov.

———

During a book reading in Munich in 1986, Aitmatov encountered an audience full of white Germanic faces, with a few Asian faces sprinkled in. Maria Aitmatova, who was accompanying her husband, thought they looked Kyrgyz. But she didn't have time to investigate because as soon as the reading was over, KGB agents from the Soviet Embassy hustled Chingiz and Maria out a back door.

Essentially bodyguards, the agents were acting on old, suspicious instincts when they hurried the couple through a service exit to a waiting car. The car sped off, with an unfamiliar white van on its tail. As if in a car chase scene in a James Bond movie, the Soviet embassy car headed out of town on side streets, with the two KGB agents constantly checking their mirrors.

When the car carrying the Aitmatovs arrived at their hotel, the white van pulled up right behind. Out stepped Azamat Altay with several Kyrgyz adults and children. The wary KGB agents rushed to block their approach. But Aitmatov halted them.

"These are my people. Let me speak with them," he said.

Aitmatov's simple gesture spoke volumes. It said, "That's enough." And with his command to the two KGB officers, fear and silence, engrained in the Kyrgyz people for decades and carried by Aitmatov himself, started to recede. It was as if Aitmatov were saying it was time to learn how to live in a normal society.

No more keeping silent. No more fear. And no more tragedies.

Yes, the fatherless Aitmatov seemed to be saying, let the next generation of Kyrgyz grow up with their fathers. And let the KGB learn another way to carry out its work.

"You can sit right beside us and listen," Aitmatov told the KGB agents.

The officers relented. As the group of Kyrgyz exiles surrounded the Aitmatovs, Altay and Aitmatov embraced. The two men then sat in the lobby and spoke for hours, catching up on the past eleven years since they had last met and talking about the changes in the Soviet Union. The personal and professional kinship was natural. As much as anyone, Altay understood the import of the momentous time and the influence Aitmatov wielded as one of the most popular writers in the Soviet Union. That understanding was informing Altay's leadership of the Kyrgyz Service at Radio Liberty.

The KGB officers sat nearby at a table, with nothing to do but listen to two venerable *aksakals* converse back and forth in Kyrgyz.[26]

12

An Expiring Ideology

On May 25, 1989, the first day of the Soviet Union's new, more democratic parliament, the atmosphere was electrifying. In the first hour deputies at the Congress of People's Deputies voted for the proceedings to be televised nationwide. From then on, Soviet citizens watched spellbound as largely unknown parliamentarians attacked sacrosanct pillars of Soviet communism, like the KGB and Red Army.

Gorbachev had designed the new congress to replace the Supreme Soviet, the Soviet Union's rubber-stamp parliament, and make a break with the dominance of the Communist Party. And even though more than 80 percent of the congress's 2,250 deputies were members of the Communist Party, elections to the new body had injected spontaneity into formerly humdrum elections, with some high-ranking party officials losing in multicandidate elections. Other reformers from the ranks of the party, like Aitmatov, streamed into the parliament to back Gorbachev. In the lead-up to the freest elections in seventy years, there were TV debates, calls for a multiparty system and coalition formation. Gorbachev himself got out on the campaign trail, preaching perestroika and glasnost in an effort to draw the public into the election process.

On that historic first day, Aitmatov, who had been elected from Kyrgyzia on a slate of candidates put forward by communist organizations, nominated Gorbachev to be president. No doubt, Aitmatov's reputation as a popular author with moral authority was instrumental in having him propose the Soviet general secretary to lead the inaugural congress. The influential writer was a weapon to beat back recalcitrant party officials who were blocking Gorbachev's reform efforts.

In making his nomination, Aitmatov offered a sober assessment of Gorbachev's virtues, lauding the Soviet leader for embarking on "a revolution of the mind." "He took this on not out of vanity," Aitmatov continued, "but because he saw the progressing disease in society, the mounting degradation of the Party under totalitarian dogma and the economic crisis, rising more and more like a visible iceberg out of the stagnant past." Coloring his speech with additional metaphors, the writer likened Gorbachev's position to a boat in rough seas being battered by high winds. "The waves are turning on the very creator of this historical moment" (see figure 12.1).[1]

In line with previous elections, deputies expected a pro forma vote with Gorbachev as the only candidate. But before the vote, Alexander Obolensky, a construction engineer from a town north of Leningrad, surprised everyone in the hall by nominating himself as an alternative candidate. Obolensky's speech laid out a progressive agenda, including the formation of a more independent judiciary and cutting the power of ministries. In the end, deputies voted down multicandidate elections, and Gorbachev was elected.

Figure 12.1: Chingiz Aitmatov making a speech at the Congress of People's Deputies, Gorbachev's new, more democratic parliament, in 1989. Source: Central State Archives of the Kyrgyz Republic.

Obolensky's bold challenge set the tone for a raucous congress over the next two weeks. On that first day, a deputy from Leningrad questioned Gorbachev on the building of a dacha in Crimea for his use. Recalling Gorbachev's all-powerful Soviet predecessors, others pressed Gorbachev to give up his post as general secretary of the Communist Party if he wanted to head the government. Gorbachev responded in a civil way to the unprecedented barrage of questions: "I am in favor of dialogue," he said. "All of us today are just learning democracy. We are just now shaping our political culture."[2]

It was political soap opera, playing on TV for six to eight hours a day across eleven time zones.

From his seat in the hall of the congress, Aitmatov watched Gorbachev develop into a skilled political operator. At times, the Soviet leader listened thoughtfully; other times he interjected his opinion. As Aitmatov observed how the Soviet leader balanced between rabble-rousing nationalists and backward-looking conservatives, he became more convinced that Gorbachev was the kind of new political leader that the country needed—a man from within the system able to manipulate the divide between conservatives and reformers to push reform at a gradual pace.

In the face of a barrage of questions, Gorbachev retained his composure. The venerable American statesman Paul Nitze once remarked that watching the balding Gorbachev under fire reminded him of the imperturbable Buddha. The Soviet leader seemed to be fulfilling those memorable lines from Rudyard Kipling's poem *If*:

> If you can keep your head when all about you
>   Are losing theirs and blaming it on you;
> If you can trust yourself when all men doubt you,
>   But make allowance for their doubting too:[3]

Above all, Gorbachev was determined, and after four years at the helm of the Soviet Union he had become inseparable from his reform plans.[4] Aitmatov got a firsthand look at the perplexing nature of Gorbachev's reforms just a week before the congress when he accompanied Gorbachev on a trip to China. The Soviet leader's visit had been meant to mend ties between the two communist neighbors after several decades of cold relations. But hundreds of thousands of students massing in Tiananmen Square to protest the Chinese Communist Party's authoritarian rule had other ideas. Tent cities on the square forced a grand welcoming ceremony for the Soviet leader, complete with honor guard and a twenty-one-gun salute, to be moved to the airport. The Chinese students even held their own welcoming placards for the Soviet leader. "We salute the ambassador of democracy" read one poster. Another crowed, "In the Soviet Union they have Gorbachev, but what do we have in China?"[5]

Aitmatov, who was traveling with Gorbachev as a member of the official Soviet delegation, saw up close the paradox of the Soviet leader. Besieged at home, Gorbachev was greeted as the father of a reform process in the Soviet Union that was dramatically reducing global tension and inspiring people around the world. During the Soviet leader's stay, demonstrators appealed to Gorbachev to address them. Imploring Gorbachev to leave his official interlocutors, one banner said: "Gorbachev! The people are here and not there!" The request carried via radio and TV stations put Gorbachev in a quandary. Some advisers urged caution, saying that any address about reform in the Soviet Union would only rile up the student protestors and, thus, further embarrass his Chinese hosts. In the end, the Soviet leader declined to meet with the students, sending a letter instead.

The irony of the situation was not lost on Aitmatov: Gorbachev sitting inside a building, in sight of a half million Chinese citizens inspired by his ideas but unable to meet with them. Two weeks later in what came to be known as the Tiananmen massacre, the Chinese government brutally cracked down on the student demonstrators. The violent suppression of the student protests underscored the two countries' different approaches toward reform. The Chinese were moving forward economically while strictly controlling the political space, while in the Soviet Union political openness was racing ahead while the Soviet economy spiraled downward.

As new political forces became more vocal in the Soviet Union, breathing what Aitmatov himself called "the intoxicating air of democracy," Aitmatov would, in fact, grow pessimistic about Gorbachev's prospects for survival as a leader. In private, he would intimate to the Soviet leader that his days were numbered.

The conversation took place before a meeting at the Kremlin, Aitmatov recalled some years later. Gorbachev invited him into his office for a chat about the situation in Soviet Central Asia. After relating his views, Aitmatov, ever the storyteller, told the Soviet leader a parable about a king who has promised his subjects freedom. But along comes a traveler who tells the king that once he gives his subjects freedom, he shouldn't expect gratitude or appreciation. In fact, the traveler warns the king, the people will badmouth him and in the end be satisfied only when they drive him from power. "So, while it's still not too late, think hard," the traveler advises the king. "You are at a crossroads: Give your people freedom or don't let go of your power." The king's guards haul the man away for his impertinent comments while the king cogitates on the traveler's advice. The king's guards are ready to chop off the traveler's head when the king intervenes. "Give this man a reward in my name," he orders. "Let him go on his way."

It was a chilling tale, and it indicates how familiar Aitmatov and Gorbachev were with one another in the late perestroika period. After hearing the parable, Gorbachev's face paled, but he quickly gathered himself. "Chingiz Törökulovich, I will not retreat," he said. "Since I have promised to give people freedom, I will insist on this until the end. I am prepared to go forward, even if I lose power or even my head."[6]

―――

Over the course of the ten-day congress, Aitmatov smoothed the Soviet leader's path. Bearing a gentle countenance with bushy eyebrows and salt and pepper hair standing on top of a high forehead, the sixty-one-year-old Aitmatov acted like a father figure. Protective of Gorbachev's "baby of democracy," he counseled speakers against overly emotional speeches and urged them to offer solutions to the problems they raised. He cautioned the radical reformers not to squander the historic opportunity for reform by demanding too much. Don't "pour oil on the fire" of conservative forces in the hall, he told them.[7]

By supporting Gorbachev, Aitmatov was staying true to gradualist inclinations. While he wanted reforms in the Soviet Union, such as more freedom for the constituent republics, he believed they had to be undertaken gradually, not in a rush to independence. Aware of how much

Kyrgyzia depended on subsidies from the Soviet Government, Aitmatov was convinced that trade ties and economic linkages between the republics had to be preserved. If they weren't, then the republics would suffer economically and living standards would plummet.

That, in turn, could put at risk the Soviet Union's prized achievement—the multinational culture of different peoples linked by the Russian language. Aitmatov himself was a case in point. He enjoyed long-standing friendships across the breadth of the Soviet Union that had been facilitated by use of the lingua franca of Russian. As a child of mixed parentage and an author whose books were printed in the languages of all fifteen republics, Aitmatov himself was both a product and beneficiary of the cross-pollination of cultures in the Soviet Union. He wanted with all his heart to preserve it.

But the juggernaut of political expression rolled on, and the Soviet republics, led by Lithuania, Estonia, and Latvia, craved more freedom. It was as if that featherless chicken hiding under Stalin's leg had suddenly ventured out and found that it wasn't too hot or cold. In fact, there was no more leg to hide under. At the historic congress, there were attacks on the KGB as a "threat to democracy" as well as an unprecedented grilling of a Soviet general for the actions of troops who had reportedly killed at least nineteen peaceful demonstrators in Tbilisi, Georgia, two months earlier.

Reformers at the congress were led by Andrei Sakharov, the subject of the letter Aitmatov had signed in the KGB-inspired campaign in 1973. By 1989, Sakharov was white-haired and bent with age. But what he lacked in youthful vigor, Sakharov made up for with moral gravitas, having weathered propaganda campaigns, harassment of his family, and six years in internal exile in the city of Gorky. During the congress, Sakharov took aim at the Soviet invasion of Afghanistan, which he called "a terrible sin." He also pushed relentlessly for a multiparty system through the repeal of the article in the Soviet Constitution guaranteeing the Communist Party a monopoly on power. Sakharov's calls to overhaul the political system, coming at a time when Gorbachev thought he himself was already pushing the envelope, put the Soviet leader over the edge. Even Buddhas can boil over. When on the last day Sakharov exceeded his allotted time in detailing his reform program, a frustrated Gorbachev cut off his microphone.

At the congress, while he urged deputies from the Soviet republics not to rush to sovereignty, Aitmatov proposed concrete steps that would increase independence. He argued that the so-called secondary languages of the Soviet Union, meaning those languages that took a backseat to Russian in their home republics—such as Kyrgyz—should be given more support. "It is important to acknowledge that each people constitutes itself as a people as long as it is able to master its own language— this is its cultural sovereignty," he said.[8]

But even while he argued for a more prominent role for the Kyrgyz language, he knew that knowledge of Russian would always be key to his people's survival. This was Aitmatov's acknowledgment of reality. The Kyrgyz were a small people, whose window onto the outside world faced north through Russia, not east to China or south to the Muslim world. Aitmatov's life itself was witness to how education, electricity and exposure to the different peoples of the Soviet Union had come to the Kyrgyz people through the Russian language.

On the language issue, Aitmatov was in lockstep with the Kremlin, which understood the importance of rebalancing language policy throughout the Soviet republics. To that end, the Kremlin was supporting reform of language legislation across the Soviet Union, including in Kyrgyzia. Several months after the congress, on September 23, 1989, the Supreme Soviet of Kyrgyzia declared Kyrgyz to be the state language of the republic. From a paltry 4 percent of all schools in Frunze, the number of Kyrgyz schools and kindergartens started to grow. Russian-speaking schools in the republic started to teach Kyrgyz as well as the history and geography of the Kyrgyz people.[9]

Aitmatov's advocacy on behalf of the language law may have had the support of the Kremlin, but it put him in the crosshairs of the KGB. According to his wife, Maria, KGB Chief Kryuchkov dispatched agents to track Aitmatov and eventually arrest him. But when Gorbachev got wind of the KGB's intentions, he stopped the operation in its tracks. "Don't arrest him," Gorbachev reportedly told Kryuchkov. "We will be embarrassed in front of the whole world."[10]

To the Kyrgyz KGB, Aitmatov was part and parcel of dangerous trends that were eroding the KGB's control over Soviet society. In the conspiratorial minds of the KGB, so-called politically harmful nationalism was on the loose, led on the inside by men like Aitmatov and abetted on the outside by Altay. Indeed, wielding authority as the Moscow-backed head of the Kyrgyz Writers Union, in December 1988 Aitmatov had convinced the Kyrgyz Communist Party to allow research on Kasym Tynystanov's works and publish new editions of his books. The new language law boosting the position of Kyrgyz followed Tynystanov's rehabilitation.

Intended to be a rebalancing, the new law marked a retreat of Russian cultural hegemony and the rise of the Kyrgyz as a people. It also portended a corresponding shift in economic and political power as local elites assumed prominent political positions. Ethnic Russians signaled their displeasure by departing the country in droves. From 1989 through 1992, approximately ten percent of the Slavic population, or about ninety thousand people, departed Kyrgyzstan, most for Russia.[11]

Indeed, change was happening at a whirlwind speed inside the Soviet Union, with Aitmatov himself leading the way in Soviet Central Asia, if not in the Soviet Union writ large. He hacked away at barriers separating the Soviet Union from the West, openly thanking the United States and Great Britain in 1988 for helping the Soviet Union during World War II, a subject that had been suppressed by Soviet authorities. Soviet citizens, he wrote in the Communist Party's newspaper in Kyrgyzia, should be grateful for the efforts of brave American pilots who had flown food and other goods into the war-ravaged Soviet Union.[12]

With the Swiss publisher Unionsverlag churning out German editions of his major works, Aitmatov was breaking down geographical barriers as well. In 1989, Unionsverlag's Leitess booked Aitmatov on his first road show. It was a bit like a turtle emerging from its shell when the Kyrgyz author showed up at book fairs in German-speaking countries. Like many Soviet citizens encountering the West, Aitmatov had never encountered free markets like book fairs, where publishers set up stalls and "hawked their wares." Guided by Leitess, Aitmatov left behind the Soviet world of reliable print runs and staid commentary for the unfamiliar world of transactions and marketing.

A product of the largely noncash Soviet economy, Aitmatov had to learn to deal with "real" money for the first time in his life. Leitess explained to Aitmatov how money was stored in bank accounts, transferred with checks, and even used virtually in the form of a credit card. For a man who called himself "retrograde"—he didn't drive and still wrote his books by longhand—it was a big adjustment.

But Aitmatov's literary works spoke for themselves. German-speaking fans would queue for hours for the author's signature, to snap pictures and give him flowers. Readers in the eastern part of recently unified Germany were especially thankful, saying his books provided guidance and support in difficult times. For a people still traumatized by the war their fathers and grandfathers had loosed upon Europe, there seemed to be a visceral connection with the writer from the Kyrgyz steppes. They sensed in Aitmatov a writer, who, though he was on the side of the victors, portrayed World War II as the cause of immense suffering. There was no gloating over heroic endeavor. Just the human loss experienced by mother Tolgonai, deserter Ismail, or POW Abutalip.[13]

—⁓—

Nearing the age of seventy, Azamat Altay had set 1989 as his retirement year, ten years after Radio Liberty had interrupted his initial attempt to retire. This time, though, he wouldn't be deterred. He groomed his deputy Hakim Özgen to replace him as director of the Kyrgyz Service. A generation younger than Altay, Özgen had grown up in Turkey, the son of Kyrgyz who had fled to China in the 1920s. Tall and gregarious, Özgen was the opposite in many ways of the reticent and serious Altay. Significantly, Özgen had never lived in the Soviet Union and didn't speak Russian. He also didn't bear Altay's stigma of being an anti-Soviet renegade.

But Özgen shared with his mentor a respect for Aitmatov, and he quickly cemented the Kyrgyz Service's close relationship with Aitmatov. Taking advantage of one of Aitmatov's frequent trips to Germany, Özgen invited the Kyrgyz writer in June 1989 to preside at a celebration marking the birth of his son. In line with Kyrgyz tradition, in which a respected elder is called on to name a newborn baby, Aitmatov named Özgen's son Noyon, after a character in the *Manas* epic.

The gathering at Özgen's Munich apartment was another celebration to cement Altay and Aitmatov's friendship. While Aitmatov, as the honored guest sat at the head of the table and was given the lamb's head to eat, Altay sat to his immediate left as the oldest Kyrgyz in the room (see figure 12.2). The atmosphere was jovial and to cap it off, Aitmatov signed the first volume of a collection of his books for Altay during his visit. "To dear Azamat Altay, who lived in foreign countries all his life and thought of the Kyrgyz people always," he wrote.

In September 1989, courtesy of an invitation from Aitmatov himself, Özgen made the first visit ever to the Soviet Union by a Radio Liberty journalist. The sociable Özgen thrived in the land of his forefathers. He met with Kyrgyz officials, made inquiries about the possibility of opening up a Radio Liberty office in Frunze, and spoke with potential stringers about filing reports to Munich.[14] It was an astonishing turn of events given that just two years earlier Kyrgyz Communist Party head Masaliev had accused Radio Liberty of spreading "nationalistic ideas."

Figure 12.2: Chingiz Aitmatov (*center*) and Azamat Altay in Munich at the celebration of the birth of Radio Liberty correspondent Hakim Ozgen's son in June 1989. Ozgen is standing. Source: Photo courtesy of Gulnara Turganbaeva.

Steadily over the next few years, Radio Liberty transformed from pariah to accepted member of the media corps in Kyrgyzia. In the free-wheeling atmosphere, the voices of naysayers and critics were muted, mostly because members of the Kyrgyz elite could finally admit—without fear of retribution—that they, too, were Radio Liberty listeners. Chingiz Aitmatov himself would give voice years later to a common sentiment when he said, "We could not live without listening daily to Radio Azattyk."[15]

On his trip, Özgen did not forget Altay. He visited Lake Issyk Kul, where he bathed in sulfur springs famous for their curative abilities. He then made a stop at Altay's home village, where he was greeted like a respected emissary. He spoke with village elders—Altay's former school-mates and fellow soldiers—who remembered Kudaibergen Kojomber-diev warmly. Altay's childhood home was long gone, but Özgen saw the poplar trees that had been planted by Altay and his father in the early 1930s. The trees stood straight and tall, like sentinels to the turbulent history that had transpired below in Altay's absence. The poplars had edged higher during the war, shaken in the wind in the liberalizing Khrushchev years, and now they waved above the village in the perestroika period that was remaking the Soviet landscape so rapidly that a former enemy broadcasting station was being greeted with open arms.

Özgen's visit to Frunze followed like a sequel to Aitmatov's Issyk Kul Forum held a few years earlier. It was another sign that Kyrgyzia was opening to the world. In fact, by 1989 Radio Liberty's signal was coming through clearer than ever since the Soviet Union, in a sign of improving relations with the United States, had stopped jamming broadcasts in November 1988.

―――

One can point to many moments in the mid-to-late 1980s when So-viet communism started to expire—the Red Army's withdrawal from Afghanistan, raucous sessions at the Congress of People's Deputies, or maybe even Chingiz Aitmatov's halting of KGB agents in their tracks in Munich, Germany. Mikhail Gorbachev added another in October 1989 on a visit to the Soviet client state East Germany. In the months previ-ous to Gorbachev's visit, taking advantage of newly opened borders in

Hungary and Czechoslovakia, thousands of East Germans had fled to West Germany. The dam was starting to break in one of the most repressive communist dictatorships in Europe.

In a touch of bitter irony, Gorbachev himself had set the stage for the exodus a year earlier at the United Nations. Affirming a commitment to freedom of choice for all nations, he had declared that the Soviet Union would no longer intervene militarily to keep control of its Eastern European satellites. He backed up his pledge at the UN General Assembly by announcing that the Soviet Union would unilaterally withdraw fifty thousand troops and five thousand tanks from Eastern Europe.[16] But surely he didn't foresee mass exodus.

During his visit to East Germany on October 6 and 7, Gorbachev remained respectful of his hosts, but behind the scenes he issued a stern warning to the inflexible East German leadership: it could reform or be defeated. "Life itself punishes those who delay," Gorbachev told his hosts.[17] But the calcified East German leadership ignored the new reality, placing the East German army on full alert to suppress widening protests. In several cities, police attacked demonstrators who were chanting "Gorby, Gorby, Gorby" in scenes reminiscent of Tiananmen Square earlier in the year. But there would be no massive crackdown in East Germany. The tide turned in Leipzig on October 9, when local communist leaders refused to attack seventy thousand marchers parading through the streets. Reading between the lines, citizens as well as communist officials understood that Moscow would not intervene to support East Germany, as it had done in Hungary in 1956 and Czechoslovakia in 1968. The protests gained momentum.

After Gorbachev told paralyzed East German leaders that the border with West Germany had to be opened to prevent unrest, the East German Communist Party relaxed the country's absolute travel ban. On November 9, once the crossing points were opened, residents of East Berlin crossed over to West Berlin, where they were met by West Germans offering them champagne and shooting off fireworks. The Berlin Wall collapsed soon after, hacked to pieces by delirious German citizens.[18]

Sitting in Moscow, Chingiz Aitmatov welcomed Gorbachev's decision not to use force. "This time historical wisdom was shown by not moving the tanks in."[19] Aitmatov sensed communism was dying but knew there would be no quick way forward. Just the hard process of the traumatized Soviet people learning patience and respect towards one another. On a trip to London in September 1989, he had outlined his prescription for spiritual healing. "I think that the only way towards a regeneration of the spirit lies in recognition of the importance of freedom to the human spirit," he said. "This freedom must be won not through revolution or cataclysmic change, but through peaceful means. When people understand the importance of freedom of the spirit to human life, then they will experience the sought-for regeneration. I think the road to democracy is, in effect, the path to salvation."[20]

PART FOUR

PART FOUR

13

The Wheels of Truth

When he retired from Radio Liberty in August 1989, Azamat Altay closed out a distinguished career that had spanned four decades. Called in to resurrect the Kyrgyz Service in the late 1970s, he had weathered a bombing, Soviet KGB spies and blistering propaganda campaigns. Under his leadership, the Kyrgyz Service had developed into a flagship department at Radio Liberty, infused with the mission to keep culture and traditions alive in Kyrgyzia despite Sovietization. In November 1989, Altay was awarded a certificate of honor "for his dedicated service and great contribution to Radio Liberty and the cause of freedom."

Altay left behind the hustle and bustle of daily journalism and headed back to resume life with his wife in their adopted home of New York City. Their neighborhood, which had continued to change in the decade they were away, had come to contain a good number of Russian-speaking immigrants. There was even a community of Bukharan Jews from Central Asia who had settled in Queens. Altay didn't have to walk far from his house to buy a Russian-language newspaper or treats from Central Asia. But with the Soviet Union cracking open, connecting with family members in Kyrgyzia became uppermost in his mind. For decades he had purposefully avoided communicating with his sisters because he didn't want to subject them to retribution from communist authorities. That silence, in addition to erroneous information, actually led Altay's relatives in Kyrgyzia to believe he had died.

A Kyrgyz artist who had traveled to Switzerland in 1980 as a member of the same artistic troupe that included Minzhilkiev told Altay's family members in Frunze upon his return that Altay had passed away. Given that it was around the time a propaganda campaign was being launched against Altay, the artist had possibly been spooked or provoked by the KGB. Not having been able to co-opt or scare Altay, the KGB may well have tried to wish him away. With members of the troupe who had met with Altay remaining silent about their rendezvous, relatives started to doubt that he was alive.

Özgen's historic trip reassured the family that Altay was alive and well in New York. In fact, during the trip Altay's nephew Toichubek, the son of his sister Gulshara, saw Özgen being interviewed on TV and immediately jumped in a car and drove ten hours from the family village on Lake Issyk Kul to meet Özgen. When Toichubek identified himself amidst a gathering crowd, Özgen pulled Toichubek forward through throngs of curious Kyrgyz. When face-to-face with Özgen, Toichubek had a short message for the Radio Liberty journalist to convey back to his uncle: "Tell him about us."

Despite Özgen's connection with his family, Altay proceeded cautiously. Wary of disrupting the lives of his relatives and unsure himself of how far perestroika had extended in Kyrgyzia, he first wrote letters to his sisters that were hand-delivered by trusted couriers. In March of 1990 he spoke by phone with Gulshara for the first time in fifty years. As soon as he could, he sent money. The big break came when Gulshara along with her two children, Toichubek and his sister Gulnara, were allowed to visit the United States in the fall of 1990. Altay sent the family plane tickets he had purchased in the United States, and they picked up their visas at the American embassy in Moscow. Indeed, with the Cold War petering out, bureaucratic walls were crumbling. Improved relations between the United States and Soviet Union meant that a simple village woman could accept an invitation to visit her "traitor" brother in New York City. And she didn't need a KGB escort.

So, on an October day in 1990, a nervous Altay awaited the arrival of his relatives at Kennedy Airport, unsure if he would recognize them. He didn't have to.

"There's our uncle," Toichubek exclaimed as he entered the airport reception hall.

—⁓—

At the airport, in place of the youthful conscript the family had sent off to Lithuania in 1940, Gulshara saw a white-haired man bent by age.

Memories of lost years raced through Gulshara's mind. The family had waited in vain for Kudaibergen to return from the war. Gulshara had been ready to nurse his war injuries and to care for him if he had been crippled. Instead, with the news that he had jumped lines, she heard him cursed as a traitor, betrayer, and spy. She got married, moved away from her home village, and took her husband's name.

And yet here her brother stood, with the same restrained smile and penetrating eyes as she had. But that's where the similarities ended. A formal man by nature, Altay likely wore a coat and tie, his work uniform as a professional journalist that made him look like a Western business-man. Gulshara, in contrast, couldn't hide her diffident plainness. She was dressed simply in a heavy winter coat, leather boots, and a shawl to cover her head, befitting of the Kyrgyz village woman she was. Two lives diverged radically on the path of history, wrenched apart for more than eighteen thousand days. And, now, incredibly, the separation was over for the aging siblings. Joy mixed with intense sadness as brother and sister embraced. "It seemed to me the tears flowing down his cheeks were tears of his bygone youth and childhood," Gulshara said of their airport reunion.

Gulshara's two-month trip in the United States—her first trip out-side the Soviet Union—bowled her over. She met her brother's friends, toured New York, and visited Washington. When asked a few months later by a Kyrgyz journalist to describe her memories, she stuck to hard facts—the standard of living and apparent societal harmony Americans enjoyed. "Roads running by the river, washing machines which wash and dry, bread in cellophane packets, and a black soldier happy to take a picture with me." Fifty years of Soviet propaganda was washed away in fifty-two days.[1]

Not long after Gulshara's epiphany in the United States, the tectonic plates of history were shifting in Frunze. There, a reform-minded KGB officer was uncovering Soviet Kyrgyzia's most notorious secret—the location of a mass grave for victims of Stalin's purges. Born during Khrushchev's thaw in 1957, Bolot Abdrakhmanov had lived through the early years of perestroika in Moscow as a student at the prestigious Higher KGB School. He had witnessed the pulse of change moving through the Soviet Union—demands for rehabilitation of Stalin's victims and rallies calling for more openness and democracy—and considered himself a member of a "new" generation of KGB officers.

So when Adrakhmanov got a tip about an elderly woman wanting to disclose a state secret, he followed up quickly. On a snowy day in December 1990, the burly Abdrakhmanov drove to a house on the outskirts of Frunze to investigate. "Is Bübüira eje home?" he inquired at the front door, using the respectful term for older women in Kyrgyz society. Bübüira Kydyralieva, a wizened woman in her early sixties, invited Abdrakhmanov inside. The Kyrgyz grandmother then began her story, the words tumbling out after years of being locked up inside.

Kydyralieva had grown up in nearby Chong Tash village on the site of an NKVD rest house. Her father had been the caretaker of the property, and in the 1930s the family had lived in a small house on the grounds. The compound came alive on weekends when NKVD employees brought their families from the city to enjoy the fresh air and open space. It was like festival time, and her father Abykan worked during the week to make sure the grass was cut, the bushes trimmed, and the flowers in bloom. The visitors laid picnics out in the shade of the pine trees. Children ran among the groups, laughing and chasing each other.

It was incongruous—such playfulness while fathers took a break from their grim work of "harvesting" so-called enemies of the people. But living in her child's world, eight-year-old Bübüira knew nothing of that. She would often join in a game of hide and seek with the visiting children, racing to her favorite spot on the second floor of a brick kiln at the top of a knoll. From the roof of the kiln, she would take in the panoramic view spreading below: yellow wheat fields, neighboring villages, and the outskirts of Frunze in the distance. Behind her rose the snowy peaks of the Ala-Too Mountains. It was a perfect hiding place, peaceful and quiet.

Grizzly reality soon intruded on Bübüira's games. One night after work in November 1938 Abykan told his wife to prepare the family to vacate the compound immediately and go stay with a friend in the nearby village of Kashka-suu. When she objected that there was no room at the friend's house, Abykan responded sharply: "These are the boss's orders. No one should stay here." When the time came to return to the compound three weeks later, Abykan warned his family: "Don't ask questions if you see anything different. Pretend like you don't notice."

But young Bübüira did notice. The brick kiln was gone, and in its place stood a mound of upturned soil. The family tried to settle back into life, but something was irrevocably changed. Bübüira used to watch through the window as her father, with a Koran slipped under his arm, would exit the house under cover of darkness and read prayers at the site of the vanished kiln. The worst time was spring, when a stench from the mound carried over the compound. Villagers plugged holes in their windows with felt to keep out the smell.

The years passed. Abykan went off to war. Bübüira grew up, raised a family, and cared for her parents. No one spoke of those November nights until thirty-five years later when a weakened Abykan called his daughter to his bedside in 1973. Sensing that death was near, Abykan unburdened himself. "Do you remember where you used to play, near that brick factory?" Abykan asked. "That's where the victims of the purges are buried."

Abykan recalled the nights that had haunted him ever since. He spoke of villagers ordered to stay inside their houses, of military transport vehicles arriving from Frunze, and of truck motors running during the frigid nights. And he spoke of the "evil silence" that then descended over Soviet society. For decades the heavy totalitarian hand of the state and self-censorship on the part of a cowed population blanketed Soviet Kyrgyzia like a heavy snowfall. Keeping silent out of fear for his family's safety, Abykan drove the horrible memories inside himself. "I hope one day things will change for the better, and you can tell people about the innocent victims," he told his daughter. "Tell the children of those murdered that their fathers are buried under that hill."

But the "evil silence" was too suffocating in the 1970s. Then in 1985, with the start of glasnost, Kydyralieva contacted journalists in Frunze about her story, but they didn't show interest. Some said they didn't believe her story; most were reluctant to take up such a controversial topic. It was better, they said, "to let sleeping dogs lie."

At the end of their two-hour talk, her eyes moist from crying, Kydyralieva had a question for the KGB officer. "Do you promise to help me?"[2]

In late April 1991, once the snows had melted, Abdrakhmanov and two KGB colleagues drove Kydyralieva to the old NKVD compound. A review of KGB files had indicated a burial site twenty to thirty kilometers outside of Frunze but didn't provide an exact location. If evidence of the brick kiln could be found at Chong Tash, Abdrakhmanov reasoned, then they would be on the trail of finding the mass grave. Kydyralieva was visibly nervous as the car approached the site, which she hadn't visited in fifty years. But once the group started walking, she regained her composure. Like a tour guide, she pointed out vanished markers of her distant childhood. "Here was the sidewalk to the NKVD rest house," Kydyralieva said. "Over there was the freezer room, made from blocks of ice, and there stood my parents' house."

The group soon arrived at the site of the brick kiln that had marked the bitter contrasts of Bübüira's youth—games of hide and seek and her family's gruesome secret. The mound of soil was long gone, washed away by more than a half century of winter snows and spring rains. While the men combed the area at the top of the hill for evidence of the kiln, Kydyralieva walked around the grassy hilltop, bending down to examine some colored chips. They turned out to be flakes from red bricks. "Yes, the brick kiln had to be here," she said.

Before departing, Kydyralieva and the KGB officers picked red poppies from the surrounding fields and laid the flowers on the site of the brick kiln. "We are on the right path to truth," Abdrakhmanov told himself.[3]

—⁓—

Abdrakhmanov's direct superiors in the KGB objected to his report on the location of the mass grave. Reluctance to unearth the distant past was not surprising: the NKVD, the KGB's predecessor, had played a prominent role in the purges, and it was an open secret to men like Abdrakhmanov that KGB leadership in Frunze opposed the policies of glasnost and perestroika. Why dig this up now and create problems? Better not to touch it. Even if it turns out to be a mass grave site, there will be no way to identify the bodies, skeptics in the Kyrgyz KGB said.

Undeterred, Abdrakhmanov argued that, with Kyrgyzia becoming more independent, there needed to be a clean break with the NKVD's sordid history. More than twenty years later, Abdrakhmanov would describe his frame of mind in those heady days when he confronted the KGB leadership head-on: "Each man in his life has turning points or epiphanies. That's what happened to me at this time, more as a person than as a KGB officer. I understood that I had to carry this work though to its end."[4]

With the quiet support of the KGB head Jumabek Asankulov, arguably the most powerful man in Soviet Kyrgyzia, Abdrakhmanov pressed forward with his own investigation. It's not entirely clear why Asankulov, a direct appointee of KGB head and avowed orthodox communist Vladimir Kryuchkov, encouraged his young subordinate. Perhaps Asankulov knew of the existence of burial sites and had decided, with Kydyralieva coming forward, that it was time to uncover the past.

Without sanction from his direct KGB bosses, Abdrakhmanov found an archaeologist at a university in Frunze to direct the exhumation. A few weeks later, in mid-June, an excavation team uncovered a wall of the brick kiln. Then twelve inches below ground they unearthed a skull with two perforations that Abdrakhmanov knew were bullet holes. Faced with a fait accompli, the Kyrgyz KGB went public with the story after the skull was found. Under the direction of a state commission, the dig continued, with journalists recording the historic unearthing of seven skulls on June 12, 1991. The next day ten more skulls were found.

The deeper the team dug, the more personal items they found. Using knives and brushes, diggers discovered Soviet coins from the 1920s and 1930s, combs, spoons, packages of matches, and even a little bundle. When workers untied the bundle's knot, a hardened piece of bread and a wooden spoon revealed themselves, brittle reminders of human lives lost tragically. Seven feet into the dig, the excavating team started to unearth clothing. Hats, vests, parts of military uniforms, and leather boots emerged remarkably intact because, evidently, at that depth the conditions in the submerged kiln had been dry enough to preserve material.

The "wheels of truth" were turning, as Abdrakhmanov would later put it.

With information appearing in local newspapers about the mass grave, families who had lost relatives in the purges called for positive identification of the remains. But thus far no identifying marks or documentation had been found that could help determine who exactly the 137 victims were. Like other members of his family, Chingiz Aitmatov suspected his father's bones were among the jumble of skeletons. But he was stumped: how would it be possible to identify the victims without biographic information to link the remains to KGB files? Would the mass grave remain a common burial site akin to a tomb of the unknown soldier? Other questions loomed as well: would the KGB be open in pursuing all leads and truthful in its disclosures? Would openness prevail over secrecy?

Chingiz Aitmatov learned about the Chong Tash discovery while he was serving as Soviet ambassador to Luxembourg. Aitmatov's abrupt switch to diplomacy in November 1990 had caught many people by surprise. Though he was an accomplished writer and public figure, he had never lived in a foreign country, nor did he speak a language used outside the Soviet Union. But Aitmatov was exhausted from high-level politics and keen to get back to writing. As a top aide to Gorbachev—he had been appointed a member of Gorbachev's presidential council in March 1990—he had been drained by the demands of perestroika.[5] In particular, bloody conflict in his native Kyrgyzia in June 1990 had shaken him to the core.

The trigger for the conflict had been a dispute over land rights in the southern city of Osh. Situated in the eastern tip of the Ferghana Valley, Osh, even though located in Kyrgyzia, was—and still is—populated mostly by ethnic Uzbeks. Under the Soviet iron hand, the two related ethnic groups—they shared a similar language, religion, and customs—had lived in relative peace. Uzbeks kept to commerce in populated centers, while Kyrgyz largely maintained a rural lifestyle in the mountains or on the outskirts of cities. But a loosening of the authority of the Communist Party and the rise of nationalist sentiment spurred demands by mostly rural Kyrgyz who felt marginalized. In a shortsighted move, Kyrgyz party officials in Osh in May 1990 allocated territory in the middle of an Uzbek collective farm to a group of young Kyrgyz demanding plots of land for housing. Locals Uzbeks responded violently.[6]

The conflict was stoked by Kyrgyz resentment of Uzbek commercial prowess and by Uzbek dissatisfaction with dominant political representation of Kyrgyz in government institutions, including the police, army, and security services. In March, alarm bells were set off when a group of Uzbek members of the Kyrgyz Communist Party had demanded the establishment of an Uzbek autonomous region in Kyrgyzia that would be more closely linked to neighboring Uzbekistan, Kyrgyzia's far larger neighbor to the west.[7]

A developed democratic society, through mechanisms of transparent elections and accountable government along with forums for mediation and negotiation, might have been able to weather the conflict without significant loss of life. But Kyrgyzia was hardly that. Instead, it was a society careening headlong into an uncertain future, like an inexperienced driver at the wheel of a fast car. The irony was that dictates from the central government about who would rule the country—people from the north or the south—had prevented discontent and smoothed contradictions. But a loosening of Soviet control revealed deep schisms in Kyrgyz society. Simply put, the all-encompassing Soviet system may have curtailed basic human rights, but it also put a lid on potential strife.

So, despite seventy years of Soviet propaganda about one Soviet society living harmoniously, Soviet Kyrgyzia split along ethnic lines. Kyrgyz and Uzbeks, who had lived side by side for centuries, descended into ethnic warfare. Following the first altercation on June 4, young Kyrgyz males started streaming down from the mountains to help their ethnic kin. Clashes spread, engulfing more cities in the south, where ethnic Uzbeks lived in compact communities. The weakened Kyrgyz Communist Party was powerless to stem the violence. There were alarming rumors that tens of thousands of Uzbeks from nearby Uzbekistan were preparing to cross the border to defend their Uzbek brethren. That could risk a conflagration, with Uzbeks overwhelming the Kyrgyz in an ethnic civil war.

As Gorbachev's unofficial adviser on Central Asia, Aitmatov was keeping careful watch from Moscow on the worsening situation. He was committed to helping Gorbachev in a time of need, and in the absence of any strong authority in Kyrgyzia, he felt compelled to put his influence on the line. If Aitmatov, the most popular writer and possibly the most influential figure in Central Asia at the time, couldn't bring peace between fellow Turkic peoples, who could? "Let me go to Osh," he appealed to Gorbachev. "I want to be there to try to figure out what's going on and help if I can."

—〰—

With the situation fast deteriorating, Gorbachev assented, organizing a military transport plane to fly Aitmatov to Uzbekistan. In Tashkent, Aitmatov urged Islam Karimov, Uzbek Communist Party general secretary, to preempt any movement of Uzbeks across the border. After discussing the Osh situation with a group of Uzbek writers, Aitmatov and two Uzbek writers flew to Osh the next day. Fighting was still raging, and savage killing was taking part on both sides. Aitmatov would later use the phrase "streaming rivers of blood" to describe the situation.[8]

On a tour of Osh, Aitmatov was taken to a house that had been attacked by mobs. He fainted at the sight of the bodies of a woman, her husband, their children, and a visiting niece, who had been slaughtered in cold blood. An ambulance took Aitmatov to a clinic, where he was revived with the help of an intravenous infusion. An American writer who spent time with Aitmatov the next year recalled Aitmatov as still being "shaken to the ground" by the savagery months after the conflict.[9]

On June 5, Aitmatov appeared on local TV with the Uzbek writers to try to calm the situation. With his address, Aitmatov hoped to head off a wider conflict. Timing was critical: Soviet troops airlifted to the region were holding back thousands of Uzbeks intent on crossing the border to attack the Kyrgyz. Aware that the Kyrgyz were vastly outnumbered by Uzbeks in the Ferghana Valley, Aitmatov made a strategic decision to address his Kyrgyz compatriots first. "Kyrgyz, who have taken up arms against the Uzbek people, against their Uzbek brothers, are the same as Kyrgyz who attack their own people, who attack Kyrgyz," Aitmatov said in the broadcast. "Kyrgyz people! Don't commit bad acts, don't give into anger, and don't believe rumor-mongers." Then Aitmatov appealed to the Uzbeks.[10]

In a testament to the gravity of the situation, the clashes in Osh became a top issue in the CIA's daily briefing of President George H. W. Bush. For several days, the CIA feared the clashes might spiral out of control and spread across Central Asia, thus imperiling Gorbachev's reform efforts. In a sign that the United States wanted to preserve stability to help Gorbachev, Radio Liberty broadcast Aitmatov's Osh appeal on June 6 and then rebroadcast it on June 7.[11]

—∿∿—

Aimatov flew to Frunze, where he delivered the same controversial speech on TV urging restraint first of all on the part of the Kyrgyz population. Then, like a fireman racing from fire to fire, he helped dissuade thousands of Kyrgyz gathered on the main square from going to Osh to avenge the deaths of ethnic kin. The clashes finally subsided after six days, likely a result of the introduction of 2,850 Soviet troops. Official estimates are that close to 600 people were killed, with the majority being Uzbek, but observers say the number killed could have been as high as 1,500.[12]

Aitmatov acted nobly in both Osh and Frunze, and the general consensus is that his interventions helped stem the bloodshed. But in the tense, nationalistic atmosphere that prevailed after the clashes, he was vilified by some Kyrgyz for what they saw as a biased appeal in favor of Uzbeks. In their view, Aitmatov was a Moscow-influenced, Sovietized Kyrgyz who had abandoned his people. The outrageous accusation made Aitmatov sound like a *mankurt*. Nearly two decades later, Elmira Ibraimova, a respected Kyrgyz female politician, captured the ambivalent way a number of Kyrgyz remember Aitmatov's peacemaking role in 1990: "Many were discouraged by his words to southerners in Osh. He betrayed the Kyrgyz position, siding with Uzbeks," the stateswoman said in 2009, before adding: "I appreciated his words. We are Kyrgyz, and we have to make the lives of other groups comfortable."[13]

Regrettably for the Kyrgyz and Uzbeks, official studies of the conflict were classified. As a result of a widespread belief that ethnic relations were not appropriate for public discussions, few attempts were made to address the conflict's root causes, and unresolved historical wounds would fester for the next two decades.[14]

—∿∿—

Upon returning to Moscow from his peacemaking efforts in Kyrgyzia, Chingiz Aitmatov threw himself into hot political battles, from the frying pan of Osh into the fire of Moscow. There was a sense of urgency among Gorbachev supporters, as if time was running out. In early June, just about the time the clashes in Osh sparked, the Soviet leader himself had admitted to US president George H. W. Bush that 1990 was the "make or break" year for his reform policies.[15]

A loyal supporter, Aitmatov defended Gorbachev's policies against attacks from conservatives. In July 1990, building upon his speeches at the Congress of People's Deputies the year before, Aitmatov skewered the communist opposition for wanting to keep alive a "repulsive" ideology."[16] He soldiered on despite health issues. The emergency trip to Central Asia seemed to have aggravated his diabetes, and his blood pressure spiked. But the pace of political life in Moscow didn't permit the sixty-one-year-old Aitmatov to rest, and, with Gorbachev's reform policies in a crucible, the stakes were too high.

Indeed, the first years of perestroika had delivered mixed results. The Soviet leader had succeeded in weakening the Communist Party's grip on Soviet society by creating rival political institutions outside party control, such as the Congress of People's Deputies and the Soviet presidency. In a sign of the Communist Party's dwindling power, Gorbachev himself had discarded the title of general secretary of the Communist Party, preferring to be addressed as president of the Soviet Union.[17]

In foreign relations, on top of achieving historic nuclear arms deals with the United States, Gorbachev had allowed the Soviet Union's Eastern Europe satellites to break free from Moscow's control. Largely for those achievements, he was awarded the Nobel Peace Prize in 1990. But that pull back—along with Western accolades—fueled the conservatives' fire. The hardline opposition also knew that economic conditions in the country were reaching an explosive point. Living standards were dropping, factory managers were struggling to pay their workers, and trade links between republics were being disrupted.

Those with a stake in the continuation of the communist system, like the military and KGB, were in open rebellion against reforms that were curtailing their influence. The military was particularly upset by the way Gorbachev seemed to be "giving up" Soviet military influence in Eastern Europe and by the humiliation of having to house in temporary barracks

Soviet soldiers and their families returning from decommissioned bases in East Germany.

Among his many problems in those days, Gorbachev was most worried about a possible breakup of the Soviet Union. With the loosening of the Communist Party's control on society, age-old conflicts, kept in check for the most part by communism's heavy hand, had resurfaced. Osh was the latest—and by some accounts the most violent—manifestation. It had followed ethnic clashes in Azerbaijan between Azerbaijanis and Armenians over an ethnic Armenian enclave that declared it wanted to be part of Armenia. In the Baltic republics, there was increasing support for leaving the Soviet Union.

<hr>

On the heels of the Osh conflict, political struggle in Soviet Kyrgyzia heated up. In an effort to deflect pressure from its failings, particularly in Osh, the Kyrgyz Communist Party had agreed to concessions, like instituting the post of president. It was an echo of what had happened in Moscow in March 1990, when Gorbachev was elected president of the Soviet Union. The election for president in October 1990 ended inconclusively, with no communist-supported candidate receiving the required number of votes from deputies in the Kyrgyz Supreme Soviet. This gave an opening to reformers to propose their own candidate if they could secure a new round of voting.

A grassroots political movement, called the Democratic Movement of Kyrgyzstan, or DDK, got to work. Employing techniques learned in other Soviet republics pressing for change, like Ukraine and the Baltic republics, young Kyrgyz rallied against the Communist Party. Then in late October, 140 people undertook a weeklong hunger strike on the main square of Frunze to demand another round of presidential elections with a new slate of candidates.

The pressure worked. A block of deputies from southern Kyrgyzia caved. Instead of supporting a nationwide referendum featuring then-current Communist Party head Masaliev as the lone candidate, the deputies backed another round of voting. The excitement was palpable: a democratic movement was turning politics on its head, allowing the Kyrgyz people to imagine a future without Communist Party rule.

Though not present, Aitmatov was looming above the historic turns. As the man who had made Kyrgyzia known far beyond its borders, he was a natural choice for president. During the rallies outside the parliament building, some youth had carried posters saying "Aitmatov for president." In fact, at the time Aitmatov's support in society was broad and deep. Both ends of the Kyrgyz political spectrum—the KGB and reformers—supported his candidacy.

But Aitmatov wasn't interested in political office. By that time, he was hatching a plan with Gorbachev to exit Moscow for Europe. Not even a personal appeal from KGB head Asankulov, who had reportedly flown to Moscow to try to persuade the writer to be president, could sway Aitmatov. At the meeting with Asankulov in the lobby of the Moscow Hotel, Aitmatov demurred, saying it was time for the younger generation to take the lead.[18] It was a curious move for the conservative KGB chairman—reaching out to an open critic—to support Aitmatov. But Asankulov's appeal was likely the result of a shrewd assessment that the gradualist Aitmatov represented a better choice than any so-called radical reformers from DDK. The KGB head's flight to Moscow was also a sign of how much the KGB was losing leverage in society, from failing to halt Tynystanov's rehabilitation to allowing the Chong Tash excavation to proceed.

Aitmatov had the same answer for the democratic reformers when they called at about 10 p.m. one night in late October. He listened attentively as Kazat Akmatov, the head of DDK, made his pitch, declaring that the Kyrgyz people needed their most celebrated writer at the critical juncture in the country's democratic development.

"Do you really think that a person should become president because he is famous?" Aitmatov replied. "I am not prepared, nor do I have the desire, to be president."

"But you will have many advisers," Akmatov replied.

"The advisers will just spoil me," Aitmatov refused to budge. "Thank you a thousand times for your trust in me. I don't want to exchange my writing career for a high government position. I have some creative ideas, and let's hope I can bring them to fruition."

When asked whom he would recommend, Aitmatov reportedly mentioned Kyrgyzia's up and coming politicians. One in particular, a physicist named Askar Akaev, struck him as suitable. Aitmatov had worked side by side with Akaev as a deputy in the historic Congress of People's Deputies session in May and June 1989. Formerly head of the Kyrgyz Academy of Sciences, Akaev had reformist credentials as a man who had worked outside the party bureaucracy and who had formed a strong bond in Moscow with Andrei Sakharov. "How about Akaev?" Aitmatov offered. "He's educated, honest, and erudite. With time, he'll become a real leader."

On October 27 the Kyrgyz Supreme Soviet elected Askar Akaev to be the first president of Kyrgyzia, thus inaugurating the republic's postcommunist journey.[19]

During the hectic years of perestroika, between official duties in Moscow and Frunze and trips abroad, Chingiz Aitmatov contented himself with spurts of writing that added to his previous works. Though limited in scope, the additions showed that Aitmatov had been stifled time and again by party censors. In 1989 he added thirty pages to his 1950s novella *Face to Face*. At the time, Aitmatov said the new pages ended the story in the authentic way he had originally wanted. As to the reasons those sections had been excluded in the 1950s, Aitmatov cited "the conditions prevailing in society" in the 1950s.[20]

A new episode showed war deserter Ismail grieving for his mother on top of a hillock because he couldn't risk being seen in public at her funeral. It was further development of Aitmatov's controversial theme that deserters have feelings, too. Aitmatov's most controversial passage, though, involved his criticism of forced collectivization that apparently had proved too risky to print even during Khrushchev's Thaw. In the introduced passage, Aitmatov showed how rich peasants, like Ismail's brothers-in-law, had fled to the mountains to avoid exile or worse. Aitmatov's point was that the brothers, who had committed no crime, had been unfairly cast out from Soviet society.

The following year Aitmatov published a new chapter for his seminal work *The Day Lasts Longer Than a Century*. In the new chapter, Aitmatov resurrected the original ending that he had shelved a decade earlier in the spirit of "self-preservation." The ending weaved a folktale about Mongol leader Genghis Khan losing the Mandate of Heaven—a white cloud that floated over his caravan of warriors—for enacting cruel policies toward his subjects. At the time, Aitmatov decided not to risk provoking Soviet censors, who would likely connect the aging khan to the septuagenarian and octogenarian leaders ruling the Soviet Union in the early 1980s.

Aitmatov's "new" chapter, which lengthened the original book by nearly a quarter, broadened the scope of *The Day* and underscored its condemnation of Soviet authoritarianism as a whole. The most damaging inclusion in the new additions was the suicide of Abutalip, the harmless schoolteacher hounded by the KGB for being captured as a POW and fighting with Yugoslav partisans during World War II—and the character whom Aitmatov had linked to Altay in 1988.

In the original version published in 1980, Abutalip's fate mirrors that of Aitmatov's father, a point driven home by Aitmatov's heartbreaking description of Abutalip glimpsing his family from the train window as the train passed through his village on the way to the labor camps—just as Aitmatov imagined his father had done on the way to Frunze prison in 1937. In that version, Abutalip died in the custody of the Soviet penal system, just as Törökul Aitmatov had. But in the belated chapter, Abutalip takes his own life after days of torture by the KGB. The suicide serves to place blame squarely on the KGB for ruining the lives of innocent people and destroying their families. Aitmatov scholar Joseph Mozur called the new chapter "an unrelentingly dark parable of Soviet totalitarianism."[21]

Aitmatov's new additions seemed like finishing touches to his Soviet-era works, farewell gestures that stamped him as an authentic reformer. It was time to move on. Having agreed with Gorbachev that he would serve as Soviet ambassador to Luxembourg, Aitmatov wrapped up his affairs in Moscow. He stepped down as Gorbachev's adviser and resigned editorships and positions on prestigious literary boards—it was as if he were closing the book on that part of his life. In November 1990, Aitmatov headed for a new life in the Grand Duchy of Luxembourg, as far from the roiling political cauldron of the Soviet Union as one could imagine.

14

New Beginnings

Through June and into July 1991, Bolot Abdrakhmanov worked at the Chong Tash site full-time, supervising barebacked diggers, shoveling himself and reporting back to his bosses at the KGB. The team unearthed the remains of about ten to twelve people a day in the twelve-by-twelve-foot mass grave. Digging carefully and then using small brushes, excavators discovered skulls with bullet holes, bones, and personal items. Undoing the jumble of bones and personal items was enervating. To Abdrakhmanov, it was as if the bodies had been thrown into a hole "like dogs." Most skulls had the same signature bullet hole—in the back of the head—and then an exit hole in the forehead or jaw. At night, faceless victims would visit Abdrakhmanov in his dreams, asking him why he was disturbing their peace "Let us bury you in a humane way," Abdrakhmanov would answer.

In July the excavating team unearthed the last skeletons. Archaeological work would eventually determine that 137 people had been executed on those frigid nights in early November 1938. Some people called it Kyrgyzia's Katyn Massacre.[1] One day, while peering into the deepening hole, Abdrakhmanov spotted cloth material about ten feet below the surface. Workers cleared off the dirt and carefully raised what turned out to be a man's quilted jacket. Bones fell out of the material. Under dirt nearby they found a piece of paper. Abdrakhmanov and his colleagues deciphered names on the torn piece of paper. It turned out to be the sentencing letter for Jusup Abdrakhmanov, the top-ranking government figure in Kyrgyzia in the early 1930s and Törökul Aitmatov's trusted colleague.

Here, finally, was proof of identification. That it turned out to be Ab-drakhmanov meant that others in the grave were likely high-ranking officials. Dry conditions at the bottom of the kiln had miraculously preserved the paper.[2] In atheistic Kyrgyzia, providence was lending a hand. Shortly thereafter, the team dusted off another document, also re-markably intact after more than five decades underground. Three discol-ored sheets were double-folded and had two visible perforations. When opened, the document turned out to be another sentencing letter. At the top was the date: November 5, 1938; the charge: anti-Soviet activity; and the name of the guilty party: Törökul Aitmatov.

On July 27, 1991, at the KGB building in downtown Frunze, the KGB head Asankulov informed Ilgiz Aitmatov of the discovery of the sentenc-ing letter bearing his father's name. Fifty-three years earlier, Asankulov's predecessor had overseen Törökul Aitmatov's execution. Now the KGB chief himself was hosting an Aitmatov family member in his office. He explained to Ilgiz that the two holes in Törökul Aitmatov's sentencing letter had been made by bullets. While most victims had been executed with a gunshot to the head, Törökul had been shot through the heart.[3] Asankulov seemed genuinely contrite. He would say to the press about the meetings with families of the victims: "My office has never seen so many tears and such sorrow."[4]

The KGB was backed into a corner and had to follow the paper trail to the end. Using information gleaned from the sentencing documents, the Kyrgyz KGB identified the rest of the victims by checking files in the KGB archives. There was no room for stonewalling or dissembling. The time for unearthing the truth had come at last. The sentencing let-ters, still readable after more than fifty years underground, were the key to unlocking the mystery of the republic's sordid past—what Aitmatov himself called "the intellectual genocide of a nation" in a powerful inter-view in *Literaturnaya Gazeta* in early September.[5]

The victims were largely of Asian ethnicity, between the ages of forty and sixty, and represented the diversity of Kyrgyzia in the 1930s. There were the educated and famous—officials like Abdrakhmanov, Aitmatov, and, yes, Tynystanov, Kyrgyzia's beloved writer whose name could at last be spoken freely thanks to the efforts of Chingiz Aitmatov. But there were also laborers, peasants, and petty criminals. The bones of Kyrgyz mixed with those of Jews, Koreans, ethnic Germans, Russians, Tatars, Uighurs, Ukrainians, and Uzbeks. There was even an Iranian, a Turk, a Chinese, a Pole, and an Estonian—all with the same bad fortune to be swept up in Stalin's deadly purges.

On July 31, the Kyrgyz president Askar Akaev addressed the families of the victims at the Kyrgyz White House. Leaning forward with his fingers pressing into the table, a solemn Akaev read the names of the victims, one by one. In the audience relatives rested their chins in the palms of their hands or turned away to look out the window. Some clutched their heads in their hands. Save for the occasional whimper or sob, the room was silent (see figure 14.1).

Members of the Aitmatov family attended the meeting in the Kyrgyz White House. Like the others, they were astounded by the turn of events. A half century of searching—of vain inquiries and KGB lies— had finally been put to rest. Maria Aitmatova had called Chingiz shortly

Figure 14.1: Members of families of victims of the Stalinist purges in Kyrgyzia in the 1930s listen to President Akaev in July 1991 as he reads off names of bodies discovered in a mass grave outside Bishkek. Source: Central State Archives of the Kyrgyz Republic.

after she got a briefing from General Asankulov in early August. When his wife told him of the discovery of the sentencing letter, Chingiz had fallen silent. But this was not the "evil" silence of the past. It was the silence of redemption. "Everything disappeared, disintegrated—the bodies of the unfortunate people, their shoes, clothes," Aitmatov would say a few weeks later, "except this paper, this document from that era, with the name of Törökul Aitmatov, which remained intact enough to read."[6]

Dry conditions had preserved the documents, but the Aitmatov family knew that something else was at work in solving the gruesome mystery. And so did many other Kyrgyz. "There is in the world some higher justice, timeless and absolute." Aitmatov said, "something maybe beyond our everyday existence."[7]

When the Kyrgyz Government announced August 23 as the date for the reburial of the bones, Chingiz Aitmatov planned his flight from Luxembourg back to Frunze. The reburial would take place at Chong Tash, which was to be remade into a national memorial. A killing field would be transformed into hallowed ground.

On August 19, General Asankulov took Maria Aitmatov on a tour of Chong Tash. They drove in Asankulov's government-issued car, complete with chauffeur and phone. They were an odd couple, the KGB veteran and the wife of the famous writer who had fingered the KGB in The Day for much that had gone wrong in the Soviet Union. Asankulov seemed to value Aitmatov, as was evidenced by his appeal to the writer to become president a year earlier, or perhaps, well aware of Aitmatov's influence in Moscow, he was being shrewdly opportunistic. In any case, in the car with Maria decent human sentiment prevailed.

On their return to Frunze, Asankulov took a call from KGB headquarters in Moscow. "Something is happening in Moscow," Asankulov said out loud. "There are tanks in the streets."[8] The coup against Soviet leader Gorbachev had begun. Tanks and soldiers had surrounded the parliament building on the Moscow River, where President of Russia Yeltsin was holed up. People waited on edge, watching CNN and BBC to see what would be the fate of the Soviet Union. Listeners inside the

Soviet Union tuned into the continuous coverage of the events from Radio Liberty and Voice of America.

The day before, conservative opponents had put the Soviet president under house arrest at his summer residence in the Crimea and assumed control of the Soviet Government. Asankulov's direct boss, Vladimir Kryuchkov, chairman of the Soviet KGB, was the driving force behind the coup. The trigger for the coup was the upcoming signing of a new union treaty on August 20, which the coup plotters believed heralded the breakup of the Soviet Union. They were determined to keep the union intact, with Moscow in control of the republics. That meant blunting the rise of Boris Yeltsin, the recently elected president of Russia who the plotters believed was undermining the foundations of the Soviet Union by building an independent Russia.

In their minds, the coup plotters didn't want to give up the Cold War struggle. In thinking indicative of the conservatives' mind-set, one of the coup plotters would later remark, "We were just not ready to become dependent on the USA, politically, economically or militarily."[9]

In Kyrgyzia, on the morning of the coup, Roza Aitmatova took a public bus from the family's dacha into town. The radio was not working at the dacha, so she first heard about the coup from three women talking excitedly, almost gleefully, on the bus. They explained to her what had happened. Roza's stomach churned. She immediately thought of her two brothers, who both supported Gorbachev's reform efforts. Would they become victims just like their father?

"Why are you happy?" Roza asked them.

"You mean you think it's bad?" answered one of the women.

"Of course," a concerned Roza replied. "The year 1937 is beginning again."

"Let it begin," added another of the women. "We don't care. We actually need a 1937 year now."[10]

After the announcement of the coup in Moscow, the Kyrgyz KGB moved to assert itself. Clearly acting on orders from Moscow, KGB Chairman Asankulov declared to Akaev that the two men would work together to carry out the orders of the coup plotters representing their self-proclaimed State Committee for the Emergency Situation.[11] Asankulov presented a more assured front than the coup leaders in Moscow. At a hastily convened press conference the evening of August 19, Gennady Yanayev, the designated spokesman for the State Committee, addressed news outlets from around the globe. But far from projecting confidence, Yanayev came across as a bumbling court jester. Images of his quavering hands flashed around the world, leaving a lasting impression of an ill-organized coup. Yanayev, it turned out, had been drinking heavily since the day before.

By the evening of August 20, declarations of support for resistance to the coup were pouring into Yeltsin's headquarters in the parliament building. The leaders of Kazakhstan and Ukraine called to say they were not fulfilling the coup leaders' orders. Estonia and Latvia declared their independence during the coup. During the night of August 20 defenders outside the parliament building prevented the military from storming the building. Tens of thousands of people manning makeshift barricades chanted "Pozor, Pozor!" (Shame, shame!) and "Rossiya, Rossiya!" at the troops surrounding them. The attempted coup unraveled quickly.

After a tense night, during which three protestors were killed trying to halt armored personnel carriers, the first tanks headed back to their bases around 11 a.m. on August 21. Soon after, huge convoys of tanks and armored personnel carriers turned around and followed. By August 22, most of the coup leaders were under arrest. Two days later, Gorbachev dissolved the Central Committee of the Communist Party, and in November Yeltsin banned the Soviet Communist Party completely.

—✳—

In Kyrgyzia, President Askar Akaev acted decisively. When leaders of other Soviet republics were prevaricating, he signaled support for Gorbachev early on.[12] Late in the day on August 19, he addressed Kyrgyz citizens by radio, choosing his words carefully: "With concern and unease, I inform you about the emergency situation that has been declared in the country."[13]

But behind the scenes Akaev was marshaling forces to quell the coup on the ground. He arrested Asankulov just a few hours after the

KGB chairman's visit to his office, thus depriving the coup plotters' of their chief instigator in Kyrgyzia. Before the outcome of the coup was clear, he ordered TV and radio stations to broadcast Yeltsin's appeal for resistance.[14]

Despite the upheaval, forensic work on remains from Chong Tash continued. Scientists did their best to match bones to names in preparation for the reburial ceremony. But with the announcement of the coup, Asankulov didn't want the work to continue.[15] It was as if the backward-looking stalwarts were trying to keep the bones silent in the abandoned kiln. There is reason to believe that if the coup had succeeded, the reburial ceremony would have been canceled, and one of the darkest chapters in Kyrgyz history would have remained buried. But with revanchist forces discredited in Moscow and Frunze, the search for closure resumed. The reburial was shifted to August 30.

—⁓—

During the tense days of the coup, Chingiz Aitmatov kept a low profile in Luxembourg, careful not to incriminate himself through traceable conversations. In phone conversations with family members in Frunze, he was guarded, saying only that the Soviet Foreign Ministry had asked him to remain in Luxembourg. But with the triumph of reform forces, he got on his way. On the flight to Frunze on August 23, he had time to reflect on his first year in Luxembourg. His diplomatic duties as Soviet ambassador had been manageable since Luxembourg was a small country with minimal strategic importance.

However, inside the embassy, things were boiling. Like the rest of Soviet society, embassy staff were divided between Gorbachev supporters and those who sided with Yeltsin. Although he was a Gorbachev supporter, the new ambassador avoided taking sides, but his actions spoke for the changes he wanted to see. In an effort to break down the walls that kept Soviet diplomats cut off from their host country, Aitmatov instituted a policy allowing embassy employees to leave the embassy premises without having to ask for permission. He opened the doors of the embassy to dissidents like world-famous cellist Mstislav Rostropovich.[16]

Besides his diplomatic duties in Luxembourg, Aitmatov found time, if not for much actual writing, then for promotion of his books. With

Leitess and translator Freidrich Hitzer, he did three to four speaking tours a year across Germany, Switzerland and Austria. *Executioner's Block* and the revised version of *Face to Face* sold well not only in the former East Germany, a traditional market for popular Soviet writers, but also in the other Germanic countries. A year's worth of touring netted about 100,000 to 110,000 books sold.[17]

Indeed, the move to Europe had revived Aitmatov, so much so that he called it a "second childhood."[18] To his delight, he was feted as a writer. In March 1991, the National Library of Luxembourg had honored him with a special evening of presentations. The evening's speaker spoke of Aitmatov's universal significance: "This writer," the local scholar remarked of Aitmatov, "has become the conscience of the Soviet Union. Maybe he will become our conscience, too."[19] But as the flight headed southeast to Frunze, Chingiz Aitmatov's thoughts turned to matters at hand. In the weeks since the discovery of the sentencing letter, he knew that a special team of researchers had shared the contents of Törökul Aitmatov's KGB file with family members in Frunze. Now, he would get a chance to fathom the event that had singularly changed his life and propelled him to become a writer.

Spread in front of Chingiz Aitmatov, the contents of folder 4418 unraveled the mystery of his father's disappearance fifty-three years earlier. Arrest papers, transcripts of judicial proceedings, and execution orders were grim markers of a secretive murder machine exposed for its brutality and chilling efficiency. The trial documents revealed miscarriages of justice characteristic of the Stalin era. Like many of his unfortunate compatriots during the Great Purges, Törökul faced an unjust legal system based on forced confessions, often obtained by torture, and on loose interpretations of article 58 of the Russian Soviet Federated Socialist Republic Penal Code, which dealt with counterrevolutionary crimes. Due legal process, as defined by Soviet law in force at the time, was replaced with summary proceedings by military tribunals or NKVD trials.

In Törökul's case, his trial on November 5, 1938 had been closed: no witnesses testified, and no evidence was presented. The only people in the room were three military judges and the accused. The arrest warrant had charged him with being active in the Socialist Turan Party, which, by most accounts, had never existed as an organized party. Last, the NKVD had labeled him the son of a "prominent kulak," a fabrication that the NKVD concocted, likely because their case against Törökul was weak.[20]

That was Soviet justice during the purges.

In the face of cold and calculating evil, Chingiz saw how Törökul had retained his personal integrity. At his trial, Törökul had recanted his previous confession. No, he told the judge, he had not tried to overthrow Soviet power. Nor had he recruited others or willfully harmed agricultural work in the south. The transcripts revealed how Törökul had refused to implicate any others. The faithful servant of Soviet communism still harbored hope for justice. In his last recorded words in the trial transcripts Törökul said, "I ask for a just verdict."

What more could a boy hope for from his father?

According to the transcripts, at 11:25 p.m., after a trial lasting twenty minutes, the judge pronounced Törökul guilty and sentenced him to death, with the punishment to be carried out immediately. Törökul Aitmatov was executed at midnight at the Frunze Prison with two gunshots to the heart, the bullets penetrating the sentencing letter he had folded in his breast pocket. Trucks then transported forty-three bodies to Chong Tash in the early morning of November 6.[21]

In a dose of bitter irony, the next day, November 7, 1938, was the eve of the twenty-first anniversary of the Bolshevik Revolution. A holiday had been declared, and stores in Frunze were filled with goodies. A train wagon of champagne arrived in the capital, flower stores were stocked with special bouquets, and the circus came to town. In Moscow, Molotov, chairman of the Council of People's Commissars, assured the Soviet people that "the Soviet path to freedom" was making progress. "As for people of other countries," he added, "the socialist revolution is the only true road to liberation from the oppression of capitalism."[22]

After the holiday was over, a vanguard of that socialist revolution— judges and prison guards—continued the bloody purges in Frunze. Fifty-three more people were executed and their bodies dumped into the mass grave, more innocent victims piled on top of Törökul Aitmatov's corpse. But lies live on for only so long. A half century later light was shining on the dark spots of history. The plucked chicken in the elder's fable was growing back feathers and marching toward the sun.

—⁓—

The reburial ceremony on August 30, 1991 began on Frunze's main square on a clear summer morning. As speakers rose to address a crowd of thousands, military transport trucks stood by, loaded with 137 boxes of human remains. The boxes were white, with a dark border, and a bouquet of flowers graced each. Two soldiers stood at attention to carry each box to its final resting place at Chong Tash.

Chingiz Aitmatov spoke after President Akaev, the hero of recent days. Akaev had the political mandate; Aitmatov held moral sway. With a loosened collar, and his tie hanging in a relaxed manner, Aitmatov read his speech from handwritten notes he held in his left hand. Behind him stood a cross section of Kyrgyzia: high-ranking government officials, a Muslim cleric, a woman, an older man and ethnic Russians. Just a few people away, a grizzled man held a photo of a victim, and next to him a woman clutched a framed portrait of Törökul Aitmatov.

Thoughts and images whirled as Aitmatov prepared to address the crowd. There was his childhood teacher, who had told him, "Never lower your eyes when someone pronounces your father's name." The face of Aunt Karakyz, who had refused to kowtow to Stalin. The old man who had dissuaded him from enacting revenge for the family's stolen cow in the winter of 1942. "This world is just," the nameless man had said.

And Chingiz Aitmatov remembered his father's dignity at the trial, his moral backbone in the face of terror. In the Soviet Union, there had been far too much inhumanity and far too little moral backbone. Now Kyrgyzia had a chance to start afresh. The new era would begin with the Kyrgyz people reclaiming their national history and burying their fathers with the dignity they deserved. The cemetery would consecrate not just the 137 victims thrown into the mass grave but would become a symbolic resting place for the thousands of residents of Kyrgyzia who had disappeared during the purges.[23]

In his speech, Aitmatov named the reburial site "Resting Place of our Fathers," or Ata Beyit in Kyrgyz. It was a fitting rebuttal to Stalin's bloody purges which had plunged thousands of families in Soviet Kyrgyzia into silent grief. And it echoed the name of the cemetery in *The Day*—Ana Beit, or "Resting Place of our Mothers"—Aitmatov's pièce de résistance that had memorialized the term *mankurt,* which was helping to fuel independence movements across the Soviet Union.

With the military transport trucks in the lead, the funeral procession set off. Under the late-morning sun, thousands of people followed the trucks as they headed down newly renamed Manas Prospekt. A human river flowed toward the mountains. Marchers bore pictures of the deceased, clutched flowers, and carried children in their arms. Young and old, men and women, healthy and ill, from all over Soviet Kirgizia walked the fifteen miles to Chong Tash. As they processed, they passed well-wishers lining the route like spectators at a marathon.

———

At Chong Tash, the coffins were laid in the ground. An imam recited funeral prayers. Family members threw in the customary handfuls of dirt. Dutiful soldiers finished the job. A composed Aitmatov laid flowers on his father's coffin. He then picked up some soil and sprinkled it onto the coffin with the remains of his father. Thirty years ago, he had honored his lost father with a short story. "Father, I don't know where you are buried," he had written in the epigraph. "I dedicate this story to you."

This time, all he had to say was "Father, I have found you at last after fifty-three years."[24]

The sensitive son had steeled himself and learned how to oppose injustice, just as his father had wished. The link between Ana Beit and Ata Beyit—the fictional and the living, the mothers interchangeable with the fathers—brought the purpose of Chingiz Aitmatov's life into clear focus. He had carved out a personal freedom in the fettered Soviet world. Yes, there had been compromises along the way: joining the same Communist Party that had presided over his father's death, voicing platitudes about Soviet communism, and signing the letter criticizing Sakharov. In September 1989, Aitmatov himself had publicly regretted his participation in the KGB-led campaign against the scientist. "I am ashamed," he had said.[25]

Compromise had been the dear price of Aitmatov's inner freedom. But he was leaving shame and accommodation behind to become the voice of his people. He had written for his people—about their history and tragedies—with the hope of redemption, whenever that time might come. Well, it had come, in unexpected quirks of fate that tied an old woman's story to the desire of a young KGB officer to break with the past. Coupled with the miracle of the preserved sentencing letters, Chingiz Aitmatov now knew where his father was buried. Lies were being uncovered, and the Kyrgyz people were embarking on a new chapter in their troubled history. Aitmatov's spirited characters were present at the burial site as well—in the hearts of the Kyrgyz people for whom they had become inspirations—Jamilya, Tolgonai, Tanabai, Edigei, and Avdi.

———

In a fitting coda to the reburial ceremony, on the next day, August 31, the Kyrgyz Parliament voted to declare independence. It was an abrupt turnabout. Just six months earlier, in March 1991 during a Soviet-wide referendum, more than 90 percent of voters in Soviet Kyrgyzia had voted to preserve the Soviet Union, albeit in a reformed version that promised to give the constituent republics considerably more power. But after the failed coup, with the republics usurping Soviet political and economic structures, Kyrgyzia made its break, thus ending seventy-four years as part of the Soviet Union.

The independence from Moscow that had been sought by Kyrgyzia's purged elite in the 1920s was on the horizon. With those forefathers properly buried, Kyrgyzia was ready to realize their dreams. That fall, President Akaev declared 1995 to be the year of the thousandth anniversary of Manas. It would be a long awaited celebration of the epos which, through the long years of Soviet totalitarianism, had carried the hopes of the Kyrgyz people for freedom and more independence.

Like a giant on clay legs, the Soviet Union collapsed just a few months later. The immediate cause of the collapse was the formation on December 21 of the Commonwealth of Independent States (CIS). Comprising eleven former Soviet republics, the CIS effectively replaced the Soviet Union. On December 25, 1991, Mikhail Gorbachev, president by that time of a shell of a country, announced his resignation on nationwide TV. "This country was going nowhere, and we couldn't possibly live the way we did," a somber Gorbachev said. "We had to change everything radically."[26]

For Aitmatov in Luxembourg, the news was a punch to the gut. Even though he had become a strong critic of the communist system, he, like Gorbachev, maintained that the best way forward was a reformed Soviet Union that kept the republics together but more loosely. But that was not to be. Aitmatov, a product of the Soviet Union's multiethnic melting pot, was left adrift. With dreams of a reformed union gone, it was as if he were losing a parent, again.

15

Times of Tumult

In New York, Altay greeted the news of the Soviet Union's collapse with cautious optimism. Kyrgyzia was finally free to pursue its own destiny, but, as a realist schooled in hard knocks, Altay knew the road ahead would be difficult. He did all he could to help his family members weather the economic downturn. Because mail links were not sufficiently established and bank transfers were nonexistent between the United States and Kyrgyzia, he sent packets of US dollars with personal couriers during the early years after the collapse of the Soviet Union.[1] The money Altay sent was a lifeline, helping his two sisters with food purchases during a time when inflation topped 1,200 percent in 1992. When his family's needs became greater—like moving to Frunze for better job prospects, education, and access to consumer goods—Altay sent larger sums of money. To assure their safe delivery, he turned to Aitmatov, who by then was serving as Russia's ambassador in Luxembourg. Using Aitmatov as a conduit, in 1993 Altay transferred $5,000 to help his sisters build a house on the outskirts of Bishkek, the new name for Frunze as of 1992.[2]

That Aitmatov was willing to use his official position to help Altay send thousands of dollars to Kyrgyzia was a testament to the strong connection that existed between the two men. Though actual face-to-face meetings had been infrequent, a bond of trust had developed over the decades. It had been kindled in New York in the 1970s, strengthened in the 1980s, and was able to be expressed openly in the 1990s.

Altay didn't limit his largesse to his family during the economic crisis. Acting like a one-man development organization, he sent money to an aging writer with Parkinson's disease, newly established cultural organizations, and a struggling literary journal. All told, Altay sent thousands of dollars of his savings across the ocean during Kyrgyzstan's early years of independence.

—⁓—

Faced with a 40 percent gap in the country's budget, President Akaev curried favor with the world's financial institutions by opening up Kyrgyzstan to the world and touting its democratic progress, including his election as president in nationwide balloting in October 1991. The World Bank, International Monetary Fund (IMF), and other development banks extended loans to what appeared to be an island of democracy in Central Asia. By 1994, the infant country had attracted more than $500 million in foreign aid, with the lion's share coming from an IMF loan package and the Islamic Development Bank.[3] Boosted by international support, Akaev's vision was that Kyrgyzstan would prosper by attracting tourists to its mountains and lakes and by developing its substantial gold reserves. The most optimistic observers called mountainous Kyrgyzstan the "Switzerland of Central Asia."

But the bare truth was that landlocked Kyrgyzstan had few advantages when it started its journey as an independent country. Designed to function as a cog in the Soviet planned economy, Kyrgyzstan was plugged into an energy network outside its borders and therefore heavily dependent on other former Soviet republics for oil and gas. When subsidies from Moscow, particularly in the form of underpriced fuel, were cut in 1992 as part of Russia's "shock therapy" economic reform, the effects cascaded like a dam breaking. There were shortages of sugar and milk as production facilities struggled with rising costs themselves. Over the next several years, the industrial economy of Kyrgyzstan would all but collapse. To be sure, some of the factories had no future, like the sugar refinery in northern Kyrgyzstan that was engineered to produce sugar from tropical cane from communist ally Cuba rather than local beetroot.

—⁓—

Where was the great Aitmatov during his country's crucible, some asked? Others sniped, recalling the comment of a reformist politician in Moscow about Aitmatov directing "his lifeboat to the shores of

Luxembourg."[4] The truth was that the writer who had chronicled his people's lives and championed their history was consumed by his own predicament. At the height of Aitmatov's popularity in the 1980s, his books had been printed in dozens of languages of the peoples of the Soviet Union, not to mention in more than a hundred foreign languages outside Soviet borders. His print runs ran in the millions.

But after the collapse of the Soviet Union, instead of writing for a massive market covering one-sixth of the earth, Aitmatov became a writer from a struggling country in innermost Asia. It was like a professional cellist all of a sudden being forced to go back and play in her small town orchestra. And that orchestra didn't even have proper instruments. In 1991 the Writers Union of Kyrgyzstan had published more than 150 books. In 1992, it had not been able to publish a single book because of the exorbitant cost of paper. The bitter irony was that the land that had produced Aitmatov couldn't afford books. And even if printing presses had been able to print books, it's not certain readers would have found reading them a good use of their time. They had other things on their mind.

In an era of tabloids and cheap detective novels, Aitmatov had lost his audience. "I feel as if my readers have moved to some other planet, to some other dimension," he said in September 1991. "The people, as well as the milieu in which I was accustomed to work, have changed." The paradox of Aitmatov was that, however much he had railed against the Soviet system and in spite of his move to Europe, he was and would always be a Soviet man—bred in the vibrant multinational culture of the Soviet Union, buoyed by its rich intellectual currents, and comfortable in its milieu.

Aitmatov's calculated opposition to the system's inhumanity had been driven by uniquely Soviet phenomena—his father's disappearance at the hands of Stalinism, the misguided policy of collectivization, and the errant drive to "engineer" a Soviet man. Groomed to oppose injustice, he had matured over time from a believer to a compromiser to a fiery critic. Now the totalitarian system that had defined his life's mission had crumbled.

Lines from Shelley's poem "Ozymandias" about a decaying monument to an ancient king come to mind:

"My name is Ozymandias, king of kings:
Look on my works, ye Mighty, and despair!"
Nothing beside remains. Round the decay
Of that colossal wreck, boundless and bare
The lone and level sands stretch far away."[5]

Of the Soviet Union, another colossal wreck, nothing remained. There
was nothing left to oppose.

In April 1991, Aitmatov described himself as a man standing "in con-
fusion before a vast plain."[6] He sounded like he was ready to yield the
road to new writers in post-Soviet Central Asia. "Young people should
ride fresh horses," he said. Build bridges to Europe, learn languages of
the West, he advised young writers.[7]

—⁕—

Aitmatov's only novel of the era, published in 1994 in German, seemed
to underscore the distance between the author and his country. It was
unlike anything else he had written. For one, *The Mark of Cassandra*
was set in the United States, with the main characters being an American philosopher and a Russian cosmonaut. With the book, Aitmatov
seemed to be reaching farther and farther into space, unhinged from the
terrestrial quotidian that had defined his realist writings. The plot was
convoluted, echoing America's abortion wars, except that in Aitmatov's
book fetuses refused to be born because of endless cycles of violence in
the world. The cosmonaut was a renegade messenger, announcing in a
letter to the pope that he had discovered a method by which he could
determine whether or not fetuses—or so called Cassandra embryos—
wanted to be born.[8]

The plot stumbled because of simplistic descriptions of Americans
and American politics. But on a deeper level, *The Mark of Cassandra*
resonated as Aitmatov's answer to Francis Fukuyama's celebrated book
The End of History. While Fukuyama posited that mankind's political
development was on an upward trajectory because of the triumph of
liberal democracy over totalitarianism, Aitmatov sounded a warning
about man's failure to evolve into a higher moral being.

Aitmatov wrote the book at the time when religious enmity between
Catholics, Orthodox Christians, and Muslims was tearing up the Bal-
kans. To halt the profusion of religious-based wars in history, Aitmatov's

American hero declares that the world needs to look past specific religious identity and embrace a values-based approach to living—what he called polyreligiosity. It was the same kind of thinking that would have Aitmatov say in his dialogues with Japanese Buddhist thinker Daisuke Ikeda that Christian missionaries should help Muslims become better Muslims.

The Mark of Cassandra rose to number three on the best seller list in Germany in 1994. But it didn't sell well in Russia and was never translated into English. For those in Kyrgyzstan inclined against Aitmatov—opportunistic politicians, disenchanted youth, and even some in the Akaev administration who were wary of the writer's gravitas and privileged position—Aitmatov's latest novel was confirmation that he had found a new life, a new home, and new subjects to write about. In their eyes, Aitmatov had chosen Europe over his homeland and writing over the hopes of his people. That was a legacy he would never shake.

—⁓—

But there were deeper grievances against the famous writer. They concerned Aitmatov's reported connection to a man many Kyrgyz associated with all that was going wrong in the country's rocky transition to a free market system. Boris Birshtein arrived in Kyrgyzia in the summer of 1991. Born in Soviet Lithuania in 1947, Birshtein ran a textile factory before immigrating to Israel in the late 1970s. He then left for Canada. But instead of starting anew in his adopted country like many immigrants, Birshtein looked back to where he had come from.

Birshtein's timing in Kyrgyzstan was perfect. With the country transitioning to a more market-driven economy, President Akaev's government needed help navigating the world of international business. In particular, the Kyrgyz government needed someone to help them exploit the country's gold reserves, most of which were trapped deep under ice in the mountains ringing Lake Issyk Kul. Some estimates at the time put the worth of the gold deposits on the lake's south shore at $5 billion.

Established in October 1991 by a decree signed by President Akaev, Birshtein's joint venture with the Kyrgyz government, called Seabeco Kyrgyzstan, received preferential treatment, including a tax exemption.[9] The company's private jets reportedly paid their airport fees in devaluing rubles rather than dollars.[10] In December 1991, Akaev named Birshtein head of the committee for the economic reconstruction of Kyrgyzstan, thus making him one of the country's top economic advisers even though he was not a Kyrgyz citizen. Birshtein was given an office on the seventh floor of the Kyrgyz White House, allowing him regular access to high-ranking Kyrgyz officials. In late December, with Birshtein ensconced in an office across the hall, Akaev signed a decree arrogating to himself unilateral control over the country's gold resources.

Akaev's decree pointed to a larger problem with reform: the fruits were being captured by a privileged few. As was the case across most of the former Soviet Union, former Communist Party officials and factory directors were concentrating wealth in their hands by engineering government contracts and privatization schemes to work to their advantage. Millionaire elites would rise to power in Kyrgyzstan over the next decade while living standards among average Kyrgyz plummeted.

In due time, Birshtein introduced the Kyrgyz government to Cameco Corporation, a Canadian mining company. At the time, Cameco was one of the world's leading uranium producers but had less experience mining gold.[11]

While details remain murky, it appears Chingiz Aitmatov's eldest son, Sanjar, who worked for Seabeco before being named Kyrgyz consul general in Zurich, Switzerland, introduced Birshtein to top officials in the Kyrgyz government in 1991.[12] Some speculate that Sanjar got an assist from his famous father in opening doors in the White House, maybe even to President Akaev.[13] Those speculations fueled a rumor mill in Kyrgyzstan: Aitmatov was living like a king in Europe, had a hand in shady business dealings, and was helping his children line their pockets.

—〰—

The gold scandal broke into the open in late 1993 and ultimately led to the downfall of the government of Prime Minister Tursun Chyngyshev. A report by a Kyrgyz parliamentary committee, which was published in 1994, implicated Sanjar Aitmatov and others in nefarious dealings. According to the parliamentary report, in August 1992, acting upon Akaev's instructions, Chyngyshev reportedly had authorized Sanjar Aitmatov, then working as Kyrgyzstan's consul general in Zurich, to take gold out of the country for refining and cleaning in Switzerland. To be sure, it was an odd job for a diplomat.[14]

On that trip, Sanjar Aitmatov accompanied 146 kilograms of unprocessed gold—with a value of at least a million dollars—to Zurich.[15] That shipment, however, was just a small part of the 1.6 tons of gold ferried out of Kyrgyzstan on Seabeco's planes between January 1992 and December 1993. Many of those shipments, which allegedly bypassed Kyrgyz customs at the airport, were declared to be illegal by the parliamentary committee.[16] "The wealth and financial resources," the committee charged, "have been appropriated by 'scoundrels,' whom our government gave shelter to."[17]

Determined to get to the bottom of the rumors, Kamil Bayalinov, an intrepid Kyrgyz journalist, showed up at the Kyrgyz embassy in Luxembourg in November 1993. The Kyrgyzstan correspondent for the Moscow-based newspaper Komsomolskaya Pravda asked Aitmatov point blank about the gold scandal which was then roiling Kyrgyzstan. Aitmatov was gracious, but it was not an easy interview.

"They say you brought Boris Birshtein to Kyrgyzstan," Bayalinov said.

"Who says that?" Aitmatov responded. "I met him once at a big banquet in Zurich. Someone introduced us, and we exchanged a few inconsequential words."

"But how about your son Sanjar?" Bayalinov pressed Aitmatov.

"He's forty years old, an adult," Aitmatov answered. "Yes, he worked at Seabeco, but that was before my cursory meeting with Birshtein. I had a serious conversation with Sanjar, and he assured me all was OK. But if he with his actions did something to hurt Kyrgyzstan and this will be proved, then my son will answer for this as a simple citizen according to the law."[18]

—◦◦◦—

The gold scandal exposed Kyrgyzstan's weak governmental institutions and self-serving officials, who if they didn't benefit from illegal gold transfers themselves, flew on Seabeco's private jets, skirted their own customs rules, and cozied up to a private businessman in an unseemly manner. The scandal cast a dark shadow over nontransparent dealings with the country's natural resources and eroded confidence in the new political structures of independent Kyrgyzstan.[19]

At a time when Kyrgyzstan was rewriting the orders of engagement for business and investment, Boris Birshtein's fast rise blurred lines between government and private sector that have stayed blurred for subsequent years. Like a heavy load, official corruption has weighed down Kyrgyzstan's transition to more equitable and transparent governance ever since the collapse of the Soviet Union.

16

Holy Ground

The collapse of the Soviet Union sluiced away the ideological divide between the East and the West. With the rise of fifteen independent countries in 1991, travel restrictions crumbled like aging fence posts. Kyrgyzstan—or the Kyrgyz Republic, as it became known officially—opened embassies and consulates around the world.

In 1994, Azamat Altay stopped in at the Kyrgyz diplomatic mission in UN Plaza in Manhattan. He felt a rush of pride when he spotted Kyrgyzstan's red and gold flag—with the yurt's centerpiece in the middle like a sun—rippling among the flags of other UN member nations.[1] Newly arrived Kyrgyz Ambassador Askar Aitmatov greeted Altay in Kyrgyz, just as his father had done nineteen years earlier in a New York City hotel. Started during détente, that friendship between Altay and Chingiz Aitmatov had outlasted the Soviet Union. Now, Askar Aitmatov, taller than his father but with the same thoughtful manner, had an invitation for the venerable Altay. "Why don't you come to the thousand-year celebration of Manas next year?"

Indeed, the hard ice of the Cold War was thawing. In independent Kyrgyzstan a visible sign was Altay's burnished image. Starting in 1991, newspapers freed from the control of the Communist Party provided a stream of information about the "American Kyrgyz."[2] Articles showed that, contrary to the misrepresentation and lies of the communist years, Altay's story had something unique to say to a Kyrgyz people casting about after the discrediting of communism. They carried headlines like "The candle of truth is kindled" and "A laborious and long road of truth."

One writer in particular grasped Altay's importance as a symbol of hope for the Kyrgyz people. Beksultan Jakiev had been one of the young writers in the audience in 1959 when Kazakh writer Mukhtar Auezov had recounted his meeting in New York City with Altay. From that day on he was Altay's silent champion, bristling whenever Soviet propaganda campaigns blackened Altay's name. In front of his students at the Kyrgyz Institute of Art, he would push back: "This man is very educated. That's the opinion of Mukhtar Auezov."[3] The bond grew only closer after Jakiev discovered their houses were just three streets away from each other in their native village on the south shore of Lake Issyk Kul. Same village, same tribe.

In the early 1990s, Jakiev and Altay started corresponding about the aging *aksakal* visiting Kyrgyzstan. For several months, they went back and forth on the sensitive topic, with Jakiev trying to convince Altay to return.

"I am homesick, but I will never return," Altay responded. "The smear campaigns have left a bad taste in my mouth."

"Your fate is not alien to us here," Jakiev answered. "Your life is like bitter tears that are part of Kyrgyz history. If you don't bring your story with you, God won't forgive you; if we don't invite you, God won't forgive us."

Unwilling to budge, Altay invited Jakiev to visit him in the United States. "I will tell you my story."

—·—

Jakiev's stay in the United States in October 1991 convinced him that Altay's story had to be told. At a time when infant Kyrgyzstan was beginning to open to the world, here was a transplanted Kyrgyz who had "made it" in the West, a shunned man who had managed to retain his Kyrgyz identity—the language, love of literature, and national pride—at the same time that he had adjusted to American life. Altay was living proof that becoming Westernized didn't mean having to give up one's culture (see figure 16.1).

Upon his return from New York in November 1991, Jakiev began work on a biography of Altay. Basing his account on personal archives that

Figure 16.1: Azamat Altay with Beksultan Jakiev, the writer who told Atlay's story back in Kyrgyzstan, during Jakiev's visit to New York in 1991. Source: Photo courtesy of Gulnara Turganbaeva.

Altay had entrusted to him, Jakiev replaced the one-sided Soviet narrative, introducing the Altay he had gotten to know in New York, the man who had paid a heavy price for freedom.

His first morning in New York, Jakiev himself had witnessed the toll years of separation had taken on Altay. Awakened by the sounds of familiar *komuz* melodies—they were songs from the record he had given Altay upon his arrival the previous night—Jakiev followed the music to the living room. There he found Altay listening to the melodies, with moistened eyes, his tears bespeaking years of living with unanswerable questions: Would he ever be accepted in his homeland again? Would he pass on without paying respects to his father's grave? Would he set eyes on his two sisters again? Or on Lake Issyk Kul?

Cut off from his family, his tribe, and his people for half a century, this was a man who deserved sympathy, not scorn. If enough people in Kyrgyzstan empathized with their distant countryman, then maybe, thought Jakiev, one day Altay could be convinced to return home. But Altay still grated from the cutting words that he was a traitor. The wounds were fresh, with just a few years having passed since the last propaganda campaign, which had been spearheaded by Kyrgyz General Secretary Masaliev himself. When Jakiev broached the subject toward the end of his stay in New York, Altay refused. "I would even turn down an offer to visit from Chingiz Aitmatov," he said.

—∿—

In the three years between Jakiev's visit and Askar Aitmatov's invitation in 1994, Jakiev's popularization of Altay's life, newspaper articles, and Altay's own philanthropy helped change public opinion. Instead of insults, Altay encountered understanding and gratitude. In September 1991, a World War II veteran living in Bishkek who had fought all the way to Germany supported Altay's decision to jump lines. The veteran cited the awful fate that had awaited Soviet POWs back home. "Prison and the distant Siberian taiga" is how he put it.[4]

After Altay had sent $1,000 to support the foundering *Ala Too* journal, Chingiz Aitmatov himself had publically thanked Altay in February 1992 in a letter printed in a local Kyrgyz newspaper. "Wherever he is, he helps his people and his homeland," Aitmatov had written. "Our aksakal would help in any way he can, and for this I want to thank him very much on behalf of myself and the Kyrgyz people."[5]

The word *aksakal* conveyed Aitmatov's sentiments toward his respected elder. Indeed, *Ala Too* was one of the journals that had lined Altay's bookshelves at home when Aitmatov had visited in 1975. It had printed Kyrgyz-language versions of Aitmatov's stories over the years and, therefore, connected Altay to his homeland's greatest writer during the Cold War. But following the collapse of the Soviet Union, the journal had fallen on hard times, with subscriptions plummeting by more than 40 percent. Altay's donation, Aitmatov noted in his letter, would help the journal pay off debts it had incurred because of the skyrocketing cost of newsprint.

Like icing on the cake, Altay was asked to join a group of honored *aksakals* a few months later. The group, which included Aitmatov, was a sort of Hall of Fame of the country's elders and included a famous *manaschi* from across the border in China. Change was certainly afoot: in 1975, Altay had had to meet with the Kyrgyz elite sans fanfare; now he could be acknowledged openly (see figure 16.2).

Figure 16.2: Azamat Altay at his home in Queens, New York, in the early 1990s.
Source: Photo courtesy of Kathleen Kuehnast.

With his reputation in independent Kyrgyzstan much improved, Azamat Altay was receptive when the UN office in Bishkek proposed that he
visit in 1994 as part of a cultural exchange. Altay's itinerary called for him
to arrive in August 1994 and spend a month giving talks at universities
on topics like Kyrgyzia in the 1920s and 1930s, his work at Radio Liberty,
and, in line with the upcoming national festival, the *Manas* epic. At about
the same time, the wheels were turning in Kyrgyzstan's judicial system.
Kyrgyzstan's Supreme Court had closed the criminal case against Altay
for desertion, concluding that there was no evidence to convict Altay of
treason, and, therefore, he was free to return.

But Altay wasn't satisfied. "Why is this sentence still hanging over me
if the Soviet Union is gone?" he wrote to Aitmatov in Luxembourg in July
1994. The truth was Altay had no faith in the justice system and imagined
being hounded by security types if he returned: "The USSR collapses,
but the laws are still there." Altay wanted complete exoneration, meaning he wanted the charge of treason against him to be dismissed. He was
innocent, he insisted, not because of lack of evidence but because of lack

of a crime. It was vintage Altay. Scrupulous, insistent, and always wary. For a man who had successfully escaped three times from the Germans, Altay didn't want his "final escape" from Soviet injustice to fall short. He asked Aitmatov to look into the matter.

Altay ended up waiting a year for the Kyrgyz legal system to adjudicate his case. It traveled from the general prosecutor to the prime minister to the supreme court, which exonerated him of any crimes. That meant Altay's UN-sponsored trip could take place during the thousand-year celebration of the *Manas* epic. Serendipity—and a personal invitation from Askar Aitmatov—schemed to help the old man be at his young country's crowning festival.

On a hot day in August 1995, Azamat Altay boarded a plane at New York's Kennedy Airport and began the long flight home via Tashkent, Uzbekistan. In his hands he gripped his American passport stamped with a visa to the independent Kyrgyz Republic, not the Kyrgyz Soviet Socialist Republic.

Azamat Altay had outlasted the enemy.

Accompanying Altay on his historic flight home was Askar Aitmatov—the son somehow destined to carry forth the work of his father in connecting Altay to his homeland. The two men transited through Tashkent and then traveled on to Kyrgyzstan. Upon arrival at Manas International Airport on August 21, Azamat Altay descended the plane via mobile stairs. Once on the tarmac, he bent down and kissed the ground. Tears streamed down his face. He hugged his sister Gulshara and, when offered, raised a bowl of *kymyz* to his lips.

Among the journalists, family members, and well-wishers waiting on the tarmac stood Cholpon Baekova, who, as chairwoman of Kyrgyzstan's Constitutional Court, was the highest-ranking government official to meet Altay. She was also symbolic proof that Altay was on the right side of the law. Steadying himself on Baekova's arm, Altay asked, "Am I really home after fifty years?"

The simple question posed from the land he had last seen more than a half century ago left onlookers awestruck. How could they possibly understand all that had happened to turn this smooth-faced Red Army recruit into the aged man before them? Fighting on the front lines of World War II, suffering in German prison camps, fleeing to the West, and weathering Soviet propaganda campaigns had all taken their toll.

With Baekova on one arm and Gulshara on the other, Altay waded into the crowd. Like a modern-day Rip Van Winkle, Altay recognized faces now fifty years older than when he had last seen them. One journalist said it was like "Gagarin returning to earth." A TV journalist, too emotionally shaken to address Altay himself, asked Jakiev to pose his question.

To make it back to Bishkek in time for the opening ceremony of the *Manas* celebration on August 26, Jakiev and Altay set off in Jakiev's rickety Zhiguli car for their native village on the south shore of Lake Issyk Kul. A TV crew followed them, ready to capture Altay's return. Three hours from Bishkek, the lake's blue waters and snowcapped mountains came into view. The emotionally exhausted Altay was overcome. "If I die now, I will be the happiest man on earth," he told Jakiev. "Please don't die at Issyk Kul," Jakiev jokingly retorted. Hold on at least until we get to the village.

Villages along the way had gotten word of Altay's arrival, and well-wishers waved the car on. In fact, for many rural Kyrgyz Altay was their first encounter with the West, that faraway mystery land they had been taught to loathe and now were supposed to embrace. In the topsy-turvy time of hope, when Kyrgyzstan was shedding its heavy Soviet cloak of isolation, Altay was not only a curiosity—a village Kyrgyz who had been Americanized—but also a bridge to new horizons. He was a testament to the possibility of change.

Journalists played into the narrative of a larger-than-life character. They called Altay head of the Turkic section at Columbia University's library when, in fact, he had worked as a clerk. And they liked to refer to him as a founder of Radio Liberty's Kyrgyz Service when, in actuality, he had merely been one of the first employees. It was as if the Kyrgyz yearned for an inflated example to bolster their own climb out of obscurity into nationhood.

Dusk settled as Jakiev and Altay approached their home village, which had been absorbed into the city of Bokonbaevo over the years. Residents lined the streets with lighters and tossed flowers on Jakiev's gray Zhiguli as it wound its way through narrow streets. People were pressing forward so much that neither Jakiev nor Altay could open the doors of the tiny boxcar. Eventually, they came to a stop. Inhaling deeply to catch his breath, Altay exited the car into lines of people.

On foot, after asking directions several times, the group found its way to the poplar trees Altay and his father had planted in the 1930s. Like Altay, they had matured over the decades, weathering seasons of joy and sorrow. Except the trees had had each other for company. Gazing at the starry sky above, Altay was transported back to his days as a young shepherd, when he had scrambled up cliff faces while his sheep were grazing. He embraced the trees and cried one last time. Tears of his bygone youth—as his sister had remarked when she met him after fifty years. Later, Altay read prayers from the Koran at his father's grave, fulfilling his filial duty after decades. Mother Earth lay firmly underfoot, and long-awaited closure calmed Azamat Altay's restless heart.

In the morning, like a homecoming hero, Altay walked down a main street, but he couldn't make much headway. There were children to kiss, old faces to embrace, and tears to wipe away. He wore a suit and tie and a kalpak. Altay, Jakiev and a few others walked to the lake. With his tie knotted to the top button, Altay looked out of place as the group descended grassy banks to the enormous inland sea spreading in front of them. The waves of Issyk Kul rolled gently onto the shore. Nearing the lakeshore, Altay spread his hands out in supplication, bent down, and scooped up water. The other men did the same, and, as if in unison, they washed their faces with the sacred water.

The taste of *kymyz*, the poplar trees, and the waters of Lake Issyk Kul—Azamat Altay had finally come home.[6]

When the Manas 1000 festival opened on Saturday, August 26, Altay and Jakiev were among the crowds greeted by colorful banners, oversized yurts, and patterned walkways at the Manas village on the outskirts of Bishkek. It was a true national party for the Kyrgyz people—a celebration of their legendary hero who had overcome trials and tribulations to unite the Kyrgyz tribes. Theaters ran shows glorifying the legendary

Manas, symposia featured *Manas* specialists from around the world, and horse acrobats and dancers reenacted scenes from the epic. For a week, a nation beset by economic woes reclaimed its heritage.

In an event that could never have taken place in the Soviet Union, President Akaev welcomed the leaders of five Turkic governments. The gathering of the heads of state of Azerbaijan, Kazakhstan, Kyrgyzstan, Turkey, Turkmenistan, and Uzbekistan may well have been the most international showing of pan-Turkism since Turkic tribes had massed to defend their land against the Mongol hordes passing through Central Asia seven hundred years earlier. Indeed, the Manas festival celebrated a small country's survival amid bigger powers. Had it not been for the traveling bards reciting the epic to pockets of Kyrgyz in their mountain hamlets, the Kyrgyz language itself might have dissipated into the languages of conquerors. "The spirit of our nation is forever encoded in this epic," Akaev declared grandly. "Every one of us carries a piece of it in his or her heart."[7]

In 1991 at the consecration of Ata Beyit cemetery, Chingiz Aitmatov had ridden high as the moral conscience of his people, a Kyrgyz citizen who had not only suffered personal loss but also had given voice to the aspirations of his people for freedom. On the opening day of the *Manas* celebration four years later, Aitmatov gave a speech citing *Manas* as the humanistic bedrock of the Kyrgyz as they embarked on national rebirth. "Practice will show how capable we are of taking advantage of this new phase of development," the venerated writer said.[8]

It was a fitting tribute to have Aitmatov speak for he himself had played a significant role in popularizing and sustaining the *Manas* epic during the last decades of the Soviet Union. He had overseen the twenty-five-year project to publish the most complete versions of the epic. The version of Sayakbai Karalaev, whose spellbinding recitation in pouring rain Aitmatov would long recall, alone took up five volumes. During the 1970s, it was Aitmatov who had pushed a reluctant Kyrgyz Communist Party to consider a *Manas* celebration. Those efforts, many believed, had sown the seeds for the 1995 celebration. Some even considered Aitmatov the godfather of the Manas 1000 festival. And, of course, he had canonized the term *mankurt*, which had roots in the epic.

But in 1995 it was Altay, the "American Kyrgyz," who was celebrated. Indeed, at a ceremony at the Kyrgyz National Library, Aitmatov formally welcomed the "renegade" Altay in a fitting tribute to the two men's decades-long friendship. What better way to celebrate the epic than to welcome back Altay—a living antidote to the *mankurt*—as a man who had respected his cultural heritage despite being alienated from his country for more than half a century? "Azamat Altay, you are in your homeland again during these good days," Aitmatov wrote on that very day in an edition of *The Mark of Cassandra* that he gave to Altay.

In seeing a picture of the two *aksakals* shaking hands at the library, one can't help but think that Aitmatov himself deserved the highest accolades among living Kyrgyz. For he had persevered and given the Kyrgyz people, including dissident Altay, multiple reasons to be proud. Indeed, to Altay himself Aitmatov was the "symbol of the nation" (see figure 16.3).[9]

Figure 16.3: Altay's farewell at Manas airport in Bishkek in September 1995 following his return to Kyrgyzstan after fifty-five years. Altay is in the center in the grey suit. Chingiz Aitmatov is to his right in a light suit, and Askar Aitmatov is on the far left in a dark suit. Source: Photo courtesy of Gulnara Turganbaeva.

It was as if the tide of history had outrun Aitmatov in time to catch up with Altay. In a testament to the vagaries of fate, their lives in independent Kyrgyzstan seemed to be inverse arcs: the man who had fled his country was feted while the writer who had chronicled his people's struggles for freedom was disregarded.

In New York, Altay became a sort of sage for the Kyrgyz in his later years, and his house in Queens, first visited by Aitmatov in 1975, became a stop on the itineraries of Kyrgyz visiting America. Presidential advisers, ministers, academics, journalists, students, and wayfarers who found themselves in New York City would pay their respects to the man who had paved the way for Kyrgyz in America. If Kyrgyz visitors were late in arriving or didn't speak proper Kyrgyz, Altay, his legendary temper rising to the surface, would scold them. "You are in a foreign country," he would say. "Don't shame the Kyrgyz people with your behavior."[10]

But invariably the meetings were welcoming affairs. There would be a traditional greeting in Kyrgyz, an introduction, and tea or a meal around the wooden table in Altay's kitchen. Then Altay would usually hand the visitor a $50 or $100 bill. It was his way of saying, "We are brothers, and it's my duty as the respected elder to help you along your way in this unfamiliar land." The reversal in his fortunes didn't escape Altay. ""Before people ran away from me, thinking I was an enemy of the people," he said in 2005. "Now they all want to say hello to me."[11]

Meanwhile, despite his official stature as Kyrgyzstan's ambassador to the Benelux countries, NATO, and the European Union, Aitmatov the writer—the persona he cared most about—was in an existential vacuum. "Literature is a story by a man about mankind, and so writers, including me, who found their paths in the Soviet era, are in difficult straits," Aitmatov said in 1997. "No one bothers us. Personally, no one bothers me. On the contrary, I have been given complete freedom, but this freedom has turned out to be empty."[12]

Aitmatov put his angst into his writing. After expounding on the drug subculture of the Soviet Union in *The Executioner's Block* and the cosmic powers of a renegade monk in *The Mark of Cassandra*, in his last book Aitmatov came back to what had made him famous—writing about the people of Kyrgyzstan against the backdrop of their natural surroundings.

The plot of *When the Mountains Fall* turns on the demise of Soviet-era journalist Arsen Samanchin, who can't find his way in the chaotic, market-driven world of independent Kyrgyzstan. True to his connection with the animal world, Aitmatov introduces an aging snow leopard named Jhabars as a mirror of his ill-equipped protagonist. With the book, Aitmatov revealed himself as crestfallen at Kyrgyzstan's post-Soviet predicament: a free but destitute people, largely defenseless against an impersonal and globalized economy and prone to violence to resolve problems.

The manuscript came into being during a time of rootlessness for Aitmatov. After the publication of *The Mark of Cassandra* in 1994, he had wandered for nearly a decade in a literary desert, penning disconnected parts of a story that would come together only after he suffered a stroke in 2004. As if propelled by his own mortality, Aitmatov hurriedly completed *When the Mountains Fall* in several months after recovering from heart surgery. Fueled by a health-conscious diet of apples and the occasional sneaked chocolate, Aitmatov would wake early, hours before his work as a diplomat would commence. In a room in the narrow, four-story house that served as his official residence in Brussels, he would lose himself in the world of his fast-changing homeland. On lined notepads, in his distinctive looping script, he wrote chapters of the novel that would become his final testament.

―⁓―

The title of *When the Mountains Fall* evokes Aunt Karakyz's cry from decades earlier when a mother sheep inexplicably rejected her lamb, upsetting the natural order of things. In the post-Soviet world Aitmatov describes in the novel, there is much to decry: crass commercialization where all is seemingly for sale, including traditional gifts of honey and flowers being hawked by the roadside all over Kyrgyzstan. The degradation extends to Arsen Samanchin's fiancée, Aidana, an opera singer who "sells" herself into the entertainment industry, and encroaches on the snow leopard, whose forefathers had wandered the Kyrgyz wilderness for centuries and whose very name conveyed its connection to nature.

In the crux of the plot, rich Arab sheiks come to Kyrgyzstan to hunt the snow leopard in the mountains above Lake Issyk Kul. Jhabar's fate as an endangered species pales in comparison to the payday that Arsen's entrepreneurial uncle will receive for corralling Jhabars into the gun sights of the oil barons.

And there is, of course, Arsen Samanchin, Aitmatov's alter ego, who, when unable to find steady work in journalism, is forced to help his uncle host the Arab sheiks, thus becoming complicit in destroying the very nature he reveres. It is a tale of oligarchs, money, power, dirty games, and desperation. Aitmatov's overriding concern—one that carries through from his novels of the 1970s—was that human greed and recklessness are destroying the natural world. It was a spiritual and emotional out-pouring of sentiments that had been stirring over the previous decade. "My personal pain I have put into words," Aitmatov told a close friend in 2007.[13]

The writer who had so vividly chronicled his people's journey through communism to independence had become superfluous, not because he had changed but because the circumstances surrounding him had trans-formed. He fell from the perch he had enjoyed during Soviet times, and his voice became muted by growing irrelevance. Aitmatov, indeed, felt himself to be Arsen, quaintly moral and disposable in a society that no longer had sufficient interest, time, or energy to pay much attention to its greatest writer.

By the time *When the Mountains Fall* was published in 2006, Askar Akaev was gone from the Kyrgyz political scene, chased from power by a largely peaceful uprising in March 2005 that had surprised even the Kyr-gyz who had led it. Akaev, who had come to power on a wave of genuine democratic sentiment in the early 1990s, had over the years consolidated power, allowed his family to get involved in running the country, and continually prolonged his terms in office through referendums. When he tried to finagle his son and daughter into parliament in 2005, the Kyrgyz people finally said "no more."

The Tulip Revolution in Kyrgyzstan—so called because opposition leaders carried tulips in their hands as they marched to protest at the

main square on March 24, 2005—came on the heels of similar events in
Georgia in 2003 and Ukraine in 2004. In those former Soviet republics,
long-standing autocratic governments were dispensed with in the Rose
Revolution and Orange Revolution, respectively, leading commentators
to speak of a wave of "colored revolutions" sweeping the former Soviet
states.

On March 24, 2005, the day of the historic events back home, Chingiz Aitmatov had a morning doctor's appointment in Brussels. By the
time he returned to the Kyrgyz embassy, Kyrgyz living in Belgium and
nearby countries were protesting in front of the embassy building. Quick
thinking—and possibly sympathetic—diplomats inside the embassy
opened the doors of the embassy, after first informing Aitmatov. "Do as
you see fit," he told them. "I am for it."[14] Aitmatov reportedly shed his
cautious approach after his staff showed him photos of protests in front
of Kyrgyz embassies around the world, including in Washington, DC,
where his daughter Shirin had joined demonstrators. "You and Shirin
are heroes," he said laconically.

Given the green light, embassy staffers in Brussels announced to the
demonstrators as they streamed in that "all their demands had been
met."[15] Once inside the embassy compound, the demonstrators—still
incredulous that they had been invited inside—and embassy staffers
sat glued to the TV. Once the demonstrators learned that protestors in
Bishkek had climbed over the protective fence surrounding the Kyrgyz
White House and stormed the building, a celebration broke out.

In the wake of Akaev's sudden departure from power, Aitmatov spoke
up, giving an interview to the Russian news agency ITAR-TASS that
evening. Calling the day's events "an authentic revolution," he went on
to say that the main reason for the uprising was pervasive corruption,
which had infected all levels of government. "The regime, which existed
until the last day and last hour, had exhausted itself," Aitmatov added.
"Dissatisfaction piled up, and expectations of reform were stifled for too
long."[16] Comments below an article carrying Aitmatov's assessment of
the March 24 events spoke volumes: "Where were you earlier, Chingiz
Törökulovich?"[17]

Aitmatov remained in Brussels for three years after the Tulip Revolution, but they were difficult ones. His comments on March 24, 2005,

notwithstanding, Aitmatov was considered an artifact of the Akaev regime by the new government, which was headed by a former prime minister, Kurmanbek Bakiev, with whom Aitmatov had little connection.
Ready to leave, Aitmatov wasn't sure where to go: Kyrgyzstan, Russia,
or some other place that might welcome him. Things came to a head in
the spring of 2008, when Aitmatov was unceremoniously recalled to
Bishkek. A government decree forced the Aitmatov family to vacate the
official residence and leave Brussels. Not bothering to call, the Kyrgyz
government sent the decree by fax to the embassy. It was, said a close
confidant of Aitmatov's, like a "knife in the back."[18]

Adding insult to injury, some embassy staffers turned away from the
Aitmatov family as they prepared to leave their Brussels home of fourteen years. One Kyrgyz diplomat didn't want to sign papers confirming
that their family belongings were diplomatic cargo, and part of the family's shipment disappeared in Belarus. Aitmatov's farewell dinner ended
up being hosted by the Kazakhs and Russians, not his own country.[19]

Epilogue

Azamat Altay's last years were spent mostly confined to his home, caring for his wife Saniye, who had developed Alzheimer's, and dealing with the onset of Parkinson's disease himself. From his favorite chair in the living room and during sleepless nights, he followed events in Kyrgyzstan. That news mostly disappointed him. At least for the economic troubles, he could be proactive by sending money. But there was little he could do about the psychic toll years of neglect had taken on the Kyrgyz people. There was the soullessness bred during the Soviet years that Altay believed had left little space for honesty and kindheartedness in the Kyrgyz. On his 1995 trip to Kyrgyzstan, Altay had noticed a people prone to drink, forgetful of their national traditions and disinclined to hard work. His feared the Kyrgyz people were squandering their chance for freedom.

During the first decade of Kyrgyzstan's independence, as the country struggled to establish itself as a sovereign state, Altay would come to the conclusion that, with the peaceful collapse of the Soviet Union, the Kyrgyz people had received their independence too easily, as if it had fallen from the skies. "If we had had to spill blood to gain our liberty, then we would understand the true worth of our land," he would say.[1] Not surprisingly, Altay's negative sentiments created a stir when reported in the Kyrgyz press. His friends and relatives felt betrayed: "How could our national hero talk in such a way about us when we welcomed him so warmly?" On one occasion, Altay upbraided a journalist for printing his unflattering comments. But Venera Djumataeva, then a reporter for Radio Liberty's Kyrgyz Service based in Bishkek, didn't flinch. "Someone

like you has to tell the truth to the Kyrgyz people," she said. "If the Kyrgyz are losing their national characteristics, you are the one they expect
to tell the truth."[2]

After a stay in a New York hospital, Azamat Altay passed away at the
age of eighty-five on May 23, 2006. Unable to recover from an operation to remove a tumor from his stomach, Altay's weakened body succumbed, but not before a final wish. The attending doctor expected to
hear Altay say something about his family or his grand-niece who had
been born two years earlier, the one he had once sat with for six hours
straight, afraid that if he left the room she might fall. But, no, his final
thoughts were not personal. They were on his people, as they had been
throughout his long life. "What else can I hope for than to be helpful to
my people?" he said.

A few days after news of Altay's death reached Kyrgyzstan, an obituary appeared in the state-owned newspaper *Slovo Kyrgyzstana* that noted
Altay's advocacy "for the idea of freedom and democracy and his speaking up in defense of human rights, freedom of speech and freedom of
the press on Kyrgyz soil." The names of eighty-four prominent citizens
appeared underneath the obituary—high-ranking government officials,
members of parliament, journalists, and human rights activists. They
represented all sides of the political spectrum and hailed from the north
and south of Kyrgyzstan, perhaps the best barometer of popular acclaim
in the riven country. Tucked in the middle of the pack was the signature
of Iskhak Masaliev, the head of the Kyrgyz Communist Party. Ishak was
the son of Absamat Masaliev, the last Communist Party general secretary of Soviet Kyrgyzia who had lashed out at Altay in 1987 for being a
nationalist. It seemed even the communists could find something to like
in Altay's remarkable life.[3]

Altay had made his own funeral arrangements at an Islamic Funeral
Home in Queens and had a friend bring soil from Kyrgyzstan—from the
Ata Beyit national memorial—to be sprinkled on his grave. He was in-
terred next to his wife in the Muslim plot of a cemetery outside New York
City on May 29. Under sunny skies and surrounded by expansive fields
of green grass, Kyrgyz men hoisted shovels to fill in the grave, just like
they do in Kyrgyzstan. Many of the eighty or so attendees had crossed
the threshold of Altay's house and received advice and a bit of spending

money, courtesy of Altay. Now, they were back—some even traveling from as Canada—to pay their respects to the "American Kyrgyz."

Urmat Alimkulov, one of the many Kyrgyz whom Altay had helped in the 1990s, served as the master of ceremonies at the funeral home in Queens. Standing beside Altay's coffin, with a portrait of Altay behind him, Alimkulov wore a kalpak and a black traditional robe with gold embroidery. Alimkulov was, in many ways, the kind of Kyrgyz who made Altay proud. He had learned English well and retrained himself to work as a nurse. He also happened to be Chingiz Aitmatov's nephew, the son of his sister Roza.

After short speeches by elders in attendance, Alimkulov read a message from his uncle in Brussels, which he had taken over the phone earlier that morning. In the message, Chingiz Aitmatov spoke of an hour of deep mourning for the Kyrgyz people and of Altay as a "great patriot" who had survived World War II and then worked in Radio Liberty's Kyrgyz Service. And Aitmatov recalled his 1975 meeting with Altay. "This event for me was unforgettable," he said. "Much of what we talked about then came true according to his predictions. He was wise and had a huge soul."[4]

It was justified praise coming from Aitmatov, for if anyone had slain the *mankurt*, it was Altay. Beginning from simple rural roots every Kyrgyz could relate to, Altay had educated himself in the West and personally amassed an extensive collection of Central Asian and Kyrgyz history, as well as helped keep alive the history of his homeland in some of the finest libraries in America. In a final gesture of goodwill to his people he had endowed two scholarships for the brightest students at Jalalabad and Karakol universities in Kyrgyzstan, sending $500 a year to make possible their continued education.

At the burial ceremony on Long Island, a mullah read prayers from the Koran while men squatted around the freshly dug grave. Altay's body, wrapped in a white shroud, was laid into the grave, his head pointing toward Mecca. The men dropped handfuls of dirt into the grave and grabbed shovels to finish the job. Women in attendance waited at a distance according to Muslim custom. Among them was a young woman, dressed in black and wearing dark sunglasses. She, too, was a Kyrgyz making her way in America, fluent in English and studying at Sarah

Lawrence College fifteen miles north of New York City. She didn't say much, just observed in the fashion of her father, the chronicler of the Kyrgyz people in their tragic twentieth century. Shirin Aitmatova, Chingiz Aitmatov's daughter, had come to pay the family's respect.

Yes, Azamat Altay was a true Kyrgyz patriot. Neither sultan nor slave, Azamat Altay had lived and died a free man.

———

After leaving Brussels in April 2008, Chingiz Aitmatov traveled home through Turkey, Azerbaijan, and Russia, finally arriving in Bishkek in April. To some it seemed he had returned to Kyrgyzstan only to be present at the celebration of his eightieth birthday in December. In honor of that milestone, the Kyrgyz government had named 2008 the Year of Aitmatov. No doubt, sympathetic minds in the government wanted to make amends for Aitmatov's unceremonious recall. Conferences, symposia, and theater festivals were planned.

Despite a hacking cough and sore throat that he had picked up in Brussels in the hectic weeks leading up to his departure, Aitmatov set off in May with his son Eldar for Tatarstan to meet a film crew to complete a documentary film on his life. But travel to central Russia took a toll. In Almaty, before the flight to Moscow, he was fatigued, and in Moscow Aitmatov took a room at the Kyrgyz embassy to rest between flights. Despite his weakened state, Aitmatov insisted on making the trip to Tatarstan, where arrangements had been made to film in the village of his maternal grandparents.[5]

Upon arrival in the Tatar capital of Kazan, Aitmatov wanted only to sleep, asking for the key to his room and retiring early. By morning, his condition had worsened; he couldn't get up from bed and was breathing heavily. Suspecting kidney failure and pneumonia, doctors in Tatarstan recommended Aitmatov be airlifted to Germany. He hung on in a German hospital in Nuremberg for twenty-four days before expiring on June 10. The official cause of death was sepsis due to complete shutdown of his organs.

Instead of feting their most famous citizen in 2008, the Kyrgyz people ended up burying him. The naysayers and critics retreated for a time, and Chingiz Aitmatov was honored, not fatuously but in line with contemporary Kyrgyzstan's struggles. "We saw the errors and mistakes of this man, but we forget that we had the good fortune to live beside true greatness," wrote the political activist Edil Baisalov on the day of the funeral. "We are living, and we are condemned to live, in the universe of Aitmatov because the images of Aitmatov—heroes, people and tragedies—became our own life."[6]

Public opinion polls showed Aitmatov as the country's top national hero, above even Manas.[7] But it was in the minds of his readers that Aitmatov had left the biggest imprint. And there he had helped usher in a revolution, from the country's new class of political leaders to the man on the street. Not the blind, violent kind of revolution Aitmatov so abhorred but a steady percolation of his people's thinking into a faith that they were masters of their own fate. "We walk around under the impression of his works," wrote Roza Otunbayeva, one of the country's most respected leaders, who served as president of Kyrgyzstan from 2010 to 2011. "We strive to be cleaner, stronger, better."[8]

With Aitmatov's strong characters and emphasis on individual responsibility, there came a realization that there would be no deus ex machina or knight in shining armor to save the Kyrgyz people. A journalist put it well in 2013: "He gave us freedom so we can learn, each one of us, how to use this freedom independently and not believe any longer in something or someone else."[9] Added a human rights campaigner, "Every family reads him and rereads him; his books taught us to be braver. He proved to us that even a single man can change things."[10]

On June 14, 2008, twenty thousand Kyrgyz citizens streamed in to view Aitmatov's open casket in Bishkek. Then along roads lined with schoolchildren and well-wishers holding framed portraits of the writer, Aitmatov's body was transported to Ata Beyit, the memorial complex he himself had named "Resting Place of Our Fathers" in 1991. Under blue skies and searing hundred-degree heat, the Kyrgyz people laid to rest their most famous son.

Ata Beyit, the site consecrated to the memory of Kyrgyzstan's purged reformers, including Aitmatov's father, was a fitting burial place for Chingiz Aitmatov. By staying inside the Soviet Union and writing bravely, he had picked up where his father's generation had left off, carrying forward the torch of liberty and freedom in what remains an incomplete and inchoate transformation from authoritarianism to democracy.

In repose, Chingiz Aitmatov represents the unsettled conscience of his troubled nation, which two years after his death revolted against Kurmanbek Bakiev, who turned out to be more corrupt—and bloody— than his predecessor Askar Akaev. Laid to rest at a spot that symbolizes redemption, his life's work is a summons to his countrymen to remember their history, develop themselves morally and vindicate with their actions the freedom they possess.

—⟿—

Born in modest circumstances, both Aitmatov and Altay were constantly educating themselves throughout their lives, in the process building a respect for democratic traditions and the rights of the individual. They saw in each other kindred spirits in the mission to preserve their people's culture, language, and literature. They were not fueled by religious fervor or any exclusivist ideology. Rather, they cherished the promise of secular democracy and its hallmarks of freedom of religion, speech, and association. They embodied the missions of their lives *with* their lives and in their efforts on behalf of their trapped countrymen.

Yes, Aitmatov and Altay are poplar trees towering over Kyrgyzstan's tremulous landscape. During the tragedies of the twentieth century, branches were torn asunder, in the case of the disappearance of Aitmatov's father, and roots nearly drained of water, in the case of Altay's estrangement from his homeland. But the trees grew tall, and the two men stand today as fathers to their country's evolving democracy, the freest country in Central Asia with an evolving parliamentary democracy.

—⟿—

In a stirring moment in *Mother's Field*, a weary Tolgonai asks Mother Earth if wars will ever end. "The answer doesn't depend on me," Mother Earth responds. "It depends on you, on people, on your will and reason."

Likewise, the legacies of Aitmatov and Altay are dependent on the extent to which the Kyrgyz people decide to keep their life lessons alive. Amidst the changing times and challenges of the twenty-first century, the inexorable march of human beings for basic rights continues. The fight to be free and the right to assemble, worship in whichever temple (or no temple), and print what you want cannot be extinguished. These instincts live on in the Kyrgyz people like swaying poplars, buffeted by the winds of authoritarianism that have blown through Central Asia for centuries and the very real gusts of religious extremism which threaten the region today.

In the midst of it all, Aitmatov and Altay are beacons to guide those willing to bear a price to be free. They are examples of courage to the current generation and, hopefully, generations to come. They fought the fight against impressive odds. Now, it's up to their countrymen to carry on. After all, nomads were never content with being contained.

NOTES

PREFACE

1. Aitmatov's works have been translated into more than 160 languages. "UNESCO Mourns Death of Famed Kyrgyz Author," UN News Centre, http://www.un.org/apps /news/story.asp?NewsID=27037#.VtxMP8fw_ow, accessed March 6, 2016.

CHAPTER 1

1. Much of the recounting of Altay's war experiences as well as his life are drawn from his memoir *The Herald of Freedom and Democracy*, published online in Kyrgyz as *Azattyk Menen Demokatiyanin Jarchysy* in Kyrgyzstan in 2010 (available at http://www .bizdin.kg), and from an article he wrote under a pseudonym for a journal published by Institute for the Study of the USSR: Kurmanbekov Abdy, "When the Paths of the Fathers are Narrow," in *Soviet Youth: Twelve Komsomol Histories*, series 1, no. 51, July 1959, ed. Nikolai K. Novak-Deker, trans. Oliver Frederiksen (Munich: Institute for the Study of the USSR, 1959). I had Altay's memoir translated into Russian. Any discrepancies between the Kyrgyz and Russian versions are my responsibility. Page-number references to Altay's memoirs refer to my Russian translation. The platoon leader's quotation is from page 23. The Russian version of Altay's memoir was serialized in full in Kyrgyzstan in the *Respublikha* newspaper from the summer of 2016 to January 2017.

2. Throughout most of his life, Kojomberdiev was known as Azamat Altay, a name he took officially in 1961, when he became a US citizen. For simplicity's sake, I refer to him as Azamat Altay.

3. Altay, *Azattyk, Menen Demokatiyanin Jarchysy*, 56.

4. L Milov, ed., *Istoria Rossi* (Moscow: Eksmo Publishing House, 2006), 515.

5. Abdy, "When the Paths of the Fathers Are Narrow," 181.

6. For example, a resident's eyewitness account of life during war in the village of Ashmyani confirms important details of Altay's imprisonment there that are described later in chapter 4: the German army occupied the village in late 1941, and Jews marked with the Star of David on their shirts worked on labor gangs during the period of Altay's confinement, thus supporting his recollection of his escape from a work gang that

included Jewish prisoners. The eyewitness account survived the war even though its author didn't. See the diary of Hinda Daul, published online at the following website: http://www.jewishgen.org/yizkor/Oshmyany/osheo59.html. Regarding other details of Altay's life during the war, a short biography from Radio Liberty lists two escapes from the Germans, not three, as recorded in Altay's memoir and detailed in this book. But the bio also contains factual errors, thus damaging its veracity. In 1991, Altay communicated with a Kyrgyz man who claimed to be the fellow prisoner Altay had escaped with during his first incarceration. In his account the man, Mirzabek Alimov, corroborated Altay's version of events with minimal discrepancies. Letter from Azamat Altay's personal files, courtesy of Gulnara Turganbaeva.

7. Beksultan Jakiev, *Azamat Altay: Povest'-essay* (Bishkek: Ala-Too Journal, 2011).

8. "The Treatment of Soviet POWS: Starvation, Disease, and Shootings, June 1941–January 1942," United States Holocaust Memorial Museum, https://www.ushmm.org/wlc/en/article.php?ModuleId=10007183.

9. Rustam Rakhmanaliev, ed., *Aitmatov: Sobranie Sochinenii v Semi Tomakh* (Bishkek: Turkestan Publishing House, 1998), 7:35.

10. "Voice from the Republics: An Interview," *Third World Quarterly* 12(1) (1990): 195.

11. The comment about the red-haired, blue-eyed combination, which is very rare, is from Chinese sources according to A. Kakeev, ed., *Istoria Kyrgyzov i Kyrgyzstana* (Bishkek: Raritet Info Publishing House, 2007), 71.

12. J. Junushaliev, ed., *Nash Kyrgyzstan* (Bishkek: Soros Fund-Kyrgzstan, 2004), 160.

13. Ahmed Rashid, *The Resurgence of Central Asia: Islam or Nationalism?* (London: Zed Books, 1994), 141.

14. Michael Rywkin, *Moscow's Muslim Challenge: Soviet Central Asia*, (Armonk, NY: M. E. Sharpe, 1982), 16. Another source claims that by 1916, three hundred thousand of the five hundred thousand Russians in Central Asia lived in the Semirech'ie region, which encompassed the enormous alpine lake called Issyk Kul. Edward Sokol, *The Revolt of 1916 in Russian Central Asia* (1954; Baltimore: Johns Hopkins University Press, 2016), 111.

15. Sokol notes in his study that the West supported Russia's conquering of Central Asia. It was in line with Western efforts to subdue Asian and African peoples, of whom a large portion were Muslim. "The suppression of slavery, incessant wars, and anarchy was regarded as a positive achievement of Western civilization as carried forward by Russia," Sokol writes. Sokol, *Revolt of 1916 in Russian Central Asia*, 8.

16. Alexandre Bennigsen, "Soviet Minority Nationalism in Historical Perspective," in *The Last Empire: Nationality and the Soviet Future*, ed. Robert Conquest (Stanford, CA: Hoover Institution Press, 1986), 135; Sokol, *Revolt of 1916 in Russian Central Asia*, 101.

17. Sokol, *Revolt of 1916 in Russian Central Asia*, 29–32. Russian and Ukrainian settlers benefited from a ruling that maintained that all conquered lands previously belonging to the Kokand Khanate had become the tsar's property. Rywkin, *Moscow's Muslim Challenge*, 16. Overall, a distressing portrait of the Kyrgyz peasant and herder under tsarist rule is presented. They were a landless proletariat, pushed to the margins of existence and forced to hire themselves out as hired labor to rich Kyrgyz, known as *bais*, and Russian settlers.

18. Petr Kokaisl and Amirbek Usmanov, *Istoria Kyrgyzstana Cherez Glaza Ochividt-sev* (Brno, Czech Republic: Tribun EU, 2012), 71–76; Sokol, *Revolt of 1916 in Russian Central Asia*, 112–117.

19. Upon requesting documents relating to the monastery massacre, my researcher was told in June 2014 at the Kyrgyz State Archives that such texts are sensitive and could

"spark interethnic conflict between the Russian minority and Kyrgyz." Email message to author, June 8, 2014. But in commemoration of the 100th anniversary of the 1916 uprising in 2016, the Russian Government opened up access to the archives by creating a web portal of documents. See http://semirechye.rusarchives.ru.

20. Diary entry, photocopied page of redacted version of surviving monk's diary, courtesy of Vladimir Plotskikh.

21. Kokaisl and Usmanov, *Istoria Kyrgyzstana Cherez Glaza Ochividtsev*, 78–79. The massacre was visible to a young monk who had stationed himself in the morning as a lookout on the church's roof and who fled down an alley before hiding in high grasses.

22. Sokol, *Revolt of 1916 in Russian Central Asia*, 124–125.

23. Ibid., 144 and 157.

24. Dungans are Chinese Muslims with origins in Xinjiang Province, China; they settled in Turkestan in the late nineteenth century.

25. Altay, *Azattyk Menen Demokatiyanin Jarchysy*, 62.

26. Sokol, *Revolt of 1916 in Russian Central Asia*, 129–133.

27. Altay, *Azattyk Menen Demokatiyanin Jarchysy*, 40.

28. A. Kakeev, ed., *Istoria Kyrgyzov i Kyrgyzstana* (Bishkek: Raritet Info Publishing House, 2007), 179. The figures are from the foreword to Sokol, *Revolt of 1916 in Russian Central Asia*, vi.

29. From the 1950s onward, the communist government of the Soviet Union preferred to sanitize the bloody uprising of 1916 by calling it a class struggle against tsarist oppression and ignoring Kyrgyz-Russian overtones. But the collapse of the Soviet Union in 1991 triggered a reexamination of the events. In independent Kyrgyzstan, statues were erected, conferences held, and books published about Ürkün, which became a national touchstone for a newly independent people. To this day, among a number of Kyrgyz, Ürkün stirs memories of a near genocide at the hands of Russians, who happened to be serving the tsar or living under his protection. But the truth is still elusive because even today the Russian government bans access to the tsarist archives in Moscow where records of the 1916 uprising itself are housed, according to the reprint of Sokol's book, *Revolt of 1916 in Russian Central Asia*, vii.

30. Altay, *Azattyk Menen Demokatiyanin Jarchysy*, 43.

31. Called *manaps, bais*, and *biis*, those wealthy landowners and influential men wielded power in prerevolutionary Kyrgyzia, mostly in the north. *Manaps* were the wealthy leaders of tribes, with the power to judge and organize fighting units. They were gradually replaced by rich, landowning *bais* at the end of the nineteenth century. *Biis* settled disputes in nomadic Kyrgyz tribes.

32. A. Berdimurat, "Islam and Communism in Turkestan," *East Turkic Review* (Institute for the Study of the USSR, Munich), no. 1 (April 1958): 71.

33. *Kymyz*, or fermented mare's milk, is the national drink of the horse-loving Kyrgyz.

CHAPTER 2

1. Tengriism calls on people to pray to the spirits around them—the Eternal Blue Sky, the Golden Light of the Sun, and other spiritual forces of nature. In fact, the Kyrgyz call Lake Issyk Kul "God Tengri's eye on earth." For them, its moving waters contain the soul of the earth.

2. Olivier Roy, introduction to *The New Central Asia: The Creation of Nations*, (New York: NYU Press, 2000), viii.

3. In fact, Kyrgyzia remained tightly tethered to Moscow as part of the Russian Soviet Republic. Only in 1936 did it shed its status as an autonomous republic to become a Soviet republic, on par with other Central Asian republics.

4. Mustafa Chokayev, "Turkestan and the Soviet Regime," *Journal of the Royal Central Asian Society* (1931): 403–420.

5. Peter Hopkirk, *Setting the East Ablaze: Lenin's Dream of an Empire in Asia* (London: John Murray, 1984), 22.

6. Ibid., 25.

7. Chokayev, "Turkestan and the Soviet Regime," 409.

8. Likbez, the campaign to eliminate illiteracy, started in 1919. Schools were established and teachers trained all over the Soviet Union. Between 1914 and 1937, the Kyrgyz Soviet Socialist Republic had the highest percentage growth in the number of students studying in any of the fifteen Soviet republics. The number of students in schools jumped from just 7,000 in 1914 to 227,000 in 1937. By 1938 in Kyrgyzia, just twenty years after the start of Likbez, the literacy rate had jumped to 70 percent from three percent, with most students learning Russian and their native Kyrgyz, an impressive result that deserves commendation. Edward Allworth, *Central Asian Publishing and the Rise of Nationalism* (New York: New York Public Library, 1965), 20.

9. Roza Aitmatova, *Belie Stranitsi Istorii* (Bishkek: Biyitik, 2009), 242.

10. Advocating for completing the revolution inside the Soviet Union, Stalin broke with his chief opponent, Leon Trotsky, who believed it was important to foster a worldwide revolution to spur the communist transition at home. Stalin's drive to forcibly collectivize agriculture was a key part of his strategy to give priority to development of communism inside the Soviet Union. State control of agriculture, Stalin reasoned, would provide the resources—through state capture of all agricultural products—for a speeded-up industrialization process that was needed to catapult the Soviet Union into the ranks of leading industrialized countries. This policy meant that Kyrgyzia, as an agricultural area, played second fiddle to the steel mills, metallurgical plants, and factories of Russia and other republics.

11. Aitmatova, *Belie Stranitsi Istorii*, 182.

12. Kokaisl and Usmanov, *Istoria Kyrgyzstana Cherez Glaza Ochividtsev*, 206.

13. Kamoludin Abdullaev with Ravshan Nazarov, "The Ferghana Valley under Stalin," in *Ferghana Valley: The Heart of Central Asia*, ed. S. Frederick Starr. (Armonk, NY: M. E. Sharpe, 2011), 120–121.

14. Aitmatova, *Belie Stranitsi Istorii*, 253–254.

15. Zev Katz, ed., *Handbook of Major Soviet Nationalities* (New York: Free Press, 1975), 241.

16. In the 1950s as part of de-Stalinization, an investigation—which concluded that evidence in security files was weak or nonexistent—reversed criminal sentences against those accused of membership in the Socialist Turan Party. By 1989, all accused of membership in the STP had been rehabilitated. In the 1990s, the State Security Services of the independent Kyrgyz Republic concluded that the STP never existed as a party. Rather, to provide a justification for purges or for score settling on the local level, Soviet security and judicial organs conflated the disgruntlement of individuals, some of whom were openly dissatisfied with the policies of the Soviet government, into existence of the

Social Turan Party. F. Ashin, V. Alpatov, and D. Hasilov, *Repressirovanaya Turkologiya* (Moscow: Russian Academy of Sciences, 2002), 250–251.

17. Kirov, in fact, was a rival to Stalin and had polled better than Stalin at the elections to the Central Committee at the Seventeenth Party Congress in early 1934.

18. Kurmanbekov Abdy, "When the Paths of the Fathers are Narrow," 5.

19. Frunze, renamed from Pishpek by the Soviets, was the capital city of Kyrgyz Soviet Socialist Republic. It was named after the Moldovan general who subjugated the last remaining rebels there in 1920.

20. Azamat Altay, "Kyrgyzia during the Great Purges," *Central Asian Review* (1964): 103.

21. Aitmatova, *Belie Stranitsi Istorii*, 169.

22. The Institute of Red Professors was a graduate-level educational institution in the Marxist social sciences, which prepared party leaders in communist ideology.

23. Interview with Ilgiz Aitmatov, June 20, 2013.

24. The Tatars are closely linked with the Mongols, and the name eventually became synonymous with *Mongol*. Originating as a steppe tribe near present-day Mongolia, they were conquered by the Mongols, participated in the Mongol conquests of Central Asia and much of Russia in the thirteenth-century Russia, and eventually settled in Russia under the banner of the Golden Horde. Tatars, whose home republic is in the middle of Russia, were at the vanguard of the Russian expansion into Central Asia in the 1860s.

25. David MacKenzie and Michael Curran, *A History of the Soviet Union* (Chicago: Dorsey Press, 1986), 187.

26. Azamat Altay, *Kyrgyzia during the Great Purges*, 36.

27. Kurmanbekov Abdy, "When the Paths of the Fathers are Narrow," 21.

28. Aitmatova, *Belie Stranitsi Istorii*, 172.

29. Ibid., 169–173.

CHAPTER 3

1. The Sheker tribe is one of the forty rays emanating from the sun on the flag of the Kyrgyz Republic. The forty rays denote the forty tribes united by Manas in his quest to defend the Kyrgyz people from outside invaders.

2. Aitmatova, *Belie Stranitsi Istorii*, 80–81.

3. After just a few weeks in Kyrgyzia, Khodakov moved on to Siberia and the Far East, where his articles served as a signal to intensify the purges in those places as well. He was a one-man wrecking machine.

4. Kokaisl and Usmanov, *Istoria Kyrgyzstana Cherez Glaza Ochividtsev*, 242.

5. Interview with Arslan Anarbaev, December 1, 2009.

6. While letters written in Russia from inmates were censored, those written in Kyrgyz escaped censorship, thus allowing Ryskulbek to write openly about his prison conditions.

7. *Talkan* is a hard wheat-based concoction made to withstand long journeys, similar to US Civil War–era hardtack.

8. Aitmatova, *Belie Stranitsi Istorii*, 33–34.

9. MacKenzie and Curran, *A History of the Soviet Union*, 184–185.

10. Kokaisl and Usmanov, *Istoria Kyrgyzstana Cherez Glaza Ochividtsev*, 205.

11. Interview with Japarbek Dosaliev, June 22, 2013.

12. Today, in testament to its important place in the nomadic history of the Kyrgyz people, the *tunduk* makes up the center of the flag of the Kyrgyz Republic.

13. Chingiz Aitmatov, *Detstvo* (Bishkek: Turar Publishing House, 2011), 14–15.

14. Kenneth Wimmel, *Alluring Target* (Washington, DC: Trackless Sands Press, 1996), xiv.

15. Aitmatova, *Belie Stranitsi Istorii*, 202-203.

16. Aitmatov, *Aitmatov: Sobranie Sochinenii v Semi Tomakh*, 7:20.

CHAPTER 4

1. The story of the stolen cow is drawn from three sources: volume 7 of *Aitmatov: Sobranie Sochinenii v Semi Tomakh, Detstvo*, and *Belie Stranitsi Istorii*.

2. Abdyldazhan Akmataliev, *Izbrannoe* (Bishkek: Sham Publishing, 1997), 266.

3. Abdullaev and Nazarov, "Ferghana Valley under Stalin," 135–136.

4. Poem written by Azamat Altay, from Azamat Altay's personal files, courtesy of Gulnara Turganbaeva.

5. Soviet POWs were decidedly not welcome home, whether or not they had surrendered willfully. A Red Army regulation declared that Soviet soldiers taken captive against their will be considered traitors. Stalin backed this up with Order No. 270 issued on August 16, 1941—just weeks before Altay's capture—which equated surrender with desertion. The Soviet government's attitude toward its own POWs blatantly contravened international law, which states that military captivity is not a crime. To add to the misery of Soviet POWs, Stalin refused to send them food packets through the Red Cross and denied their families food rations. That's why it became common for Soviet POWs to say that captivity spelled troubled for many. See "Stalin's War against His Own Troops: The Tragic Fate of Soviet Prisoners of War in German Captivity," Institute for Historical Review, http://www.ihr.org/jhr/v14/Teplyakov.html.

6. *Istoria Rossi*, 570.

CHAPTER 5

1. Roman Gul, *Ya Unyos Rossiyu, Apologia Emigratsii, Rossiya v Amerike*, (New York: BSG Press, 2001), 3:121.

2. *Azattyk Menen Demokatiyanin Jarchysy*, 45–46.

3. "Winston Churchill's Iron Curtain Speech," http://history1900s.about.com/od/churchillwinston/a/Iron-Curtain.htm, accessed October 18, 2015.

4. These days in Russia under Vladimir Putin's control, Nikolai Berdyaev is interpreted differently—less as a freedom-seeking thinker and more as a conservative philosopher who preached the values of a strong and orderly state.

5. Chokai died mysteriously in 1941. His death came after he stopped cooperating with the Nazis on the establishment of a Nazi-supported Turkestan legion, made up of Soviet Central Asian POWs, to fight for the Germans. "Kazakhs Film Life of Mustafa Chokai, Turkestan's First Defender," Window on Eurasia, http://windowoneurasia

.blogspot.com/2008/03/window-on-eurasia-kazakhs-film-life-of.html, accessed June 29, 2017.

6. George F. Kennan, *Memoirs, 1925–1950* (New York: Pantheon Books, 1967), 354–367.

7. It's likely that the Committee for the Liberation of Turkestan received its funding from the Office of Policy Coordination (OPC), a secret agency in the US government created shortly after World War II to counter the Soviet Union. OPC was later folded into the CIA.

8. Arch Puddington, *Broadcasting Freedom* (Lexington: University Press of Kentucky, 2000), 24–29 and 165–188. Puddington writes that in a sign of the secrecy under which the anticommunist struggle was waged in the United States, no mention of CIA funding was mentioned. Radio Liberty employees were told funding came from wealthy individuals, and most listeners believed the radio station was funded by the US government. The CIA's cover story about funding held up in the United States for close to two decades because a compliant US media did not challenge the claim. When it came out that Radio Liberty was being funded by the CIA, the outcry wasn't so much over CIA funding but over deception of the US public—that US citizens had been duped into believing that Radio Liberty's contribution to keeping hope alive behind Iron Curtain was due to one source when it was actually coming from another.

9. Puddington, *Broadcasting Freedom*, 154–161; and A. Ross Johnson, *Radio Free Europe and Radio Liberty: The CIA Years and Beyond* (Stanford, CA: Stanford University Press, 2010), 33–34.

10. "Soobshchenie o sozdanii Koordinatsiyonovo Tsentra antibolshevitskoi borbi," *Turk Eli Journal*, September–October 1952, 9.

11. Puddington, *Broadcasting Freedom*, 215–217.

12. Interview with Beksultan Jakiev, June 17, 2013.

13. Puddington, *Broadcasting Freedom*, 225.

14. Stemming from restrictive US immigration policy from the late nineteenth and early twentieth century, US immigration laws in the 1950s contained quotas on the number of Asians who could immigrate to the United States. Altay may well have been caught up in that net. He also had no relatives in the United States to help him qualify to immigrate.

15. US authorities were particularly stringent about participation in the Nazi-sponsored Turkestan Legion, a collection of Soviet refugees and POWs whom the Germans trained and turned back against the Soviets as a fighting force. Those who had fought in the Turkestan Legion, including some of the men Altay knew in Europe in the post-war period, were unable to immigrate to the United States. My research turned up no evidence that Altay himself was ever in the Turkestan Legion. The fact that his indictment for desertion from the Soviet Army and Soviet propaganda attacks in the 1980s didn't include this accusation provide some support for the case he avoided being caught up in the legion.

16. "Khronika," *Novoye Russkoye Slovo*, September 12, 1956. The newspaper's Wednesday edition carried news of arrivals expected that week, including Altay. In fact, his plane from Germany was delayed a day because of weather, so he officially set foot in America on September 15, 1956.

CHAPTER 6

1. *Istoria Kyrgyzov i Kyrgyzstana*, 256–258.

2. "Entertainment in Frunze 1963–1964," *Central Asian Review* 12(4) (1964): 280–291.

3. [Eurasia] Interview with Kyrgyz President Roza Otunbayeva, https://wikileaks .org/gifiles/docs/39/3991688_-eurasia-interview-with-kyrgyz-president-roza-otunbaye va-.html, accessed January 7, 2016.

4. Proclaimed in the 1930s, socialist realism was characterized by a positive hero who, with the help and inspiration of the Communist Party, overcame obstacles to help society in some public way. Even after Stalin's death, the genre still held sway among conservative ideologues and writers, who continued to espouse its principles up until the 1980s. Joseph Mozur, *Parables from the Past: The Prose Fiction of Chingiz Aitmatov* (Pittsburgh: University of Pittsburgh Press, 1995), 180n18.

5. About the same time as other "minipurges" in the Soviet Union, the Manas purge in Kyrgyzia claimed the life of at least one victim, Tashim Baizhiev, one of the three men jailed, who died in prison in 1952. The other two men, Ziyash Bektenov and Tazabek Samanchin, were freed from prison during destalinization in the mid to late 1950s but never regained their former stature. *Repressirovanaya Turkologia*, 282–288.

6. Among those purged were Kasym Tynystanov and Russian Turkologist Evgeni Polivanov, who was arrested in August 1937. Polivanov was charged with being a Japanese spy and executed in January 1938 in Frunze. He was an unusually gifted linguist who spoke eighteen languages. He was also, for twenty-seven years, a heroin addict, whose addiction didn't seem to affect his scholarly accomplishments. Like many others unfairly imprisoned, he was tortured in captivity. Polivanov was one of several Russians who worked in Kyrgyzia as specialists in the Turkic language. They were well-respected by the Kyrgyz, and their work counters the Communist Party–influenced Kyrgyz-Russian split over language and cultural issues during the divisive years of the 1930s to 1950s. Polivanov was posthumously rehabilitated in 1963.

7. The conference in Frunze actually ended in a deadlock. Eventually the issue was resolved according to Moscow's will, and the epos was condemned by the Academy of Science of the Soviet Union for its "pan-Islamism, bourgeois-nationalism, military adventurism, and disdain for the toiling masses." The epic was manipulated for political purposes, with parts reinterpreted to undermine Kyrgyz nationalism. For example, Manas's unification of Kyrgyz tribes was compared to the unification of different nations under Soviet communism. References to Manas, or to the epic itself, as symbols of the Kyrgyz nation were forbidden, and most of the epic was removed from classrooms. But, due in part to Auezov's speech, Manas was not banned like its "blacklisted" Kazakh and Uzbek counterparts. Joseph Mozur, "Doffing Mankurt's Cap: Chingiz Aitmatov's 'The Day Lasts More Than a Hundred Years' and the Turkic National Heritage," paper written for the Carl Beck Papers in Russian and East European Studies, University of Pittsburgh Center for Russian and Eastern European Studies, September 1987, 18–19; and Ewa Wasilewska, "The Rebirth of Kyrgyzstan," *Saudi Aramco World* 47(3) (May–June 1996).

8. Interview with Chingiz Aitmatov, September 2, 2007.

9. Chingiz Aitmatov, "Ya Otkril Svoiu Zemlyu," *Literaturnie Kyrgyzstan*, June 1978, 107.

10. Reflecting his unsteady position as Soviet leader and the fact the he, too, was compromised as a former aide to Stalin who had carried out purges in the Ukraine in 1938, Khrushchev did not implicate or bring to trial anyone for the crimes he outlined in his secret speech. The personality cult, not individuals, was responsible.

11. Aitmatova, *Belie Stranitsi Istorii*, 217–218.

12. Ibid., 223.

13. Untitled biography of Chingiz Aitmatov, Hoover Institution Archives, box 11672, Editor's file, Kyrgyzstan, Personalities, Chyngyz Aitmatov.

14. Chingiz Aitmatov, *Detstvo*, 93.

15. Tvardovski was Aitmatov's patron—or patron saint—in Moscow, a man of status and respect who profoundly influenced Soviet letters in the 1950s and 1960s and who could shepherd controversial works through the Soviet system. Aitmatov called him "the conscience of the country." Chingiz Aitmatov, *Detstvo*, 96.

16. Details on *Jamilya* are from Abdyldazhan Akmataliev, *Izbrannoe* (Bishkek: Sham Publishing, 1997), 276–277.

17. Louis Aragon, "Samaya Prekrasnaya na svete povest' o lyubvi," *Kultura i Zhizn*, no. 7 (1959), 39–43.

CHAPTER 7

1. Frederick Kempe, *Berlin 1961: Kennedy, Khrushchev and the Most Dangerous Place on Earth*, (New York: Berkley Books, 2011), 18. In addition, Leon Uris's novel *Armageddon*, about the blockade of Berlin in 1948, contains graphic accounts of rapes by Soviet soldiers, whom he describes as Mongols.

2. Altay had a working knowledge of six languages—English, French, German, Kyrgyz, Russian, and Turkish—but he was always most comfortable speaking Kyrgyz. He was, in learning foreign languages, a jack of all trades but master of none.

3. Selected Books and Assorted Atomica, Conelrad Read Alert, http://www.conelrad.com/books/flyleaf.php?id=379_0_1_0_M, accessed March 17, 2015.

4. Kempe, *Berlin 1961*, xvi; Charles Bohlen, *Witness to History: 1929–1969* (New York: W. w. Norton and Co., 1973), 483–484.

5. A Kazakh doctor whom Altay befriended in the 1960s confirmed that Altay was on the Soviet blacklist. Saim Balmukhanov, an oncologist who spent six months in New York on an exchange, found out from the Soviet embassy that Altay was persona non grata, according to Altay's memoirs.

6. Some people who knew Altay contend that he was on the CIA's payroll and employed occasionally to interact with Soviet Central Asians. However, a request through the CIA's Freedom of Information Act failed to turn up any evidence he was ever a member of the agency. The search, though, was not exhaustive, as some documents still were classified, leaving the CIA to conclude that it can "neither confirm or deny the existence or nonexistence of records" related to whether Altay ever worked for the CIA. Author correspondence with information and privacy coordinator, Central Intelligence Agency, June 10, 2016.

7. Religious clerics in the Soviet Union, be they Russian Orthodox priests or Muslim preachers, were carefully monitored by the KGB, and a good number either willingly cooperated or were coerced into cooperating. It is highly likely that Jeyenbekov, to gain

permission to travel abroad—particularly to the hajj—had to have been working for the KGB. His reappearance in a Soviet propaganda campaign against Altay in the 1980s further strengthens the case for his KGB affiliation.

8. Altay's correspondence with the chairman of the collective farm is from the personal files of Venera Djumataeva.

9. Interview with Edward Kasinec, September 23, 2014, and *An Idiot System for Intelligence*, CIA Historical Review Program, release in full, September 22, 1993, accessed March 17, 2015, https://www.cia.gov/library/center-for-the-study-of-intelligence/kent -csi/vol6no4/html/v06i4a03p_0001.htm.

10. "CIA Financed Book Distribution Programs: Part One, Free Europe Committee," *Cold War Radio Vignettes* (blog), http://coldwarradios.blogspot.com, October 4, 2011, accessed February 9, 2015; Adam Bernstein, "Isaac Patch, Who Led CIA-Financed Program to Distribute Books in the Soviet Union, Dies," *Washington Post*, June 9, 2014, https://www.washingtonpost.com/entertainment/books/isaac-patch-who-led-cia -financed-program-to-distribute-books-in-the-soviet-union-dies/2014/06/09/3aea5fe2 -efdc-11e3-9ebc-2ee6f81ed217_story.html?utm_term=.0d5229a52a85, accessed June 30, 2017.

11. "George C. Minden, 85, Dies; Led a Cold War of Words," *New York Times*, April 23, 2006.

12. Bruce Pannier, "Edward Allworth: the Last of the Great Masters of Central Asian Studies," *Qishlog Ovozi* (blog), Radio Free Europe/Radio Liberty, https://www.rferl .org/a/qishloq-ovozi-scholar-wallworth-obituary-central-asia/28073914.html, accessed June 30, 2017.

13. Interview with Beksultan Jakiev, June 17, 2013.

14. Information on the pavilions at Expo 67 is drawn from: http://britton.disted .camosun.bc.ca/expo67/unitedstates.html and http://www.westland.net/expo67/map-docs/ussr.htm, accessed August 12, 2015.

15. Azamat Altay, *Azattyk Menen Demokatiyanin Jarchysy*, 78–79.

CHAPTER 8

1. Transcription from documentary film called *Chingiz Aitmatov*, directed by Izya Gershtein, Kyrgyzfilm, 1968.

2. Aitmatov, *Aitmatov: Sobranie Sochinenii v Semi Tomakh*, 6:544.

3. Vaganova (1879–1951) is best known for combining French, Italian, Russian, and Soviet ballet into what is known as the Vaganova method, one of the most popular techniques for teaching classical ballet in the world today. In her honor, the Leningrad Choreographic Institute, where she taught for thirty years, was renamed the Vaganova Academy of Russian Ballet in 1991 (see the website http://www.vaganova.ru/page_en .php?id=298&pid=272).

4. Bermet Mambetalieva, *Neyuteryannie Pisma ili Razgovor na Dzherjinke* (Bishkek: Turar Publishing House, 2010), 21–22.

5. Mambetalieva, *Neyuteryannie Pisma ili Razgovor na Dzherjinke*, 106.

6. Aitmatov closely followed the Soviet writer Mikhail Sholokov, a mentor of sorts and favorite writer. Sholokhov's novel *The Fate of a Man* also deals with the destructive side of war and its heart-wrenching toll on people affected by it.

7. Aitmatov, *Aitmatov: Sobranie Sochinenii v Semi Tomakh*, 1:375.

8. Ibid., 1:392. For a good discussion of *Materinskoe Pole*, see Mozur, *Parables from the Past*, 35–37.

9. Aitmatov, *Aitmatov: Sobranie Sochinenii v Semi Tomakh*, 1:331.

10. Ibid., 1:320.

11. Mozur, *Parables from the Past*, 34–35. According to Yevtushenko, several years after he signed the letter, Aitmatov asked Yevtushenko to forgive him. Yevtushenko believed that Aitmatov's allies in the Moscow literary establishment were able to help him fend off cultural conservatives in Kyrgyzia. Mozur, *Parables from the Past*, 180n19.

12. Edward Allworth, ed., *The Nationality Question in Soviet Central Asia* (London: Praeger Publishers, 1973), 20–23.

13. *Tamizdat*, which in Russian literally means "published there," refers to writing and works of literature published outside the Soviet Union and smuggled back in, while *samizdat*, which means "self-published," refers to writing circulated illegally inside the country, usually in typewritten copies.

14. A. Akmataliev and H. Isaev, eds., *Chingiz Aitmatov: Vsyelennaya Sotvorena Lyubovyu* (Bishkek: Chingiz Aitmatov Institute of Language and Literature, 2016), 90–91.

15. The Aral Sea would in the ensuing years recede dramatically as its water was drained off for cotton cultivation in Uzbekistan, creating one of the signature ecological disasters in the Soviet Union.

16. Aitmatov, *Aitmatov: Sobranie Sochinenii v Semi Tomakh*, 7:546.

17. Ibid., 7:545.

18. Mambetalieva, *Neyuteryannie Pisma ili Razgovor na Dzherjinke*, 168.

19. Aitmatov, *Aitmatov: Sobranie Sochinenii v Semi Tomakh*, 2:60–61.

20. Mambetalieva, *Neyuteryannie Pisma ili Razgovor na Dzherjinke*, 166.

21. Ibid., 142.

22. Aitmatov never divorced his first wife or married Beishenalieva. He existed in a guilt-plagued limbo that he tried to assuage by giving Kerez the house in Bishkek he had built with the Lenin Prize money and his car.

23. Aitmatov, *Aitmatov: Sobranie Sochinenii v Semi Tomakh*, 6:207.

24. Chingiz Aitmatov, "Nebo i Slovo," *Slovo Kyrgyzstana*, September 12, 2006, 6 and 11.

CHAPTER 9

1. Box 1, folder 1, Mirra Ginsburg Papers, Rare Book and Manuscript Library, Columbia University.

2. Joseph Mozur argues that in *The White Ship* Aitmatov is harkening back to pre-Soviet times—before the mass influx of Russians—when the Kyrgyz lived more in harmony with their surroundings. Mozur, *Parables from the Past*, 71. Mozur, the author of the best examination of Aitmatov's work to date in the United States, says that Altay himself confirmed to him when they met that Soviet censors in Moscow missed much when reviewing Aitmatov's works because of lack of knowledge of Kyrgyz. On a research trip to Bishkek in 1992, Mozur met with Kyrgyz Aitmatov scholar Abdyldazhan Akmataliev, who confirmed that informed readers could see that behind the name Orozkul was the bigger idea of the Kyrgyz's cultural and social subjugation to Russia. Akmataliev

pointed out the similarity in spelling to *orus-kul* in Kyrgyz, which means "Russian slave." The theme of subjugation would be driven home by Aitmatov a few years later with the mankurt reference in his novel *The Day Lasts Longer Than a Century*. Aitmatov would continue the pattern of signaling meaning through names in his late 1980s novel *The Executioner's Block*.

3. Tvardovski would succumb to cancer in the fall of 1971, after treatments in the same elite Moscow hospital as Beishenalieva. In fact, on visits to Moscow in 1971 Aitmatov would visit with both of them over tea in Beishenalieva's room.

4. Hedrick Smith, *The Russians* (New York: Ballantine Books, 1976), 602.

5. "Pismo v Redaktsiyu Gazeti Pravda," *Literaturnaya Gazeta*, September 5, 1973.

6. Robert Kaiser, *Russia: The People and the Power* (New York: Washington Square Press, 1984), 399.

7. Box 1, folder 1, Mirra Ginsburg Papers, Rare Book and Manuscript Library, Columbia University.

8. Information about the borough of Queens is from http://en.wikipedia.org/wiki/Flushing,_Queens

9. *Aitmatov: Sobranie Sochinenii v Semi Tomakh*, 1:183.

10. Interview with Beksultan Jakiev, June 17, 2013.

11. Mambetalieva, *Neyuteryannie Pisma ili Razgovor na Dzherjinke*, 151.

12. *Aitmatov: Sobranie Sochinenii v Semi Tomakh*, 6:546.

13. Michael Parks, "Kyrgyzia Gets Low Mark for Ideology," *Baltimore Sun*, July 3, 1973.

14. "Soviet Writer, Though Critical, Is Favored," *New York Times*, June 4, 1974.

15. "Writer in Soviet Union Defends Suicide of Story's Hero," *New York Times*, July 29, 1970.

16. *Kazakh/Kirghiz Studies Bulletin*, Central Asia Studies Program, University of Washington, accessed October 4, 2007, 3, http://depts.washington.edu/centasia/Kyrgyzbulletin.htm

17. Folder 4, Collection #C0010, Zelda Fichandler Papers, Special Collections and Archives, George Mason University Libraries.

18. Ibid.

19. Ibid.

20. Alan Schneider, "We Opened in Moscow, Then on to . . ." *New York Times*, November 18, 1973.

21. Schneider, "We opened in Moscow, then on to. . ." Section 2. P. 1.

22. Folder 4, Collection #C0010, Fichandler Papers, Special Collections and Archives, George Mason University Libraries.

23. Box 1, folder 1, Mirra Ginsburg Papers, Rare Book and Manuscript Library, Columbia University.

24. Jack Kroll, "Ascent and Dissent," *Newsweek*, June 30, 1975, 44.

25. Richard Coe, "An Absorbing 'Ascent,'" *Washington Post*, June 5, 1975, C1.

26. Interview with Zelda Fichandler, January 12, 2015.

27. Don Shirley, "Aitmatov: An Ascent at Arena," *Washington Post*, June 30, 1975.

28. Jack Kroll, "Ascent and Dissent," 44.

29. Peter Osnos, "There's More to Russia Than Americans Recognize: The Russia Americans Ignore," *Washington Post*, June 19, 1977.

30. "A New Boris Exemplifies Individuality at Bolshoi," *New York Times*, July 17, 1975.

31. Altay, *Azattyk Menen Demokatiyanin Jarchysy*, 127.

32. Ibid., 126–127.

33. *Aitmatov: Sobranie Sochinenii v Semi Tomakh*, 7:304.

34. Interview with Gulnara Turganbaeva, January 23, 2016.

35. Letter dated August 9, 1975, courtesy of Venera Djumataeva.

36. The meeting with Alapaev, including the dialogue in the prison cell, is a composite drawn from three sources: Vladimir Plotskikh, "Törökul, Otets Chingiza," in *Törökul Aitmatov* (Bishkek: Ilim Publishing House, 1993) 55; Aitmatova, *Belie Stranitsi Istorii*, 30–34; interview with Roza Aitmatov, June 16, 2013.

37. Aitmatova, *Belie Stranitsi Istorii*, 37.

CHAPTER 10

1. It's not clear why the bomb was placed outside the Czechoslovak Service when it was the broadcasts of the Romanian Service that had triggered the bomb plot. But the overall goal of striking at RFE/RL was achieved. Carlos the Jackal was reportedly paid $1 million for the operation. The bombing eventually turned out to be an embarrassment for his Hungarian hosts, and as the 1980s wore on, Carlos was forced to move from place to place before landing in Yemen in the early 1990s. He was arrested in 1994 and is serving life in prison in France. Richard Cummings, "Special Feature: The 1981 Bombing of RFE/RL," *Radio Free Europe/Radio Liberty*, February 9, 1996, accessed April 15, 2015, http://www.rferl.org/content/article/1080043.html.

2. Two more reasons soldiers from Soviet Central Asia predominated in the initial invasion forces were conscripts from Central Asia, because of a weaker grasp of Russian, were overrepresented in infantry and construction battalions, which entered Afghanistan in the first waves, and Afghanistan's proximity to Soviet Central Asia meant that it made logistical sense to send troops from military districts in Uzbekistan and Kazakhstan. Jiayi Zhou, "The Muslim Battalions: Soviet Central Asians in the Soviet-Afghan War," *Journal of Slavic Military Studies* 25 (2012): 302–328.

3. "Bektash Iliyasov: KGB tapshirmasin atkara albadim," *Radio Free Europe/Radio Liberty*, accessed April 8, 2015, http://www.azattyk.org/content/kyrgyzstan_azattyk_anniversary/24888974.html

4. "A Karavan Idyot," *Sovietskaya Kyrgyzia*, February 5, 1982 (translated from Kyrgyz to Russian).

5. "Tshchetni Potugi otshchpentstev," *Sovietskaya Kyrgyzia*, March 23, 1982 (translated from Kyrgyz to Russian).

6. "Prezrenie," *Sovietskaya Kyrgyzia*, October 29, 1982.

7. "Prime suspect in Georgi Markov 'umbrella poison' murder tracked down to Austria," *The Telegraph*, March 23, 2013, accessed January 15, 2016, http://www.telegraph.co.uk/news/uknews/crime/9949856/Prime-suspect-in-Georgi-Markov-umbrella-poison-murder-tracked-down-to-Austria.html. See also Christopher Andrew and Oleg Gordievsky, *KGB: The Inside Story* (New York: HarperCollins, 1990), 644–645.

8. "A Karavan Idyot."

9. Interview with Azamat Tynaev, June 19, 2013.

10. At the time when he was preparing to write *The Day*, Aitmatov was overseeing the publication of a version of *Manas* recited by the famous *manaschi* Sagimbai Orozbekov.

During the course of that work, he came across a passage in the epic in which Kalmyk khans, intent on preventing Manas from becoming a future leader, discuss a plan to capture and torture him by covering his head with a piece of animal hide. *Chingiz Aitmatov: Izbrannoe* (Publishing House Kyrgyzstan, Frunze, 1983), 590–591; *Chingiz Aitmatov: Sobrannie sochinii v semi tomakh*, 6:282–284.

11. For a good discussion of *The Day Lasts Longer Than a Century*, see Mozur's *Parables from the Past*, 96–129; and Peter Brampton Koelle, "Chingiz Aitmatov: A Reflection on Soviet Rule Through Memory," in *Russian Language Journal* 54, nos. 177–179 (Winter–Spring 2000): 139–160.

12. Just five years after the collapse of the Soviet Union, in a discussion with a Kazakh colleague, Aitmatov confirmed the bold stance he had taken in *The Day*. "The totalitarian regime, while it governed, put an ideological hide cap on society as a whole, on its world view, yours and mine and all of us. This was done by collaring us, with the goal of subjugating us to one ruling regime." *Chingiz Aitmatov: Sobrannie sochinii v semi tomakh*, 6:284.

13. Eugene Parta, *Discovering the Hidden Listener: An Assessment of Radio Liberty and Western Broadcasting to the USSR during the Cold War* (Stanford, CA: Hoover Institution Press, 2007), xix.

14. Arch Puddington, *Broadcasting Freedom* (Lexington: University Press of Kentucky, 2000), 174.

15. Ibid., 170.

16. Ibid., 264

17. "Sovetskaya Literatura v borbe za Kommunisma i yeyo zadachi v svete reshenie 26-ovo syezda KPSS," *Literaturnaya Gazeta*, July 1, 1981.

18. Bohdan Nahaylo and Victor Swoboda, *Soviet Disunion: A History of the Nationalities Problem in the USSR* (New York: Free Press, 1990), 214.

19. Aitmatov, *Aitmatov: Sobranie Sochinenii v Semi Tomakh*, 7:406.

20. Ibid., 7:403.

21. Interview with Osmanakun Ibraimov, June 13, 2013.

22. Aitmatov, *Aitmatov: Sobranie Sochinenii v Semi Tomakh*, 7:393.

23. Mozur makes the point in *Parables from the Past* that Aitmatov intended that the guilty party in *The Day* be the Soviet Union. Indeed, Aitmatov's subplot about the *mankurt* points to Soviet culpability for isolating itself from the world through militarized borders, jammed radio broadcasts, and control over the movements of its citizens. Before Soviet censors forced Aitmatov to rewrite the ending, the novel was supposed to conclude with the missiles firing from the Soviet steppe, sending Edigei, his camel, and his dog scurrying for cover, making the implication about Soviet responsibility clear.

24. Speech by Imretraud Gutschke at Library of Congress symposium commemorating Chingiz Aitmatov, December 4, 2008.

25. Included in the published version of *The Day* was the ending Aitmatov was forced to write—Abutalip dying of a heart attack in a jail cell. In 1990, in the more open atmosphere spawned by Gorbachev, Aitmatov published his original version, in which Abutalip is driven to suicide by his tragic predicament.

26. Interview with Beksultan Jakiev, June 17, 2013.

27. Interview with Enders Wimbush, January 30, 2015.

28. In the 1980s and 1990s, Aitmatov would explore religious themes intensively in his works, giving characters religious backgrounds and holding a dialogue with a prominent Buddhist leader in Japan, Daisuke Ikeda.

29. Chingiz Aitmatov, *The Day Lasts More Than a Hundred Years*, trans. John French (Bloomington: Indiana University Press, 1983), 342. Interestingly, in November 1983 two Kyrgyz academics lauded Aitmatov on the pages of *Izvestiya* for introducing into socialist realism "the spiritual world of the contemporary man." It was a stilted way of saying Aitmatov had made Edigei a living and breathing human being. Some years later in the 1990s, Aitmatov would say, "God is not somewhere in the clouds but in the soul of man." A. Akmataliev and H. Isaev, eds., *Chingiz Aitmatov: The Universe Created with Love* (Bishkek: Chingiz Aitmatov Institute of Language and Literature, 2016), 118.

30. Interview with Azamat Tynaev, June 19, 2013.

31. Altay did receive financial remuneration, but it was a onetime advance payment in line with the accepted practice of translating holy books, which forbids royalty payments. E-mail correspondence with Boris Arapovic, May 15, 2015.

32. Jack Weatherford, *Genghis Khan and the Making of the Modern World* (New York: Broadway Press, 2004), 29.

33. The dispute was over the true nature of Christ—whether Jesus was in the belief of the Nestorians two entirely separate people, one human and one divine, or, as the Orthodox understood, one person, human and divine at the same time.

34. V. Voropaev, ed., *Podvodnie taini i neraskretie zagadki Issyk-kulya* (Bishkek: Kyrgyz-Russian Slavyanski University, 2010), 17.

35. Azamat Altay, *Azattyk Menen Demokatiyanin Jarchysy*, 131.

36. Mikhail Gorbachev, *Perestroika I Novoe Myshlenie dlya nashei strani I dlya vsevo mira* (Moscow: Politzdat, 1987), 78.

CHAPTER 11

1. Information on Matthias Rust's flight is from Don Oberdorfer, *The Turn: From the Cold War to a New Era* (New York: Touchstone, 1991), 228–230.

2. "Tsena Prozreniya," *Ogonyok*, July 1987, no. 28, in *Aitmatov: Sobranie Sochinenii v Semi Tomakh*, 7:500–501.

3. *Aitmatov: Sobranie Sochinenii v Semi Tomakh*, 7:450.

4. Chingiz Aitmatov, *Plakha*, in *Aitmatov: Sobranie Sochinenii v Semi Tomakh*, 4:97.

5. "Miller's Russian Tale: Arthur Miller Talks to Michael Ratcliffe about Power, Gorbachov [sic] and 'The Archbishop's Ceiling,'" *Observer*, October 26, 1986, 23.

6. Ahmed Rashid, *The Resurgence of Central Asia: Islam or Nationalism?* (London: Zed Books, 1994), 141.

7. Some people contend the lake never freezes because of a high salt content produced by evaporation. With water flowing into the lake but no tributaries carrying water out, evaporation occurs naturally.

8. Mikhail Gorbachev, *Memoirs of Mikhail Gorbachev* (New York: Doubleday, 1995), 200.

9. *Aitmatov: Sobranie Sochinenii v Semi Tomakh*, 7:430.

10. Ibid., 7:496.

11. Ibid., 7:490.

12. Ibid., 6:356.

13. Nahaylo and Swoboda, *Soviet Disunion*, 236.

14. *Aitmatov: Sobranie Sochinenii v Semi Tomakh*, 7:494.

15. Mozur, "Doffing Mankurt's Cap," 12.

16. Nahaylo and Swoboda, *Soviet Disunion*, 256.

17. E. Kaptagaev, ed., *Kasym Tynystanov: Talant i Sudba* (Bishkek: Central State Archives of Kyrgyz Republic, 2011), 353–356.

18. *Istoria Kyrgyzov i Kyrgyzstana*, 275.

19. Beksultan Jakiev, "Azamat Altai: Povest/Essai," *Ala Too Journal* (2011): 42. Jakypov, who like Altay remained in Europe after the war, started to work for Radio Liberty a few years after Altay and worked there for many decades, including the 1980s when Altay returned.

20. Puddington, *Broadcasting Freedom*, 224.

21. Interview with Enders Wimbush, January 30, 2015.

22. "International Issyk-Kul Summit and Chingiz Aitmatov," RFE/RL Broadcast, November 3, 1986, box 11672, Broadcast Records, Radio Free Europe/Radio Liberty Archives, Hoover Institute, Stanford University .

23. Aliya Moldalieva, "Topical Reflections from Twenty Years Ago: Valeri Vilenski and Konstantin Orozaliev's Ailanpa: The World on Its Circles (1989), http://www .kinokultura.com/2010/29-moldalieva.shtml, accessed November 15, 2015.

24. The excerpts are from the film *Ailanpa: Mir na Krugakh svoikh* from author's transcription and translation of the Russian text.

25. The deal with Unionsverlag was Aitmatov's first foray outside the Soviet publishing industry, and the deal was nearly undercut by bigger German publishing company Bertelsmann, which had been publishing the works of Soviet writers through an exclusive arrangement with the All-Union Association of Writers (known by its Soviet acronym VAP), which had enjoyed a monopoly on sales of Soviet books abroad. But Aitmatov and Leitess broke the VAP's hold when neither Bertelsmann nor VAP could produce a contract binding Aitmatov to Bertelsmann. Interview with Lucien Leitess, August 10, 2014.

26. E-mail communication with Eldar Aitmatov, June 20, 2015.

CHAPTER 12

1. Stenographic record of the First Congress of the People's Deputies of the USSR, May 25–June 9, 1989 (Moscow: Supreme Soviet of the USSR, 1989), May 25 transcript, 56.

2. Hedrick Smith, *The New Russians* (New York: Random House, 1990), 456.

3. http://www.poemhunter.com/poem/if/, accessed May 13, 2015.

4. President George Bush noted as much in his memoirs when he remarked to his staff in December 1989, "Look, this guy is *perestroika*." Oberdorfer, *Turn*, 376.

5. James Lilley and Jeffrey Lilley, *China Hands: Nine Decades of Adventure, Espionage and Diplomacy in Asia* (New York: Public Affairs, 2004), 298–301; Diary of Teimuraz Stepanov-Mamaladze, http://digitalarchive.wilsoncenter.org/document/119287, accessed September 13, 2015. During the trip, Aitmatov himself noted that the Chinese "youth thirsts for change," http://digitalarchive.wilsoncenter.org/document/119285.

6. Aitmatov, *Aitmatov: Sobranie Sochinenii v Semi Tomakh*, 6:370–371. Aitmatov doesn't mention a specific date for the conversation, but it is likely in 1990 after he became a top adviser to Soviet leader Gorbachev.

7. Stenographic record of the First Congress, June 2 transcript, 300–301.

8. Ibid., 56.

9. Eugene Huskey, "The Politics of Language in Kyrgyzstan" (Washington, DC: National Council on Soviet and East European Research, 1995), 7–8. In reality the passage in the language law was mostly symbolic, designed to placate the majority while reassuring offended minorities, namely Russians. Officials were required to use the state language "to the extent necessary" in their dealings with the public, but in all other spheres of life either Kyrgyz or Russian could be used.

10. Interview with Maria and Eldar Aitmatov, June 24, 2013.

11. Huskey, "Politics of Language in Kyrgyzstan," 10. Implementation of the language law, however, was another story. Beset by economic crisis and a budget deficit, the governments of both Soviet Kyrgyzia and independent Kyrgyzstan could not provide the necessary resources to retrain teachers and publish textbooks. To the present day, to the good fortune of many Kyrgyz migrant laborers who earn a living in Russia, Russian remains a staple language of the Kyrgyz.

12. Chingiz Aitmatov, "Podrivayutsya Osnovi," *Sovetskaya Kyrgyzia*, May 6, 1988.

13. Friedrich Hitzer and Rahima Abduvalieva, "Chingiz Aitmatov and His German-Speaking Readers," *Discovery Guides 2012*, 12–20.

14. Interview with Tyntchtykbek Choroev, November 18, 2009.

15. Tynchtykbek Choroev and Bruce Pannier, "Kyrgyzstan: Chingiz Aitmatov, A Modern Hero, Dies," *Radio Free Europe/Radio Liberty*, June 11, 2008, http://www.rferl.org/content/article/1144589.html, accessed June 15, 2013.

16. Oberdorfer, *Turn*, 358.

17. David Remnick, *Lenin's Tomb: The Last Days of the Soviet Empire* (New York: Random House, 1993), 240.

18. Remnick, *Lenin's Tomb*, 240–241; and George Bush and Brent Scowcroft, *A World Transformed: The Collapse of the Soviet Union, the Unification of Germany, Tiananmen Square and the Gulf War* (New York: Alfred A. Knopf, 1998), 148–149.

19. Chingiz Aitmatov, "Padenie Kulturi vlechyot za soboi tragediyu," *Literaturnaya Rossiya*, July 13, 1990.

20. "Voice from the Republics," *Third World Quarterly* 12(1) (1990): 194–200.

CHAPTER 13

1. "Amerikada 52 кun: Kyrgyzurpagi Azamat Altaydin birtuugan karindashi USA dabolupkeldi," *Jashtyk Jarchysy*, January 31, 1991.

2. Kydyralieva's story is drawn from four sources: Aitmatova, *Belie Stranitsi Istorii*, 9–22; Helimskaya, *Taini Chong Tasha*, 8–18; Bolot Adrakhmanov, "Cherez Serdtse k Istinu" (paper delivered at a conference in Bishkek, Kyrgyzstan, commemorating the 110th birthday of Törökul Aitmatov, June 10, 2013); and interview with Bolot Abdrakhmanov, June 14, 2013.

3. Interview with Bolot Abdrakhmanov, June 14, 2013.

4. Abdrakhmanov, "Cherez Serdtse k Istinu."

5. In March 1990, Aitmatov's political capital soared when he was appointed to the newly formed presidential council. The creation of the council was meant to undermine the power of the Communist Party, which had previously controlled decision making in the Soviet Union through the party-dominated Politburo. The council was meant

to make Gorbachev's job of governing more manageable. As the Soviet Union's most prominent non-Russian writer, Aitmatov was one of the strongest liberal voices on the council.

6. The Ferghana Valley was ripe for conflict in 1990. Residents suffered from low levels of education, high unemployment, and lack of housing. In fact, the valley was so densely populated by a mix of Kyrgyz, Tajiks, and Uzbeks, that there was an average of just ninety-seven square feet of living space per person. National Intelligence Daily, June 8, 1990, declassified by the CIA September 1, 2009, http://www.foia.cia.gov /print/1819875, accessed December 15, 2015.

7. Valery Tishkov, Ethnicity, Nationalities and Conflict in and after the Soviet Union: The Mind Aflame (Oslo: Sage Publications, 1997), 36; and Pulat Shozimov, Baktybek Beshimov, and Khurshida Yunusova, "The Ferghana Valley during Perestroika," in Ferghana Valley: The Heart of Central Asia, ed. S. Frederick Starr (Armonk, NY: M. E. Sharpe, 2011), 194–195.

8. E-mail communication with Eldar Aitmatov, June 20, 2015.

9. Interview with Joseph Mozur, October 5, 2007.

10. Chingiz Aitmatov's address is from Chingiz Aitmatov House-Museum, July 24, 2010, https://www.facebook.com/pg/Chingiz-Aitmatov-House-Museum-132710763419195 /notes/?ref=page_internal.

11. "USSR: Moscow Fears Spread of Kirghiz Disorders," National Intelligence Daily, June 8, 1990, 1.

12. Shozimov, Beshimov, and Yunusova, "Ferghana Valley during Perestroika," 195; and International Crisis Group, The Pogroms in Kyrgyzstan (Asia Report No. 193), August 23, 2010, 1.

13. Interview with Elmira Ibraimova, July 23, 2009, Washington, DC.

14. International Crisis Group, "Pogroms in Kyrgyzstan," 2–4. See also "Comments by the Government of Kyrgyzstan in response to the report of the Kyrgyzstan Inquiry Commission into the Events in southern Kyrgyzstan in June 2010," p. 8, https://www .ndi.org/files/KG-comments-final-ENG.pdf, accessed August 8, 2015.

15. Bush and Scowcroft, World Transformed, 280.

16. Chingiz Aitmatov, ""Padenie Kulturi vlechyot za soboi tragediyu," Literaturnaya Rossiya, July 13, 1990.

17. In March 1990, the Congress of People's Deputies, the perestroika-era parliament that Gorbachev had pushed through as part of his democratic-oriented political agenda, created the position of the presidency and removed article 6 of the Soviet constitution, which had guaranteed the Communist Party's monopoly on political power. Gorbachev was duly elected.

18. E-mail communication with Eldar Aitmatov, June 20, 2015.

19. For information on Aitmatov's refusal to be a presidential nominee and on the October 1990 presidential election, I drew on Aitmatov: Sobranie Sochinenii v Semi Tomakh, 6:390–394; and interviews with Kazat Akmatov, Tynchtykbek Choroev, Osmanakun Ibraimov and Chingiz Aitmatov. In an interview with the author in 2007, Aitmatov maintained he had never been offered to be president, dismissing the talk as rumor and saying that at age sixty-two he was too old to get into politics at that level. But even if no official offer was ever made, it was clear that serious discussions had been held and that Aitmatov had not shown interest. When discussing why her brother had refused the presidency, Roza Aitmatova said in 1995, "He could not rule the country. He

is a sensitive, creative person with a child-like personality. Men with his kind of disposition cannot rule." *Kazakh/Kyrgyz Studies Bulletin*, accessed October 4, 2007, http://depts.washington.edu/centasia/Kyrgyzbulletin.html. On the question of whether he proposed Akaev, debates continue, with Aitmatov's immediate family maintaining that he just suggested to Asankulov and Akmatov that a younger person be nominated, not specifically Akaev. But in the pages cited earlier in *Aitmatov: Sobranie Sochinenii v Semi Tomakh*, Aitmatov does not refute the description of events and even appears to corroborate them. For their part, his family says it was actually brother Ilgiz who assisted Akaev, reportedly arranging for Akaev to fly in from Moscow in time for the election. Ilgiz, the Aitmatov family said, hoped to become president of the National Academy of Sciences, a post he did, indeed, hold under Akaev. Ibraimov, who by his own account worked as a high-level intermediary between Akaev and Aitmatov in the early 1990s, said Aitmatov helped Akaev become president and that the writer even spoke to Gorbachev on Akaev's behalf.

20. "Voice from the Republics," 195.

21. Mozur, *Parables from the Past*, 127.

CHAPTER 14

1. The site in present-day Belarus where in 1940 on Stalin's orders the NKVD executed four thousand Polish prisoners of war. The Soviet Union denied the massacre, blaming it on the Nazis. Only in 1992, after the collapse of the Soviet Union, did the Russian government admit the truth.

2. Although they shared the same last name, Bolot Abdrakhmanov was not related to Jusup Abdrakhmanov.

3. A shot through the heart appears to be the way the KGB finished off the highest-ranking Communist Party officials. Jusup Abdrakhmanov was also shot through the heart.

4. Helimskaya, *Taini Chong Tasha*, 21.

5. A. Akmataliev and N. Isaev, *Chingiz Aitmatov: The Universe Created with Love* (Bishkek: Chingiz Aitmatov Institute of Language and Literature, 2016), 180.

6. Plotskikh, "Törökul, Otets Chingiza," 52.

7. Akmataliev and Isaev, *Chingiz Aitmatov*, 179. A few years later, the secular Aitmatov would put a name to the discovery. "There is a God on this earth," he said in the mid-1990s. "Maybe it came late, but justice triumphed." *Aitmatov: Sobranie Sochinenii v Semi Tomakh*, 6:171.

8. Interview with Maria Aitmatova, June 24, 2013.

9. Remnick, *Lenin's Tomb*, 451. The words were spoken by Dmitry Yazov, then the Soviet minister of defense.

10. Aitmatova, *Belie Stranitsi Istorii*, 41–42.

11. Askar Akaev, *Trudnaya Dorogu k Democrati* (Moscow: International Relations Publishing House, 2002), 151.

12. Gorbachev, *Memoirs of Mikhail Gorbachev*, 640. In fact, Medetkan Sherimkulov, the speaker of the Kyrgyz parliament, was the first official to officially denounce the putsch-attempt. Akaev followed him.

13. Aitmatova, *Belie Stranitsi Istorii*, 42.

14. Dilip Hiro, *Between Marx and Muhammed: The Changing Face of Central Asia* (London: HarperCollins, 1994), 136.

15. Interview with Roza Aitmatov, June 16, 2013.

16. For Rostropovich, who was in Luxembourg to perform at the birthday party of the Grand Duke of Luxembourg, it was the first time he had set foot in a Soviet embassy since being forced to leave the Soviet Union in the 1970s.

17. Interview with Lucien Leitess, August 10, 2014.

18. Aitmatov, *Aitmatov: Sobranie Sochinenii v Semi Tomakh*, 7:538.

19. L. Stroilov, "Nash Posol v Luxembourge," *Slovo Kyrgyzstana*, March 28, 1991.

20. For the charges against Törökul Aitmatov, see Aitmatova, *Belie Stranitsi Istorii*, 191–192.

21. There are conflicting reports about where the executions took place, whether in the prison or at the site. On the basis of a reading of various sources, I have concluded that the executions took place in the prison and the bodies were then loaded onto military transport trucks for burial at Chong Tash.

22. The account of the November 7, 1938, holiday is drawn from Helimskaya, *Taini Chong Tasha*, 98–99.

23. The number of Kyrgyz who perished during the purges ranges from four thousand to forty thousand.

24. Interview with Ravil Husseinovich, March 8, 2006.

25. "Presidium Member in Interview with Post: 'Reformer Gorbachev is a Hero,'" *Jerusalem Post*, September 22, 1989.

26. Text of Soviet President Gorbachev's final speech is available at http://www.nytimes.com/1991/12/26/world/end-of-the-soviet-union-text-of-gorbachev-s-farewell-address.html.

CHAPTER 15

1. One of Altay's most trusted couriers was Kathleen Kuehnast, whom he was tutoring in Kyrgyz. Kuehnast, a graduate student at the University of Minnesota, had been traveling back and forth between the United States and Kyrgyzia since 1990, a living example of collapsing barriers. She would hand-carry gifts and money and return with photos and letters.

2. In what may be a diplomatic record, Aitmatov served as an ambassador representing three different countries in the span of four years: Soviet ambassador to Luxembourg (1990), Russian ambassador to Luxembourg (1992), and Kyrgyz ambassador to the Benelux countries (1994). Aitmatov's help to Altay in sending money to his relatives is from author's interview with Kathleen Kuehnast, February 10, 2014.

3. Eugene Huskey, *Kyrgyzstan: The Politics of Economic and Democratic Frustration* (Washington, DC: National Council for Soviet and East European Research, 1995), 13.

4. Interview with Roald Sagdeev, June 28, 2009.

5. https://www.poetryfoundation.org/resources/learning/core-poems/detail/46565, accessed July 26, 2106.

6. Mozur, *Parables from the Past*, 168–169.

7. Chingiz Aitmatov, "Ya Rad shto tipear' net ni fascisma ni kommunisma," *Slovo Kyrgyzstana*, September 15, 1992.

8. *The Mark of Cassandra* actually veered into science fiction when from his orbital station the cosmonaut sent a harmless ray to earth, which, upon encountering pregnant females, left a visible mark on the expectant mother's head indicating the wish of her embryo not to be born.

9. "The Appendix to the Information Results of Kyrgyz Republic Jogorku Kenesh Deputy Commission's work on gold," which can be accessed at the website of the Kyrgyz Committee for Human Rights (http://www.kchr.org/documents/corruption/20041015 .htm).

10. Ibid.

11. Kamil Bayalinov, "Zolotoi Sovetnik Prezidentov," *Komsomolskaya Pravda*, February 5, 1993; Leyla Boulton, "The Big Man in Kyrgyzstan: A Canadian's Connection to Gold, Scandals and a Coup in Four Former Soviet Republics," *Financial Post*, February 5, 1994.

12. Interview with Kazat Akhmatov, June 16, 2013; interview with Osmanakun Ibraimov, June 13, 2013.

13. Interview with Zamira Sydykova, April 15, 2011. Osmanakun Ibraimov, a former high-ranking official in the Akaev administration, corroborated that Chingiz Aitmatov had contacts with Birshtein. Interview with Osmanakun Ibraimov, June 13, 2013.

14. Chyngyshev became famous for reportedly saying, "Only fools and lazy people don't take bribes." See "Appendix to the Information Results."

15. Author calculation of the value of 146 kilograms of unrefined gold is an approximate value, based on the 1992 price of $344 for an ounce of gold.

16. "Appendix to the Information Results."

17. Ibid.

18. Kamil Bayalinov, "Cheteri vechera s Chingizom Aitmatovim," *Komsomolskaya Pravda*, November 6, 1993.

19. Zamira Sydykova, *Za Kulisama Demokratii no Kyrgyzski* (Bishkek: Respublikha Press, 1997), 45. Matters weren't helped by news that in 1993 Akaev's eldest daughter, Bermet, a student in the prestigious math department at Moscow State University, moved to Switzerland to study. To outsiders, it looked like the elite in Kyrgyzstan were making bad decisions and concerned about their own welfare.

CHAPTER 16

1. Kyrgyzia joined the United Nations in 1992 along with eight other former Soviet republics. The country joined under the official name Kyrgyz Republic but was commonly referred to as Kyrgyzstan.

2. In 1991, according to an unofficial tally conducted by the author, there were at least ten articles on Altay in Kyrgyz language newspapers.

3. Interview with Beksultan Jakiev, June 17, 2013.

4. Mamytbek Toktorbai Uulu, "Tagdir Kandai Tataal," *Kyrgyz Tusuu*, September 5, 1991.

5. "Letter from Chingiz Aitmatov," *Emgekchil Newspaper*, February 20, 1992.

6. Details and events surrounding Altay's return are from Jakiev's biography and assorted newspaper articles from the time period, including Altay's recounting of his trip in *Respublikha* newspaper, published in the December 9–15, 1997, edition and Jakiev's

version of Altay's return, dated September 10, 1994, and published in letter form in the appendix of Altay's personal memoir *Azattyk Menen Demokatiyanin Jarchysy*. The year 1994 is clearly a typo as Altay's trip took place in 1995.

7. Ewa Wasilewska, "The Rebirth of Kyrgyzstan," *Saudi Aramco World*, May–June 1996.

8. *Aitmatov: Sobranie Sochinenii v Semi Tomakh*, 7:200.

9. Letter from Azamat Altay to Sang-Guk Suh, November 8, 1990, personal archives of Azamat Altay, courtesy of Gulnara Turganbaeva.

10. "Ulandin Kati," Azamat Altay's memoir, *Azattyk Menen Demokatiyanin Jarchysy*, 243–245.

11. K. Makeshov, "Stalindin olumun Kyrgyz tilinde duinovo uguzgan," *Agym*, October 7, 2005, 7.

12. *Aitmatov: Sobranie Sochinenii v Semi Tomakh*, 7:531.

13. Interview with Imretraud Gutschke, December 8, 2008.

14. Interview with Nur Kerim, June 24, 2013.

15. Ibid.; interview with Joomart Ormonbekov, June 13, 2013.

16. "Chingiz Aitmatov poderzhal Kyrgyzskuyu Revoltsiyu," https://lenta.ru/news /2005/03/25/aitmatov/, accessed January 29, 2008.

17. "Chingiz Aitmatov poderzhal Kyrgyzskuyu Revoltsiyu," https://lenta.ru/news /2005/03/25/aitmatov/, accessed January 29, 2008.

18. Interview with Osmanakun Ibraimov, June 13, 2013.

19. Interview with Maria and Eldar Aitmatov, June 24, 2013.

EPILOGUE

1. "Letter from Ulan," dated August 20, 2008, and published in memoirs of Azamat Altay, *Azattyk Menen Demokatiyanin Jarchysy*, 243–245.

2. Interview with Venera Djumataeva, August 13, 2014.

3. "Azamat Altay, 1920–2006," *Slovo Kyrgyzstana*, May 26, 2006 (in Russian).

4. Video of Altay's funeral ceremony, personal archives of Azamat Altay, courtesy of Gulnara Turganbaeva.

5. Details on Aitmatov's health are from interview with Joomart Ormonbekov, June 13, 2013.

6. "Segodnya narod Kyrgyzstana skorbet and plachet," Live Journal of Edil Baisalov, http://baisalov.livejournal.com/411492.html?mode=reply, June 10, 2008.

7. Kyrgyzstan National Opinion Poll, October 2008 and May 2009, carried out by the International Republican Institute and Baltic Surveys/Gallup Organization. Author copies of polls.

8. Draft of article written by Roza Otunbayeva for Rukhaniat Association in connection with publication dedicated to the eighty-fifth birthday of Chingiz Aitmatov, provided to author by Otunbayeva in June 2013.

9. Interview with Azamat Tynaev, June 19, 2013.

10. Philip Shishkin, *Restless Valley: Revolution, Murder and Intrigue in the Heart of Heart of Central Asia*, (New Haven, CT: Yale University Press, 2013), 13.

BIBLIOGRAPHY

Abdrakhmanov, Bolot. "Cherez Serdtse k istinu." Paper delivered at a conference in Bishkek, Kyrgyzstan commemorating the 110th birthday of Törökul Aitmatov, June 10, 2013.

Abdullaev, Kamoludin, and Ravshan Nazarov. "The Ferghana Valley under Stalin." In *Ferghana Valley: The Heart of Central Asia*, ed. S. Frederick Starr. Armonk, NY: M. E. Sharpe, 2011.

Aitmatov, Chinghiz. *The Day Lasts More Than a Hundred Years*. Translated by John French. Bloomington: Indiana University Press, 1983.

———. *Detstvo*. Bishkek: Turar Publishing House, 2011.

———. *Jamilia* Translated by James Riordan. London: Telegram Books, 2007.

———. *Kogda Padayut Gori*. St. Petersburg: Azbuka-Klassika, 2006.

———. "Nebo i Slovo." *Slovo Kyrgyzstana*, September 12, 2006.

———. "Padenie Kulturi vlechyot za soboi tragediyu." *Literaturnaya Rossiya*, July 13, 1990.

———. "Podrivayutsya Osnovi." *Sovetskaya Kyrgyzia*, May 6, 1988.

———. *Time to Speak*. Moscow: Novosti Press, 1989.

———. "Ya Otkril Svoiu Zemlyu." *Literaturnie Kyrgyzstan*, June 1978.

———. "Ya Rad shto tipear' net ni fascisma ni kommunisma." *Slovo Kyrgyzstana*, September 15, 1992.

Aitmatova, Roza. *Belie Stranitsi Istori*. Bishkek: Biyitik, 2009.

Akaev, Askar. *Kyrgyz Statehood and the National Epos Manas*. New York: Global Scholarly Publications, 2003.

———. *Trudnaya Doroga k Demokrati*. Moscow: International Relations Publishing House, 2002.

"A Karavan Idyot." *Sovietskaya Kyrgyzia*, February 5, 1982.

Akiner, Shirin. *Islamic Peoples of the Soviet Union*. London: Paul Kegan International, 1983.

Akmataliev, Abdyldazhan. *Izbrannoe*. Bishkek: Sham Publishing, 1997.

Akmataliev, A., and N. Isaev, ed. *Chingiz Aitmatov: The Universe Created with Love*. Bishkek: Chingiz Aitmatov Institute of Language and Literature, 2016.

Altay, Azamat. *Azattyk Menen Demokatiyanin Jarchysy*. Bishkek: n.p. 2010. http://www.bizdin.kg.

———. "Kyrgyzia during the Great Purge." *Central Asian Review* (1964): n.p.

———. (pseud. Abdy, Kurmanbekov). "When the Paths of the Fathers Are Narrow." In *Twelve Komsomol Histories* (Institute for the Study of the USSR), series 1, No. 51, July 1959.

Allworth, Edward. *Central Asia: 130 Years of Russian Dominance: A Historical Overview.* Durham, NC: Duke University Press, 1994.

———. *Central Asian Publishing and the Rise of Nationalism.* New York: New York Public Library, 1965.

———, ed. *The Nationality Question in Soviet Central Asia.* London: Praeger Publishers, 1973.

"Amerikada 52 кun: Kyrgyzurpagi Azamat Altaydin birtuugan karindashi USA dabolup-keldi." Jashtyk Jarchysy, January 31, 1991.

Anderson, John. *Kyrgyzstan: Central Asia's Island of Democracy.* Amsterdam: Harwood Academic Publishers, 1999.

Andrew, Christopher, and Oleg Gordievsky. *KGB: The Inside Story.* New York: Harper-Collins, 1990.

"Announcement about the Creation of the Center of Anti-Bolshevik Struggle." *Turk Eli Journal,* September–October 1952.

Aragon, Louis. "Samaya Prekrasnaya na svete povest' o lyubvi." *Kultura i Zhizn,* no. 7, 1959.

Ashin, F., V. Alpatov, and D. Hasilov. *Repressirovannaya Turkologiya.* Moscow: Russian Academy of Sciences, 2002.

Axmatov, Asan. *Mech I Pero.* Bishkek: Turar, 2011.

"Azamat Altay, 1920–2006." *Slovo Kyrgyzstana,* May 26, 2006.

Bakashova, Jyldyz, ed. *Vselennaya Aitmatova: Biographicheskaya Encyklopedia.* Bishkek: National Library of Kyrgyzstan, 2009.

Bayalinov, Kamil. "Cheteri Vechera s Chinghizom Aitmatovim." *Komsomolskaya Pravda,* November 6, 1993.

Bennigsen, Alexandre. "Soviet Minority Nationalism in Historical Perspective." In *The Last Empire: Nationality and the Soviet Future,* edited by Robert Conquest, 131–150. Stanford, CA: Hoover Institution Press, 1986.

Bennigsen, Alexandre, with Marie Broxup. *The Islamic Threat to the Soviet State.* New York: St. Martin's Press, 1983.

Berdimurat, A. "Islam and Communism in Turkestan." *East Turkic Review* (Institute for the Study of the USSR) (April 1958): n.p.

Bohlen, Charles. *Witness to History: 1929–1969.* New York: W. W. Norton, 1971.

Boulton, Leyla. "The Big Man in Kyrgyzstan: A Canadian's Connections to Gold, Scandals and a Coup in Four Former Soviet Republics." *Financial Post* (Toronto), February 5, 1994.

Bush, George, and Brent Scowcroft. *A World Transformed: The Collapse of the Soviet Union, the Unification of Germany, Tiananmen Square and the Gulf War.* New York: Alfred A. Knopf, 1998.

Chadwick, Nora, and Victor Zhirmunsky. *Oral Epics of Central Asia,* Cambridge: Cambridge University Press, 1969.

Chokayev, Mustafa. "Turkestan and the Soviet Regime." *Journal of the Royal Central Asian Society* 18 (1931): 403–420.

Choroev, Tynchtykbek, and Bruce Pannier. "Kyrgyzstan: Chinghiz Aitmatov, a Modern Hero, Dies." *Radio Free Europe/Radio Liberty,* June 11, 2008.

Coe, Richard. "An Absorbing 'Ascent.'" *Washington Post,* June 5, 1975.

Cummings, Richard. "CIA Financed Book Distribution Programs: Part One, Free Europe Committee." October 4, 2011. http://coldwarradios.blogspot.com/

———. "Special Feature: The 1981 Bombing of RFE/RL." *Radio Free Europe/Radio Liberty*, February 9, 1996.

Edigeyev, Jenishbek. "Atlindi kozgoshso Nasiridinin olum siri achiluudai boloberet." *Agim*, February 20, 2007.

"Entertainment in Frunze 1963–1964." *Central Asian Review* 12(4) (1964): 280–291.

Figes, Orlando. *Natasha's Dance: A Cultural History of Russia*. London: Penguin Press, 2003.

Garrard, John, and Carol Garrard. *Inside the Soviet Writer's Union*. New York: Free Press, 1990.

"George C. Minden, 85, Dies; Led a Cold War of Words." *New York Times*, April 23, 2006.

Gorbachev, Mikhail. *Memoirs of Mikhail Gorbachev*. New York: Doubleday, 1995.

———. *Perestroika i Novoe Myshlenie dlya nashi strani i dlya vsevo mira*. Moscow: Politzdat, 1987.

Government of Kyrgyzstan. "Comments by the Government of Kyrgyzstan in Response to the Report of the Kyrgyzstan Inquiry Commission into the Events in Southern Kyrgyzstan in June 2010." https://www.ndi.org/files/KG-comments-final-ENG.pdf.

Gul, Roman. *Ya Unyos Rossiyu, Apologia Emigratsii, Rossiya v Amerike*. Vol. 3. New York: BSG Press, 2001.

Haber, Erika. *The Myth of the Non-Russian: Iskander and Aitmatov's Magical Universe*. Lanham, MD: Lexington Books, 2003.

Helimskaya, Regina. *Taini Chong Tasha*. Bishkek: Ilim, 1994.

Hiro, Dilip. *Between Marx and Muhammed: The Changing Face of Central Asia*. London: HarperCollins, 1994.

Hopkirk, Peter. *The Great Game: The Struggle for Empire in Central Asia*. New York: Kodansha, 1992.

———. *Setting the East Ablaze: Lenin's Dream of an Empire in Asia*. London: John Murray, 1984.

Hough, Jerry, and Merle Fainsod. *How the Soviet Union Is Governed*. Cambridge, MA: Harvard University Press, 1979.

Huskey, Eugene. "The Fate of Political Liberalization." In *Conflict, Cleavage and Change in Central Asia and the Caucasus*, edited by Bruce Parrott and Karen Dawisha, 242–276. Cambridge: Cambridge University Press, 1997.

———. "Kyrgyzstan: The Politics of Economic and Democratic Frustration." Washington, DC: National Council for Soviet and East European Research, 1995.

———. "The Politics of Language in Kyrgyzstan." Washington, DC: National Council on Soviet and East European Research, 1995.

Imanaliev, Kanybek. *Kyrgyzi*. Bishkek: K. Imanaliev, 2012.

Imankulov, J. *Aitmatov I Teatr*. Bishkek: Uchkun, 2003.

International Crisis Group. *The Pogroms in Kyrgyzstan*. Asia Report No. 193. August 23, 2010.

"International Issyk-Kul Summit and Chinghiz Aitmatov." *RFE/RL Broadcast*. November 3, 1986.

Jakiev, Beksultan. *Azamat Altay Povest'/Essay*. Bishkek: Ala-Too Journal, 2011.

Junushaliev, J., ed. *Nash Kyrgyzstan*. Bishkek: Soros Fund-Kyrgyzstan, 2004.

Kaiser, Robert. *Russia: The People and the Power*. New York: Washington Square Press, 1984.

Kakeev, A., ed. *Istoria Kyrgyzov i Kyrgyzstana*. Bishkek: Raritet Info Publishing House, 2007.

Kaptagaev, E., ed. *Kasym Tynystanov: Talant I Sudba*. Bishkek: Central State Archives of the Kyrgyz Republic, 2011.

Katz, Zev, ed. *Handbook of Major Soviet Nationalities*. New York: Free Press, 1975.

Kempe, Frederick. *Berlin 1961: Kennedy, Khrushchev and the Most Dangerous Place on Earth*. New York: Berkley Books, 2011.

Kennan, George. *Memoirs, 1925–1950*. New York: Pantheon Books, 1967.

"Khronika." *Novoye Russkoye Slovo*. September 12, 1956.

Kleveman, Lutz. *The New Great Game: Blood and Oil in Central Asia*. New York: Atlantic Monthly Press, 2003.

Koelle, Peter Brampton. "Chinghiz Aitmatov: A Reflection on Soviet Rule Through Memory." *Russian Language Journal* 54 (Winter–Spring 2000): 139–160.

Kokaisl, Petr, and Amirbek Usmanov. *Istoria Kyrgyzstana Glazami Ochividstev*. Brno, Czech Republic: Tribun EU, 2012.

Kotkin, Stephen. *Stalin*. New York: Penguin Press, 2014.

Kroll, Jack. "Ascent and Dissent." *Newsweek*, June 30, 1975, 44.

"Letter from Chinghiz Aitmatov." *Emgekchil Newspaper*, February 20, 1992. In *Azattyk Menen Demokatiyanin Jarchysy*. Bishkek: n.p. 2010. http://bizdin.kg/книга/азамат-алтай-азаттык-менен-демократиянын-жарчысы/. (Author commissioned translation from Kyrgyz to Russian.)

Lilley, James, with Jeffrey Lilley. *China Hands: Nine Decades of Adventure, Espionage and Diplomacy in Asia*. New York: Public Affairs, 2004.

MacKenzie, David, and Michael Curran. *A History of the Soviet Union*. Chicago: Dorsey Press, 1986.

Makeshov, K. "Stalindin olumun Kyrgyz tilinde duinovo uguzgan." *Agym*, October 7, 2005, 7.

Mambetalieva, Bermet. *Neuteryannie Pisma ili Razgovor na Dzherjinke*. Bishkek, Turar Publishing House, 2010.

May, Walter, trans. *Manas*. Vols. 1 and 2. Bishkek: Publishing House Door, 1995.

Meyer, Karl, and Shareen Blair Brysac. *Tournament of Shadows*. Washington, DC: Counterpoint, 1999.

"Miller's Russian Tale: Arthur Miller talks to Michael Ratcliffe about Power, Gorbachov [*sic*] and 'The Archbishop's Ceiling.'" (London) *Observer*, October 26, 1986.

Milov, L., ed. *Istoria Rossi*. Moscow: Eksmo Publishing House, 2006.

Mozur, Joseph. "Doffing Mankurt's Cap: Chinghiz Aitmatov's 'The Day Lasts More Than a Hundred Years' and the Turkic National Heritage." Carl Beck Papers in Russian and East European Studies No. 65, University of Pittsburgh Center for Russian and Eastern European Studies, . Pittsburgh, PA, September 1987.

———. *Parables from the Past: The Prose Fiction of Chinghiz Aitmatov*. Pittsburgh, PA: University of Pittsburgh Press, 1995.

Nahaylo, Bohdan, and Victor Swoboda. *Soviet Disunion: A History of the Nationalities Problem in the USSR*. New York: Free Press, 1990.

"A New Boris Exemplifies Individuality at Bolshoi." *New York Times*, July 17, 1975.

Novikov, Victor. *Chingiz Aitmatov on Craftsmanship*. Moscow: Raduga Publishes, 1987.

Oberdorfer, Don. *The Turn: From the Cold War to a New Era*. New York: Touchstone, 1991.

Osnos, Peter. "There's More to Russia than Americans Recognize: The Russia Americans Ignore." *Washington Post*, June 19, 1977.

Otunbayeva, Roza. "The Long Road to Democracy." *Washington Post*, March 8, 2011.

Parks, Michael, "Kyrgyzia Gets Low Mark for Ideology." *Baltimore Sun*, July 3, 1973.

Parta, Eugene. *Discovering the Hidden Listener: An Assessment of Radio Liberty and Western Broadcasting to the USSR during the Cold War*. Stanford, CA: Hoover Institution Press, 2007.

"Pismo v Redaktsiyu Gazeti Pravda." *Literaturnaya Gazeta*, September 5, 1973.

Plotskikh, Vladimir. "Törökul, Otets Chinghiza." In *Törökul Aitmatov*, 52–63. Bishkek: Ilim Publishing House, 1993.

"Presidium Member in Interview with Post: 'Reformer Gorbachev Is a Hero.'" *Jerusalem Post*, September 22, 1989.

"Prezreniya Naroda." *Sovietskaya Kyrgyzia*, October 29, 1982.

"Prime Suspect in Georgi Markov Umbrella Poison Murder Tracked Down to Austria." *Telegraph*, March 23, 2013. http://www.telegraph.co.uk/news/uknews/crime /9949856/Prime-suspect-in-Georgi-Markov-umbrella-poison-murder-tracked-down -to-Austria.html.

Pryce-Jones, David. *The Strange Death of the Soviet Empire*. New York: Henry Holt, 1995.

Puddington, Arch. *Broadcasting Freedom*. Lexington: University Press of Kentucky, 2000.

Rakhmanaliev, Rustam, ed. *Aitmatov: Sobranie Sochinenii v Semi Tomakh*. Bishkek: Turkestan Publishing House, 1998.

Rashid, Ahmed. *Descent into Chaos*. New York: Penguin Press, 2008.

———. *Jihad: The Rise of Militant Islam in Asia*. New Haven, CT: Yale University Press, 2002.

———. *The Resurgence of Central Asia: Islam or Nationalism?* London: Zed Books, 1994.

Remnick, David. *Lenin's Tomb: The Last Days of the Soviet Empire*. New York: Random House, 1993.

"Report of the Independent International Commission of Inquiry into the Events in Southern Kyrgyzstan in June 2010." http://reliefweb.int/site4s/reliefweb.int/files /resources/Full_Report_490.pdf.

Roy, Olivier. *The New Central Asia: The Creation of Nations*. New York: NYU Press, 2000.

Rywkin, Michael. *Moscow's Muslim Challenge: Soviet Central Asia*. Armonk, NY: M. E. Sharpe, 1982.

Schneider, Alan. "We opened in Moscow, then on to . . ." *New York Times*, November 18, 1973.

Shirley, Don. "Aitmatov: An Ascent at Arena." *Washington Post*, June 30, 1975.

Shishkin, Philip. *Restless Valley: Revolution, Murder and Intrigue in the Heart of Heart of Central Asia*. New Haven, CT: Yale University Press, 2013.

Shneidman, N. N. *Soviet Literature in the 1970s: Artistic Diversity and Ideological Conformity*. Toronto: University of Toronto Press, 1979.

Shozimov, Pulat, Baktybek Beshimov, and Khurshida Yunusova. "The Ferghana Valley during Perestroika." In *Ferghana Valley: The Heart of Central Asia*, edited by S. Frederick Starr, 178–204. Armonk, NY: M. E. Sharpe, 2011.

Smith, Hedrick. *The New Russians*. New York: Random House, 1990.

———. *The Russians*. New York: Ballantine Books, 1976.

Sokol, Edward. *The Revolt of 1916*. Baltimore: Johns Hopkins Press, 2016.

"Soviet Literature in the Struggle for Communism and Her Tasks in Light of the Decisions of the 26th Congress of the Communist Party of the Soviet Union." *Literaturnaya Gazeta*, July 1, 1981.

"Soviet Writer, Though Critical, Is Favored." *New York Times*, June 4, 1974.

Starr, S. Frederick. *Lost Enlightenment: Central Asia's Golden Age from the Arab Conquest to Tamerlane*. Princeton, NJ: Princeton University Press, 2013.

Stroilov, L. "Nash Posol v Luxembourge." *Slovo Kyrgyzstana*, March 28, 1991.

Sydykova, Zamira. *Godi Ozhidanii i Poter'*. Bishkek: Respublikha, 2003.

———. *Za Kulisama Demokratii no Kyrgyzski*. Bishkek: Respublikha Press, 1997.

Thorp, Meredith. *Glimpses of Village Life in Kyrgyzstan*. Bishkek: Sonun Jer, 2004.

Tishkov, Valeri. *Ethnicity, Nationalities and Conflict in and after the Soviet Union: The Mind Aflame*. London: Sage Publications, 1997.

Toktorbai Uulu, Mamytbek. "Tagdir Kandai Tataal." *Kyrgyz Tusuu*, September 5, 1991.

"Tschetni Potugi Otshepentsev." *Sovietskaya Kyrgyzia*, March 23, 1982.

"Two in New York Plead Guilty in Insurance-Claim Schemes." *New York Times*, September 4, 1993.

Ulam, Adam. *Expansion and Coexistence: Soviet Foreign Policy, 1917–1973*. New York: Holt, Rhinehart and Winston, 1974.

Urazgildeyev, Robert. *Bibisara Beishenalieva*. Frunze: Publishing House Frunze, 1970.

Vasiliev, A, ed. *Central Asia: Political and Economic Challenges in the Post-Soviet Era*. Moscow: Russian Academy of Sciences, 2001.

"Voice from the Republics." *Third World Quarterly* 12 (1990): 194–200.

Voropaev, V., ed. *Underwater Secrets and the Undiscovered Mysteries of Issyk Kul*. Bishkek: Kyrgyz-Russian Slavyanski University, 2010.

Wasilewska, Ewa. "The Rebirth of Kyrgyzstan." *Saudi Aramco World*, May–June 1996, http://archive.aramcoworld.com/issue/199603/manas.at.1000-the.rebirth.of.kyrgyzstan.htm.

Weatherford, Jack. *Genghis Khan and the Making of the Modern World*. New York: Broadway Press, 2004.

Wimmel, Kenneth. *Alluring Target*. Washington, DC: Trackless Sands Press, 1996.

"Writer in Soviet Union Defends Suicide of Story's Hero." *New York Times*, July 29, 1970.

Zhou, Jiayi. "The Muslim Battalions: Soviet Central Asians in the Soviet-Afghan War." *Journal of Slavic Military Studies* 25 (2012): 302–308.

INTERVIEWS

Interview with Abi Pazulov, August 31, 2007 and April 27, 2010, Bishkek.
Interview with Alexander Katsev, June 20, 2013, Bishkek.
Interview with Amirbek Usmanov, August 13, 2014, Prague.
Interview with Arslan Anarbaev, December 1, 2009, Washington, DC.
Interview with Asan Axmatov, June 17, 2013, Bishkek.
Interview with Askar Aitmatov, June 16, 2013, Bishkek.
Interview with Chinghiz Aitmatov, September 2, 2007, Cholpon Ata.
Interview with Azamat Tynaev, June 19, 2013, Bishkek.
Phone interview with Bakit Beshimov, June 1, 2010.
Interview with Beksultan Jakiev. June 17, 2013, Bishkek.
Interview with Brian Whitmore, August 12, 2014, Prague.
Interview with Bolot Abdrakhmanov, June 14, 2103, Bishkek.
Interview with Edward Kasinec, September 25, 2014 New York.
Interview with Elmira Ibraimova, July 23, 2009, Washington, DC.
Interview with Enders Wimbush, January 30, 2015, Washington, DC.
Interview with Gulyaim Ashakeeva, August 12, 2014, Prague.
Interview with Gulnara Turganbaeva, January 23, 2016, Queens, NY.
Interview with Ilgiz Aitmatov, June 20, 2013, Bishkek.
Interview with Imretraud Gutschke, December 8, 2008, Washington, DC.
Interview with Japarbek Dosaliev, September 11, 2007, and June 22, 2013, Sheker.
Interview with Jibek Maselbekova, September 11, 2007, Sheker.
Interview with Joomart Ormonbekov, June 13, 2013, Bishkek.
Phone interview with Joseph Mozur, October 5, 2007.
Interview with Jyldyz Bakashova, August 24, 2010, Bishkek.
Interview with Kanat Joldoshov, Aisulu Akunova and Timur Motogirov, April 25, 2010, Bishkek.
Interview with Kazat Akmatov, June 16, 2013, Bishkek.
Interview with Kathleen Kuehnast, February 10, 2014, Washington, DC.
Interview with Lucien Leitess, August 10, 2014, Zurich.
Interview with Maria and Eldar Aitmatov, June 24, 2013, Bishkek.
Interview with Nur Kerim, June 24, 2013, Bishkek.
Interview with Osmanakun Ibraimov, June 13, 2013, Bishkek.
Interview with Ravil Husseinovich, March 8, 2006, Bishkek.

Interview with Roald Sagdeev, June 28, 2009. College Park, MD.
Interview with Ross Johnson, February 24, 2015, Washington, DC.
Interview with Roza Aitmatov, June 16, 2013, Bishkek.
Phone interview with Tyntchtykbek Choroev, November 18, 2009.
Interview with Venera Djumataeva, June 11, 2013, Bishkek, and August 12, 2014, Prague.
Interview with Zamira Sydykova, April 15, 2011, Washington, DC.
Phone interview with Zelda Fichandler, January 12, 2015.

INDEX

Page numbers in italics indicate maps. Numbers followed by "*f*" indicate photos. Numbers followed by "n" indicate notes.

After witnessing the collapse of the Soviet Union as a journalist in the 1990s, Jeff Lilley moved to Central Asia in 2004. During a three-year posting in Kyrgyzstan, he started reading the works of Chinghiz Aitmatov, slept in yurts, drank fermented mare's milk, and hiked in the country's beautiful mountains. Over the following ten years, as he worked in the field of democracy and governance support in Washington, DC, and the Middle East, he continued researching Aitmatov while adding Altay's remarkable life story. He finished writing the book in 2016, shortly before returning to Kyrgyzstan to lead a British-funded parliamentary support program. Lilley is the coauthor of *China Hands: Nine Decades of Adventure, Espionage and Diplomacy* (Public Affairs, 2004).

9 780253 032447